RETHINKING THE BORDERLANDS

BETWEEN CHICANO CULTURE AND LEGAL DISCOURSE

CARL GUTIÉRREZ-JONES

D0040265

University of California Press

Berkeley · Los Angeles · London

University of California Press
Berkeley and Los Angeles, California

University of California Press, Ltd.
London, England

Library of Congress Cataloging-in-Publication Data

Gutiérrez-Jones, Carl Scott.
   Rethinking the borderlands: between Chicano culture and
legal discourse / Carl Gutiérrez-Jones.
      p.   cm.—(Latinos in American society and culture: 4)
   Includes bibliographical references and index.
   ISBN 0-520-08578-7 (alk. paper).—ISBN 0-520-08579-5
(alk. paper : pbk.)
      1. American literature—Mexican American authors—
History and criticism—Theory, etc.   2. Law and
literature—Social aspects—United States.   3. Mexican
Americans—Legal status, laws, etc.   4. Mexican
Americans—Historiography.   5. Mexican Americans in
literature.   6. Narration (Rhetoric)   I. Title.   II. Series.
PS153.M4G87   1995
305.868'72073—dc20   93-47485

Printed in the United States of America
9 8 7 6 5 4 3 2 1

For Joyce, Leslie, Marina, and Natalia

Contents

Acknowledgments

Many people have labored to produce this book. Foremost, I would like to thank Leslie Gutiérrez-Jones, who contributed stimulating ideas and criticism as well as steadfast support in myriad ways only a person living with a book-in-progress may. Her suggestions have enhanced virtually every aspect of the writing, and I could not have hoped for more engaging conversations than those I have shared with her over the eight years that this book has developed. My special thanks also to José Saldívar, whose mentorship since 1982 has been invaluable. *Rethinking the Borderlands* could not have come into being without the help and encouragement of these people.

The nucleus of this book grew out of a moonlighting project undertaken while I should have been finishing my dissertation at Cornell University. My appreciation goes out to my graduate committee, Debra Castillo, Dominick LaCapra, Jonathan Tittler, and my chair, Molly Hite, all of whom supported both undertakings with equal verve. I cannot overemphasize how much these people have shaped the thinking which led to this book. They never ceased to give an exceptional amount of their time, and I am truly indebted. I would also note that the first seeds of this work were planted in an outstanding undergraduate course, entitled "Marxism and/or Feminism," offered by Catharine MacKinnon at Stanford University in 1981.

Particular readers have had a significant impact on the manuscript versions of this book. I would like to thank my series editor, Mario García; María Herrera-Sobek; Ellen McCracken; Elliott Butler-Evans; George Lipsitz; and especially Ramón Gutiérrez, whose care and insight was exemplary. Richard Helgerson, Giles Gunn, Eric White, and Christopher Newfield, my colleagues in the English department at the University of California–Santa Barbara, also contributed important comments at a crucial early stage in the project's development. In terms of such contributions, I would also highlight the tremendous help provided by my students over the last three years, and particularly the comments and discussions shared by those students participating in my Chicano studies courses; their energy and interest quite literally sustained this project, and this book is as much theirs as it is mine. A number of graduate and undergraduate students have also joined me as research assistants and readers during the writing process, including Alma Rosa Alvárez, Wendy Avila, Cheryl Cardosa, Parker Douglas, Lisa Guerrero, Amy Rabbino, and Sarah Searcy. These friends gave far more than they were ever asked and went at the book with a sense of commitment that was a joy to behold. Special thanks are due Parker, whose efforts have been especially important in shaping the arguments offered. I also extend my gratitude to Raymond Huerta, coordinator for the Affirmative Action Office at Santa Barbara, who has provided crucial advice regarding the legal history explored in the manuscript.

A number of institutional bodies have also played a role in the development of this book. In particular, the Center for Chicano Studies has served as a home away from home, providing a very stimulating environment—including the SCR-43 study group. The Center for Cultural Studies at the University of California–Santa Cruz has also provided a much appreciated home for research and conversation. In addition, invaluable archival assistance has been made available by the Hector P. García Special Collection, State University of Texas at Corpus Christi, and by the Colección Tloque Nahuaque at the University of California–Santa Barbara; the work undertaken by the librarians at both institutions has been tremendous. A special note of thanks to the Colección scholars, including Salvador Guerena, Raquel González, and Patrick José Dawson, for their commitment to tracking down—and fielding a great variety of questions about—often difficult materials.

Parts of the first chapter of this book have appeared elsewhere in somewhat different form; these essays include "Legal Rhetoric and Cultural Critique: Notes Toward Guerrilla Writing" (*Diacritics* 20.4 [1991]:57–73) and "Rethinking the Borderlands: Between Literary and Legal Discourse" (*Dispositio* 16.41 [1993]:45–60, published by the Department of Romance Languages and Literature of the University of Michigan). My gratitude to the editors of these journals for their comments and for permission to reprint this material.

Numerous sources of financial support deserve mention. Among those, I would like to thank the Ford Foundation (Postdoctoral Fellowship, 1993–1994), the California State Legislature's SCR-43 Initiative (1992–1994), the University of California Faculty Career Development Initiative (1991), the University of California–Santa Barbara's Interdisciplinary Humanities Center (1992), and the University of California–Santa Barbara's Center for Chicano Studies (1992–1993).

The editors at the University of California Press have contributed much diligent work to the manuscript, and have offered substantial encouragement; I would like to extend my special appreciation to Laura Driussi, Dan Gunter, and Eileen McWilliam for their efforts. Finally, I will take advantage of my unique position as a writer addressing contemporary artists and critics to thank those people whose works—often constructed under particularly difficult circumstances—are the focus of this project. There are no doubt many others to whom this book owes significant debts; I offer in advance my assurance that such contributions are prized.

Introduction

> The criminalization of the Chicano resulted not from their being more criminal or violent but from a clash between conflicting and competing cultures, world views, and economic, political and judicial systems.
>
> Alfredo Mirandé, *Gringo Justice*

The process by which Chicanos have become institutionally and popularly associated with criminality has a long and complex history that is intimately related to their very construction as a social group in the United States. From the perspective of many Chicano historians, contemporary Chicano communities grew out of the 1848 signing of the Treaty of Guadalupe Hidalgo, which ended President Polk's expansionist war against Mexico. Because this document guaranteed to the former Mexican national inhabitants of the lands ceded to the United States legal rights even beyond those defined in the Constitution—rights which were not honored by the United States—it is, in the eyes of these scholars, a key to understanding the social situation in which Chicanos find themselves.[1] By contrast, the Cortina Revolt (1859), the zoot suit–U.S. servicemen's riots (1943), the Chicano Moratorium (1969), and even the King verdict riots (1992) have all acted as defining moments for the Anglo establishment, inasmuch as these legal interactions have been read in the media and the courts as symptoms of a racially defined criminal penchant.[2] Even "sympathetic" treatments of Latino criminality have generally avoided larger historical factors, a fact which may well reveal a constitutive denial of racial mechanics built into the law.[3] Sympathetic or not, such studies consistently assume a more "objective" critical approach and therefore tend to reinforce the barriers between Chicano and mainstream worldviews by re-creating what are better thought of as mock dialogues between cultures; in this manner, they strengthen deeply ingrained stereotypes about

1

Chicanos by perpetuating methods of interpretation locked into complex mechanisms of denial.

Considered from a perspective grounded in Chicano history, broad accusations of criminality—often accompanied by calls to "close" the border or to "repatriate" Chicanos and Mexicanos—demonstrate not objectivity but rather a political and economic investment on the part of Anglo institutions.[4] The cooperation between the Los Angeles Police Department and the Immigration and Naturalization Services (INS) during the 1992 King verdict riots and Police Chief Darryl Gates's subsequent inflammatory accusations against Latino immigrants are but instances of a long-standing tendency in this regard. This point was confirmed when the Hispanic Advisory Council in Los Angeles found that Chief Gates's television interviews—in which he announced that "illegal aliens played a major role in looting and violence during the rioting"—supported a larger program of intimidation that was simply not based on any substantial evidence.[5] Although the police department claimed to be using the INS personnel as translators to aid in the recovery of stolen property, the council found evidence of a systematic collaboration between the agencies, the goal of which was apparently to take advantage of the chaotic situation to inspire fear and to deport as many Latinos as possible.[6] Victor Valle and Rudy D. Torres have argued that a concomitant tendency in the media to produce a "great melodrama of race relations" has missed the extensive impact of the riots on Latinos as a larger, more diverse group, a group unique for its cultural mixing, or *mestizaje*.[7] In this study I argue that systematic institutional collaborations of the sort revealed in the King verdict riots are the norm and that they are premised on a strategic deferral of racism as a central force in U.S. history; hence the importance of "forgetting" how Mexicanos and Chicanos have been made into a malleable working class through economic, educational, and political underdevelopment, even as they have been effectively targeted as a class.[8]

Perhaps no particular incident studied here stands out as a better example of these tendencies than the conspiracy linking deportation policy and the accusations of criminality for political gain that were launched in 1934 against Los Angeles's first Spanish-speaking radio personality, Pedro González. Initially wooed by the Anglo establishment for the new Latino audiences he reached, González quickly found himself the victim of a plot to ruin his symbolic position of resistance in the Latino community. His "crime" was using his radio variety show to speak out not for his Anglo "supporters" but rather against the coercive repatriation of all persons of Mexican descent to Mexico. Falsely convicted of statutory rape—a conviction which was upheld even after the truth about the conspiracy came to light—González spent much of the rest of his life in San Quentin prison and in Mexico as a prisoner deported without pardon. Although González's treatment at the hands of the legal system, like the treatment received by numerous others, has been largely ignored in mainstream histories, stories like these continue to inform Chicano cultural critique, especially when systematic institutional collaboration is in question. However, these narratives virtually never pose blanket condemnations of U.S. institutions, including the legal system. Rather, they offer complex negotiations between the achievements gained through rights discourse activism (particularly the struggle for civil rights waged since World War II) and the legitimation and denial supported by a whole range of legal failings. Committed to securing themselves a legitimate place within the U.S. context but also wary of discrimination and coercion, Chicanos thus support the protection of civil liberties even while 70 percent (and more) of the population fears the police and legal processes in general.[9]

Both mirroring and reacting to this situation, the Chicano artists I take up in this book suggest that we must confront complex institutional problems if we are to fully comprehend the dialectical tensions which have shaped both Chicano politics and U.S. legal rhetoric. On the most explicit level, the artists considered here assume that the stereotypical ascription of "criminality" to Chicanos must be read in the context of larger U.S. institutional aims, including the maintenance of Chicanos and Mexicanos as a malleable, productive underclass.[10] Their intervention, however, also carries with it a latent though no less important "formal" critique. Hence, in the face of mainstream legal skepticism regarding claims of institutional discrimination, these artists work from the premise that legal rhetoric—especially the narrow examination of an individual's explicit intentions (the law's primary method)—cannot account for the exercise of racism in the United States or abroad. Simply put, such legal rhetoric conveniently limits the institution's ability to adjudicate issues involving groups and finally makes the problems facing groups virtually invisible because the law views their occasions as unique, individual instances.[11] By contrast, as José Saldívar has demonstrated, Chicano artists participate in a pan-American critical genealogy that understands discrimination and other forms of material and discursive underdevelopment affecting Chicanos as systematic, even though largely unacknowledged.[12] Working with this approach in mind, I will likewise consider the ways in which institutional mechanics help to maintain particular social groups in a fundamental dependency that affects political, economic, and cultural practices.

With this understanding of systematic dependency, and with the legacy of combative legal interactions which has virtually defined what has become Chicano history, this study follows the manner in which Chicano artists project their own versions of the courtroom, and of legal culture in general, as a critical arena of resistance.[13] Deconstructing the notion that crimes are deviations from an otherwise just and egalitarian code of behavior, these cultural critics take radical stances toward conventional understandings of "consensual" relations—especially where the subject of the social "contract" pertains to interpretive conventions. By reconstructing the supposedly antithetical relationship between force and consent that has been so important to apologists of mainstream legal practice, they offer instead a vision of institutional power as a dialectic between coercion and hegemony: where outright material limits fail, or where they prove inefficient, ideological discipline shapes the quiet participation of variously situated groups by legitimating the dominant class's privilege. Hence, material barriers—including unequal pay, unequal treatment by agencies of enforcement, unequal education—combine in this discriminatory society with hegemonic cultural techniques which succeed by (1) getting members of the subordinate groups to underestimate the extent of their own power and (2) extending the denial of outright discrimination, denial that effectively contains reforms that might originate "from the top down."[14]

To return to the particular position constructed for Chicanos, we should recall that an important part of the legitimation process depends on socially constructed notions of criminality. Besides being a tool that changes over time to fit particular trends and needs, this process of criminalization delegitimizes interpretive practices conceived of as threats to mainstream institutional designs.[15] This point has been painfully apparent to Chicanos and Mexicanos, whose histories relate numberless incidents of political and economic disenfranchisement in which legal definitions have been manipulated in order to favor the Anglo assumption of power in the Southwest, particularly through blatant land grabs.[16] Of course, this version of Anglo/Mexicano relations has been markedly absent from Anglo historical accounts.[17] This situation has compelled the majority of Chicano artists to pursue a complex combination of aesthetic, political, and historiographic goals; as cultural critics, they therefore often bear a strong resemblance to their Caribbean and Latin American counterparts, who likewise tend to work within a radically interdisciplinary mode that draws strong links between political engagement and formal experiment.[18] In the U.S. context, they also share an important, if heretofore unremarked, affinity with proponents of Foucauldian discourse analysis and of Critical Race Studies (in large part a reaction to Critical Legal Studies); in both of these emergent fields, one finds a subtle rethinking of political agency, a rethinking that extends the understanding of institutional power by focusing on the ideological implications of institutionally based languages. These approaches also offer a revitalized notion of the relation between theory and praxis, a notion that complements the pan-American trends identified by Saldívar and linked to what he defines as the Chicano criticism of dependency.[19]

While it is true that most of the Chicano narratives studied here were created without immediate reference to Critical Race Studies or discourse analysis, I have chosen to exploit the links for two principal reasons: first, the concepts made available by discourse analysis and Critical Race Studies not only complement those issues developed in the Chicano texts but also assist in the translation and extension of these issues to a multiplicity of institutional contexts (the media, the courts, the schools); second, Chicano studies and the attendant activist programs need to reevaluate their accepted notions of political agency as they come to terms with the difficult reality that many of the reforms undertaken during the Chicano movement of the 1960s and 1970s have not achieved the successes for which they had hoped.[20] In response to this latter situation, I propose to focus attention on the Chicano artists' interpretations of institutional dynamics while also using the most appropriate tools developed within the legal and academic spheres. In this sense, my strategy is committed, as I believe the artists' is as well, to turning hegemonic tools themselves against the designs of a society based on both material and cultural inequality.

If the complex positions assumed by Chicano artists place some significant pressures on Chicano critics for the rethinking of dependency I have described, the difficulty is all the more pressing for general readers working within the U.S. academy, especially as they try to interpret Chicano texts (at least in part) through the context of debates over canon formation, "political correctness," and multi-culturalism. In taking up a more global reading of Chicano narratives, I intend to convey the subtlety found in Chicano rereadings of historical-legal interactions; I hope to demonstrate not only the ways in which particular events are "rejudged" to challenge stereotypes (for instance, assertions of criminality) but also the ways in which legalistic interpretation itself is revised (i.e., how certain modes of counterreading call forth criminalization). The goal, then, is to move beyond what I understand to be a primary dynamic animating academic arguments about racial politics: the battle over the inclusion or exclusion of marginalized materials or (pluralistically endorsed) perspectives.[21] Instead, this project follows the process by which historical events and historiography itself are rewritten by Chicanos once they recognize the ways that specific legal rhetoric has shaped hegemonic interpretations and institutions. Because the problems defined by the artists in question often transcend those established within the academy (inasmuch as they challenge the implicit tenets of Anglo historiography as a whole), this analysis of legal rhetoric and its manipulations significantly supplants patchwork, "inclusive" efforts at redeeming literary history. My goal is not so much to improve the standing of these authors in various interpretive circles, although doing so may well be an important project. Instead, my concern is with negotiating the means by which these authors attempt to restructure important debates about enfranchisement in its broadest sense.

In what follows, then, I consider this battle over the tenets of interpretation by exploring the conflictual dialogue generated between representations of the "objective voice" of society—that is, its legal discourse—and modes of artistic discourse historically associated with the Chicano interrogation of U.S. institutions. The first chapter sets out for the study as a whole a broad institutional context that combines overviews of (1) trends in Critical Legal and Critical Race studies, (2) tendencies within Chicano studies, (3) neoconservative cultural strategy, and finally, (4) resistance strategies in Chicano art, art that attempts to negotiate and/or dialogue with the pressures revealed in (1) through (3). This chapter is an interdisciplinary bricolage that risks labyrinthine development for the sake of creating a strategically conflictive cognitive map that might more adequately accommodate the complex interventions undertaken by the artists in question. Throughout, I seek to evoke the dialectical tensions and latent rhetorical economies that constitute the very intimate relationships between Chicano resistance and the hegemonic legal culture.

The two following chapters consider, respectively, the rise of "the Spanish fantasy," as evidenced in the structure of Helen Hunt Jackson's *Ramona* (1884), and the magical realist Chicano response to dependency undertaken by Alejandro Morales in *The Brick People* (1988).[22] While the former chapter examines the displacement of Mexicanos by the "mission revival" initiated in large part by the success of Jackson's novel, the subsequent chapter studies Morales's response to such mainstream historical amnesia by exploring the possibilities of effecting a Foucauldian reversal of Anglo "disciplinary techniques" through experiments with the magical. Demonstrating in more particularized contexts the dialectical tensions proposed earlier in the study, the second and third chapters thus offer an opportunity to consider institutional dynamics as they animate closely analyzed literary texts and their rhetorical strategies.

Having thus worked through two "case studies" examining the battleground on which Chicanos have challenged Anglo legal practice, I then take up the unique contribution made by contemporary Chicana artists as they redefine the critical-legal project. Extending the reading of legal interactions in order to rethink gender, sexuality, and specific inflections of consent as an ideological paradigm, the authors addressed here—Ana Castillo, Cherríe Moraga, and Helena María Viramontes—pose broad and profound questions about the manipulation of desire and coercion. Drawing particularly on the dynamics of rape and shame, these texts significantly complicate the legal-rhetorical model offered to this point by demonstrating the diverse functions played by sexuality and gender as these affect political and resistant affiliations within communities.

The final chapter reads the implications of the Chicana critique back through two explicitly masculinist texts, Oscar Zeta Acosta's *Revolt of the Cockroach People* (1973) and Edward James Olmos's *American Me* (1992). The study takes this turn in order (1) to pursue a greater engagement between the implications of Chicana critique and the often insulated, too often misogynistic texts produced by Chicano males and (2) to build on issues of sexuality and race toward a reading of the "homosocial" dynamics that come to inform the resistant group affiliations modeled in the works. Inasmuch as these Chicano male texts appear to code the historiography they offer as a type of mourning conditioned by the law, this chapter examines the manner in which the texts stage the death of Chicanas (linguistically, politically, literally) as a constitutive event against which their own patriarchal privilege is defined. As a response to this patriarchal, homosocial dynamic, this final chapter concludes by considering examples of Chicana activist mourning, examples that project a previously elided genealogy of cultural critics. Here the wills and testimonials of Mexicanas just after the colonization are taken up, along with the fight by Beatrice Longoría in the late 1940s to have her husband buried in a previously whites-only chapel; the section turns finally to the fiction of Patricia Preciado Martín, fiction which rethinks the historiographic process itself as a retaking and reformulation of mourning by Chicanas.

The final two chapters thus work together to rectify a predominant fault identified by the Chicano cultural critic Juan Bruce-Novoa: the tendency by Chicano literary studies to maintain an "incestuous focus" on certain male authors. Overall, these chapters demonstrate that this incestuous focus is actually better thought of as homosocial—that is, as part of a larger "economy" of male desire, one fed by the legal-cultural bonds between men both within and outside of the Chicano community. Beyond this ideologically powerful bonding, we find a radically transgressive Chicana activism, an activism burdened by a unique double, if not triple, oppression, yet also benefiting from a critical position that allows a thorough, subtle engagement of the problems which Chicano history attempts to work through.

1

Legal Rhetoric and Cultural Critique
An Institutional Context for Reading Chicano Narrative

This study begins with the assumption that certain historiographic tenets impose themselves every time we propose or consider arguments about affirmative action and other socially progressive types of institutional reform. Particularly at the university level, students and faculty alike have become attuned, in terms of their perception of equity, to certain limiting expectations, not the least of which is meritocracy.[1] Developing a rhetorical-legal resistance to dominant principles like meritocracy fuels the institutional revisions undertaken by Chicano artists. Confronting particular legalistic modes of thinking, the Chicano artists considered here argue that it is impossible to approach the most obvious questions about equality without critically examining the subtle positions many people take as givens regarding how social justice itself is constructed. These artists begin by recognizing that such assumptions are very much bound up with our immersion in legal rhetoric via a seemingly endless reproduction of legal interactions in mass culture. From news reports of actual cases to Judge Wapner to Madonna's First Amendment self-aggrandizement in *Truth or Dare*, we are almost continually pummeled "politically unconscious" with concepts about the composition of social justice. Most explicitly, Chicano artists reveal the manner in which such concepts impose particular limitations on group analysis.

To follow this point out in greater detail, we may build on the work of Critical Legal Studies (CLS). Mark Kelman, for instance, has argued that liberal-legal conventions dictate the ground rules for thinking about social justice and institutional problems. According to Kelman, these liberal-legal modes of arguing about social revision encode certain parameters for considering social agency and responsibility, parameters which work at the expense of alternative methods, especially those that are group oriented. Considering this displacement, Kelman notes:

> Legal discourse ... need not bring out underlying policy or philosophical dilemmas; it may well suppress their presence through unconscious manipulation of material that allows us to believe that we are "solving" a case by applying settled or noncontroversial decision norms to "facts" that are found without reference either to norms or to a subconscious urge to avoid thorny issues. (289)

In response to such limiting ground rules, Chicano narratives challenge the presuppositions of inquiry by asking questions which present, and therefore codify, nonlegitimate problems, problems which resist legal-institutional imperatives. Thus, an author like Cherríe Moraga is able to critique the particular position imposed on Chicanas who must contend with unique forms of discrimination that simply will not be acknowledged in a courtroom because the institution strategically separates considerations of race from considerations of gender.[2] Responding to similar difficulties within the law, Kelman maintains that one of the most significant tasks facing the CLS movement is the need to look beyond the explicit workings of ideology in legal texts and instead to develop a critique of the latent mainstream rhetorical forces which radically police alternative cognitive processes (274–75).

Kelman notes that mainstream legal scholars in the United States have long depended on a model of the relation between the legal and social spheres which draws on the ideology of liberal functionalism. Laws, in this model, reflect society and develop according to transformations in mores, social conventions, and so on. CLS writers have done much to dismantle this overly simplistic notion of reflection; in doing so, they have underscored the relative autonomy of legal institutions and hence their ability to shape social thought. Although the methodologies pursued by these critics are varied, including Marxist, feminist, and deconstructive approaches, the emphasis throughout tends to fall on the legitimating force of legal culture—its ability to structure interpretive processes. Of course, the implications of such an overall finding are profound, accounting in part for the tremendous impact of CLS work (at least outside the law schools where it was initiated).

Perhaps the best of these new inquiries take the form of dialogic interactions rather than occasions to lay legal-rhetorical grids over other disciplines. Anticipating the difficulties which must be faced as we turn to the complex terrain inhabited by Chicano artistic critiques of the law, we will turn to the literary realm and John Guillory's argument about academic institutions in "Canonical and Non-Canonical: A Critique of the Current Debate," an argument that significantly complements the CLS understanding of institutional autonomy. According to Guillory, schools, like the courts, maintain social inequalities but actually "succeed by taking as their first object not the reproduction of social relations but [rather] the reproduction of the institution itself" (496). What we learn as we study such complementary processes is that the strength institutions exhibit over time rests on a sum total of complex practices which displace potentially disruptive rhetorical options by formally prohibiting such disruptive practices. Hence, certain eternal verities—often articulated in the realm of values—take a defensive posture against rhetorical strategies recognizing historical change. While both the school and the court produce a means of accessing the traditions of culture and law, these institutions perpetuate specific relations to both which differ for different people. Chicanos recognize this precise state of affairs when they both protest for better educational programs and move toward declining graduation rates, when they both support civil rights activism and express fear about legal institutions. Their experience consistently tells them that they will be treated differentially—that is, as Chicanos, not as race-neutral citizens. Even so, their concomitant awareness of the very real gains that have been won through protest and rights activism induce a certain hope and further offer a crucially important opportunity for the construction of resistant communities.[3] It is with these stakes in mind that Chicano artists most frequently struggle with legal culture; even in the most radical, most utopian experiments, what is at issue is the potential for altering institutions which perpetuate specific social relations, relations rooted in class, gender, sexuality, race, and ethnic hierarchies. In this sense, criticism of legal representation hangs in the balance, but so does an activist strategy of legal and cultural enfranchisement.

If, as I am arguing, a battle is taking place in which rhetorical options severely limit the conception and institution of reform, then perhaps no site of contestation could make a better starting point than the law school itself—a site which stands out as the most obvious juncture of the academic and judicial institutions. The contestation of ideas (especially alternative ones) and the subsequent certification of "appropriate thinking," both typical of the school in general, work together in the law school environment to ensure the continued vitality of specific legal-rhetorical tools. This situation is entirely in line with larger institutional processes of canonization, processes which celebrate key texts in order to foster certain interpretive practices (legal, literary, etc.). While reverence for the canon itself perpetuates the notion of "sacred" banks of knowledge, canonical interpretive processes at the same time validate particular historiographic approaches, often by virtue of a canon's own self-legitimating metanarrative. Precedence, both in the academy and in the court, may thus be read as an interpretive end in itself. Hence, as Kimberlé Crenshaw has noted, the law school classroom exercises an overarching Anglo, upper-class worldview that is coded as "objective" and "perspectiveless" even while it posits a history of race-neutral social interactions.[4] The process as a whole masks the clearly "interested," if denied, hegemonic foundation. In turn, minority students find their experiences and their histories displaced as they are forced by teachers and peers either to acquiesce to a properly "distanced" mode of thinking or to become sources of subjective, emotional (sometimes coded "hysterical") testimony about racial problems, which are, of course, supposedly peripheral to the larger workings of the "objective" classroom and the essentially race-neutral machinery of the law. This pedagogic situation, much like the environment created by antidiscrimination law itself, tells members of minorities that, as rhetorical participants, they may succeed only by walking a very fine line in which majority interlocutors are dangerously introduced to alternative metanarratives that challenge directly the belief in the "objective" processes which the majority holds so dear.[5]

Theories emphasizing the force of legitimation processes have been the mainstay of CLS efforts. Giving this focus his own particular twist, Kelman addresses the interplay of legitimation and rhetorical strategies at the conclusion of his recent work *A Guide to Critical Legal Studies* (1987). An introduction to "a cognitive theory of legitimation," this final chapter reframes the CLS approach, diverse as it is, by training our attention on the limits perpetuated by legalistic "rhetorical understandings of the world." Offering a set of "ways in which legal thinking is prone to be an effective justificatory ideology," Kelman thus provides a "cognitive" approach to the law which focuses on its rhetorical manipulation of thought processes. According to this approach, the power of the law to create cognitive strictures affects law students and lay people to the extent that they are "'afflicted' with legal thinking," an affliction which makes "counterhegemonic thoughts harder to think" (269). Supporting this claim, Kelman sets out six ways in which legal thinking attempts to disrupt counterhegemonic considerations:

> (1) reification; (2) conflation of the potential legal solubility of a problem with the existence of a problem; (3) synthetic individualism (a belief that social relations can be understood only as the sum of readily comprehensible individual relations); (4) "take and give" (giving the appearance that the system is less harshly oppressive or biased than it could be); (5) denial of political stress through the use of technical thought; and (6) the privileging of libertarian poles in the face of contradictory political pulls. (269)

Although Kelman identifies counterhegemonic thoughts with "critical" stances in general, his specific definitions of the six strictures implicitly align modes of resistance with "transformative thought," thought which challenges the preconditions of legal discourse's ideal notion of the world: a place of "self-determined subjects, expressing consistent, unambivalent, and unexceptionable desires, seeking their ends in a private world of voluntary transactions freed from force or nonnatural necessity by a state that imposes only clear rules against illicit force, using rules both because it fears becoming forceful itself and because people should know precisely what is expected of them" (290).

According to CLS scholars, this liberal worldview is perpetuated in the law not simply by "misdescription" but by "a system of (largely legal) thought that portrays the ideal as nothing more than the summary of routine rhetorical starting places . . . , ordinary ways of dealing with and apprehending the world" (Kelman 290). While the CLS approach to legitimation has crucially informed subsequent Critical Race Studies (CRS) theories, one finds in Kelman's typification of the CLS project the principal point of disagreement; specifically, CRS scholars take issue with what they see as an overvaluation of legal legitimation. As CRS scholars perceive the situation, CLS theories of legitimation have too quickly dismissed the role of minority worldviews. Crenshaw has offered the most thorough evaluation of this situation. In the critique she develops of the CLS tendencies in her essay "Race, Reform, and Retrenchment: Transformation and Legitimation in Antidiscrimination Law," she finds that the almost exclusive focus on discursive legitimation misses the larger dialectical processes by which hegemony and outright material coercion work together to maintain cultural and social dependency. At stake is the appropriate interpretation of Antonio Gramsci's work, an interpretation that she argues must account for the inextricable links between distinct material and ideological conditions. For Crenshaw, it is simply not sufficient to assume that legal discourse, as powerful as it may be, has the ability to totally dictate the existence of racism or minority perspectives. Hence, she takes issue with the CLS assumption that legal legitimation forces minorities literally to begin again every time they try to sustain an alternative worldview; as Crenshaw suggests, such worldviews are alive and well, informing minority activist and grassroots organizations even while material and ideological contention continues.

What is particularly troubling about the CLS elision is that it seems to repeat, although with clearly more sympathetic intentions, the law's larger denial of minority claims. As Crenshaw argues, it may well be that the CLS theory of legitimation is limited exactly to the extent that it misapprehends the rhetorical role of its own legitimation critique; thus, the emphasis on legitimation may speak far more effectively to an Anglo, upper-class audience which struggles not only against legal-cultural indoctrination but also against a basic ignorance about minority experiences and perspectives. Perhaps most important for the purposes of the study at hand is Crenshaw's argument that no understanding of legal-cultural legitimation can effectively describe the radical projects undertaken by minority artists and critics without situating itself in a dialectical process that includes explicit, material coercion. As Crenshaw and the Chicano artists and critics attempt to convey, it is only with such a dialectical outlook (legitimation and coercion working in concert) that we may properly interpret a legal system which rhetorically obscures judicial error, abuses of force, disenfranchisement, and social inequality—issues which could act as motors for social change.

Legal rhetoric most often reacts to these potential motors for change by engendering a passivity (most strongly felt in society's dominant groups) through the perpetuation of a basic confusion about how rules in society function. By portraying order in society as dependent on the continued legitimacy of rules, people come to assume "that the rules make us do good rather than that we sometimes collectively choose to do the good things we do when applying rules or even when we don't" (295). Battling such habits by which people may be induced to abdicate their power is, of course, a central concern for those who seek Chicano enfranchisement. Hence, Chicano and Mexicano activist organizations, including the League of United Latin American Citizens (LULAC) and the Mexican American Legal Defense and Education Fund (MALDEF), have used legal rights discourse against such pacifying tendencies, although such legal struggles have at times yielded uncertain results, as I will detail in the pages to come.[6]

What is certain is that the counterhegemonic collective action pursued by LULAC, and to a greater degree by MALDEF, has had a particularly resistant role in a liberal-legal system which privileges individual agency—a fact which, in a different register, echoes Crenshaw's observations. It is likewise no accident that explorations of collective action are repeatedly taken up in Chicano narratives which are keenly sensitive to the machinations of legal culture. In the taxonomy Kelman provides, "synthetic individualism," or the assumption that groups may always be reduced to their individual members, suggests the complex position that individual agency assumes as the liberal system imposes limits on Chicano conceptions of collective action. Recognizing this situation helps us to understand the difficulties of instituting affirmative action; the strictures articulated by a fully legitimated cognitive practice of synthetic individualism (strictures validating meritocracy and the creation of contracts between autonomous individuals) will of course deny claims of institutional racism that cite collective histories of segregation, discrimination, coercion, and any attendant cultural effects. Depending on entrenched oppositions between "freely" acting individuals and a "regularizing" government charged with overseeing the public, the liberal system displaces collective approaches to institutional racism by sustaining apparently self-evident rhetorical categories. Hence, despite the seeming contradiction, affirmative action itself, after only a brief tenure, may be severely limited in the courts on grounds entirely consistent with mainstream legal practice. In response to such conflicts, the CLS and the more refined CRS projects propose a working through of "the sort of confusion legalistic practice engenders" in an effort to come to terms with the highly complex mechanisms which obscure counterhegemonic interpretive strategies; the difference between the projects is finally the supposition in the CRS arguments that these legal mechanisms are but a part of a larger systematic underdevelopment carried out along a primarily racial, as opposed to legal, dynamic.

The example provided by Crenshaw's work is in line with other recent writings that may be termed part of the CRS initiative, writings which attempt both to challenge and to move beyond the historical and racial decontextualization of academic-legal discourse. For instance, Gerald López's recent book *Rebellious Lawyering: One Chicano's Vision of Progressive Law Practice* (1992) offers a thorough critique of reformist strategies which would maintain the professional distance between law office and community and thereby protect the hierarchy of power that activist lawyers may enjoy as they inadvertently set themselves up as autonomous agents of the law dispensing rights (23–24, 75). Arguing that counterhegemonic or "nonlawyerly" solutions to problems come about from nonlawyerly contact, López suggests that working with culturally specific stories of a community can help an activist lawyer step into a new role as translator (as opposed to dispenser). In such a role, lawyers may learn as well as teach, benefiting both from their acquaintance with the legal system and from the street savvy which community members bring to their understandings of the problems at hand. In the latter instance, lawyers may thus profit by utilizing the interpretive potential of Chicanos who have learned in their role as subordinates how to read their bosses' power and how to adjust for their own benefit (59). A book made up largely of exemplary stories—stories evidencing just such profitable interchanges at the community organization level—*Rebellious Lawyering* both theorizes and enacts a rhetorical strategy which builds on worldviews found within Chicano communities.

In a similar vein, Patricia Williams's *Alchemy of Race and Rights: Diary of a Law Professor* (1991) has critiqued the limiting legal rhetoric which constitutes a denial of self and authority in the African-American community. Reviewing her experiences of racism through a study of the process by which her attempts to relate those experiences were negated by journal editors, Williams attacks racial denial as it is propped up on the basis of style, on postures of neutrality and objectivity, and on the basis of verifiability.[7] Ultimately, López and Williams have chosen to pursue local, case-study approaches which, by opening both an autobiographical and a collective rhetoric, refuse to obscure the interpreter's (perhaps more properly, the translator's) role in engaging events and collective issues. Such local focus, combined with the rhetorical transgression of professional forms, in turn allows a new mobility, one that has the potential to radically disrupt institutional pursuits and thereby open the door to worldviews other than those canonically sanctioned by legal institutions.

Crenshaw also works toward defining this mobility as she takes issue with the arguments offered by Critical Legal Studies. As she notes, CLS scholars tend to approach questions of domination by considering how legitimation (the process by which the social order is accepted) restrains potentially subversive or transformative social conflicts and antagonisms ("Race, Reform, and Retrenchment" 1352). From the CLS position, reform begins with an essentially negative action, with *de*legitimation or what has been termed the "trashing" of the rights system as a whole:

> The vision of change the Critical scholars express flows directly from their focus on ideology as the major obstacle that separates the actual from the possible. Because it is ideology that prevents people from conceiving of—and hence from implementing—a freer social condition, the Critics propose the exposure of ideology as the logical first step toward social transformation. ("Race, Reform, and Retrenchment" 1354)

Convinced that the CLS approach best describes the manner in which the white dominant majority seduces itself into accepting the existence of racial coercion (1358), Crenshaw argues that a reevaluation of this ideology—including the role of civil rights discourse—needs to better accommodate the perspective of minority communities. Attempting to map out just this sort of alternative approach to rights discourse, Crenshaw finds that a much more ambivalent picture comes to the fore, one which weighs important gains for minority communities against the larger co-optation of the civil rights movement, a co-optation which has led to the increasingly popular notion that racism no longer exists in the United States.[8] In large part, Crenshaw's more complex vision of rights discourse is founded on the notion that a fundamental indeterminacy inheres in the legal rhetoric. Noting that statements defining this nation's attitudes toward racial equality have aimed primarily at reforms of a symbolic nature, Crenshaw argues that a crucial rhetorical mobility has opened up for minorities, one which should not be discounted too quickly:

> Removal of . . . public manifestations of subordination was a significant gain for all Blacks, although some benefited more than others. The eradication of formal barriers meant more to those whose oppression was primarily symbolic than to those who suffered lasting material disadvantage. Yet despite these disparate results, it would be absurd to suggest that no benefits came from these formal reforms, especially in regard to racial policies, such as segregation, that were partly material but largely symbolic. Thus, to say that the reforms were "merely symbolic" is to say a great deal. These legal reforms and the formal extension of "citizenship" were large achievements precisely because much of what characterized Black oppression was symbolic and formal. (1378)

Emphasizing that "formal equality is not the end of the story," Crenshaw is careful not to overvalue such mobility even as she is wary of treating it too pessimistically. As a critic convinced that transformation must reshape existing institutions as well as culturally constructed worldviews, Crenshaw contextualizes this mobility, proposing that minorities working on the law find themselves on a purely relational terrain. The struggle for recognition and an institution of nonmajoritarian concerns—a struggle which anchors minority power and accounts for minority discontent—must exist in the same world that activists stand against.[9] In such a shared terrain, resistance and survival itself often depend precisely on mobility because (despite the promise held by liberal-legal rhetoric) no utopian, race-neutral space exists to yield sanctuary.

In Patricia Williams's work, the rhetorical reframing of such shared terrain permits a complex psychological refiguring of her experience of language and the past, a refiguring which locates historical transformation not in the abstract, Olympian halls of the academy or the courtroom but rather in intimate locales. In this vein, she describes how her family members still carefully walk around long-vanished furniture that once stood in her grandmother's room; comparing these habits to pressures of race not acknowledged by the law, Williams evokes complex social pathologies through powerfully resonant anecdotal passages. In this manner, her strategy is analogous to López's: both rework stories in order to bring disparate worlds together—in conflict. Communities are thus understood not in terms of purifying consensus (the assimilation model) but rather in terms of conflictual renegotiations (ongoing migrations).[10]

What is implied by such a reframing of experiences of racism, especially when they are presented in intensely personal formats? As Alan Freeman has argued in "Legitimizing Racial Discrimination Through Antidiscrimination Law: A Critical Review of Supreme Court Doctrine," one conventional manner of delegitimating instances of racism as legal issues relies on a constrained notion of the perpetrator's intention (limited in time and agency) to the exclusion of the victim's or victimized group's experience, thereby seriously restricting recourse to action within the liberal system.[11] Taking up the larger CRS goal of approaching the law from the more complex orientation of the minority community, Williams's self-proclaimed "guerrilla legal writing" disrupts the stability of the conventional rhetorical configuration noted by Freeman, asserting instead the applicability of different rhetorical possibilities, of different interpretive strategies, including the politically personal perspectives of the victims of racism.

The guerrilla writing offered by Williams and López (and its theoretical elaboration in Crenshaw's work) has important corollaries in the literary realm, as evidenced in the works of minority authors who serve witness to the more pragmatic effects of the legal and educational institutions. Inasmuch as works of minority artists mirror the "guerrilla writing" I have been describing, they critically review historically situated interactions with the court and with the academy. Like the legal scholars discussed above, these artists appropriate rhetorical options in order to alter a cognitive framework and in so doing recondition reception itself. Academic interaction between literary studies (or more conventionally cultural contexts) and the law has, of course, taken off during the recent years. It is possible to conjecture a variety of reasons for the emergence of the legal sphere as a central component of U.S. culture (including the consolidation of the academy's role as a perpetuator of nationalism in the face of a displacement by mass culture). Whatever the reasons, these comparative analyses now suggest a dialogue between legal and literary institutions which previously was hindered by the supposedly distinct reading strategies of these disciplines. As suggested by Kelman, Crenshaw, and Guillory, one outcome of this dialogue includes a rethinking of canonicity and tradition and their role in reproducing a particular rhetorical constellation crucial to an institution's functioning. At stake are definitions of inequity that pit the experience of systematic injustice apart from the experience of merely "accidental" or "coincidental" injuries, as might occur when certain groups of students or particular types of works fail to meet assumedly neutral standards of excellence.

In large part, the film *Stand and Deliver* (1988) is about exactly this sort of rethinking. A narrative detailing the unorthodox yet highly successful teaching methods of a math instructor at East Los Angeles's Garfield High School, this docudrama (directed by Ramón Menendez) tells how the Educational Testing Service attempted in 1982 to disallow an entire class's exceptional Advanced Placement scores on the grounds that a conspiracy must have occurred for the Chicano students to have all performed so uniformly well. As the film reveals, the scores were reinstated when the Educational Testing Service was forced to admit that it was Jaime Escalante's unique, noncanonical pedagogy, and not an unfair advantage, that affected the scores. If we think of the narratives Escalante wove into his math lessons—for instance, his contextualizing of "zero" as a concept originating in pre-Columbian culture—we begin to appreciate the power of guerrilla tactics. Such stories have an impact not simply because they rewrite history for Chicano students, although this fact surely empowers the students by making the math their own. The very incorporation of the culturally specific stories radically remakes canonical education for these students; living history becomes part of a supposedly cold and distant knowledge, even as history itself transgresses its traditional boundaries.

A history of this retaking of historiography, *Stand and Deliver* is an example of guerrilla tactics, one which approaches the question of neutral standards in order to demonstrate that, even with an educational system so biased toward the worldview of Anglo upper-class children, it is possible to create successful rhetorical alternatives.

By positing a crucial distinction between reading institutional histories in order to recover elided participants, events, and perspectives, and reading the histories in order to explore how they might rethink historiography and the battle over historical rhetoric itself, I argue throughout the course of this study that more attention should be devoted to the ways in which Chicano historiographic assertions (complete with their own notions of effective change) challenge canonical interpretive practices and the broader effects of underdevelopment. Such study may be engaged fully only if we understand the ways in which the academic framework is ideologically structured around liberal-legal notions of agency, notions that give priority to understanding struggles between individualistically vested interests and pluralistically based consensus rather than to understanding historically and culturally situated conflicts as they pertain to the dependency of social groups.

To sketch the limitations of institutional change as they have affected Chicano studies specifically, I will begin this chapter by examining arguments regarding Chicano canon formation; by doing so, we may both consider the structures which underlie conventional rhetorics of race and pose the following interrelated problems: (1) What pressures have come to bear in the process of defining a Chicano alternative to the canon? (2) What rhetorical conventions from traditional literary history are worthy of appropriation? (3) What new methods of organization should be explored? As a bridge to this more specific approach, it will be helpful to consider the larger context of race as a criterion within U.S. literary studies. Henry Louis Gates, Jr., points out that race has remained a "persistent yet implicit presence" in twentieth-century literary criticism.[12] According to Gates, the peripheral existence of racial issues should not be taken as a sign of their unimportance as viable categories of interpretation; instead, the status of racial issues "on the border" of literary studies must be regarded as a sign of their assumed status (8–9). Although mostly unrecognized, this borderline quality does in fact play a crucial role in the production of the canonical identity. Insofar as racial issues have acted as the impure elements to be purged or sacrificed, they admit a certain cultural demarcation between the "legal" and the "illegal," between sociopsychically ingestible and noningestible subjects.[13] However, the ritual sacrifice has had its price. In *The Poetics and Politics of Transgression* (1986), Peter Stallybrass and Allon White have formulated this debt in terms of "a psychological dependence (on the part of the sociosymbolically high, or the hegemonic culture) upon precisely those others who are being rigorously opposed and excluded at the social level." According to Stallybrass and White, the core culture incorporates the peripheral symbolically, "as a primary eroticized constituent of its own fantasy life," and it is in this sense that "what is socially peripheral is so frequently symbolically central" (5). With such a conception, we may start to rethink the often contradictory forces that affect the reception of race and racially coded subjects.

Stallybrass and White's theory is particularly useful for examining conventional adoptions of Chicano material in hegemonic contexts inasmuch as it helps explain the apparent contradiction posed by the production of highly popular cinematic stereotypes—including seductive yet criminally prone Chicanos—within a society that politically underdevelops their real-life counterparts. Once identified as part of a larger sociosymbolic "contract" described by Stallybrass and White, this figurative exploitation begins to reveal key elements, or constitutive relations, inherent in the construction of the hegemonic worldview (and hegemonic subjectivity generally). These constitutive relations, including the "criminal" scapegoating of Chicanos, purposefully negate the potentially transformative aspects to be found in Chicano narrative practices by legitimating particular types of reading practices. Resistant practices are thus selectively underdeveloped while stereotypes of the culture, ones which satisfy a certain token and erotic function, are fostered. Given that the academy's reading of Chicano resistance must face similar pressures, more dialogues need to be undertaken which will encourage an explicit self-examination of the academy's complicity; among the critical levers which would assist such debates, the implications for canon formation posed by Chicano works remain indispensable.

CHICANO CANON FORMATION

> When the validity itself of the applicability of the term Chicano is under severe question not only in the community but also among writers, can we rightfully expect there not to be a questioning of what the value of ethnicity is in a text or even of which values are more or less authentic?
>
> Juan Bruce-Novoa, "Canonical and Noncanonical Texts"

Published in 1986, at a time when reevaluation of the Chicano movement was in full swing, Juan Bruce-Novoa's article "Canonical and Noncanonical Texts" stands out as a landmark attempt to sketch a history of Chicano canon formation. While acknowledging the need to recognize institutional and particularly canonical processes affecting Chicano literature's reception (an inevitable result of editorial and curriculum decisions), Bruce-Novoa finds little in the way of a contemporary critical consensus capable of answering the basic questions which confront Chicano cultural studies. According to Bruce-Novoa, these questions include (1) how should the literature be differentiated from mainstream literature? (2) how will the recognition of Chicana writers redefine the literature? and (3) how should specifically alternative literary institutions be developed? The first issue—that most thoroughly treated by Bruce-Novoa—imposed itself with some force after the disclosure of racial impersonation by Daniel James, who published the award-winning novel *Famous All over Town* as "Danny Santiago," a supposedly Chicano writer, in 1983. A crucial moment for the burgeoning field of Chicano literature, this scandal brought national attention to the process of defining Chicano identity. Even so, it is far from clear that an improvement in the general understanding of Chicano issues has been achieved, especially given the responses by prominent members of the academy, most notably Roberto González Echevarría's claim that no harm had been done since literature is about lying anyway.[14] On other occasions, however, sincere efforts have been made to understand the status of non-Chicano writers who are quite successful at conveying a sensitivity to Chicano perspectives. For instance, Antonio Márquez has argued that John Nichols's novel *The Milagro Beanfield War* (1974) deserves "insider" status even though the author "fails the blood test" (qtd. in Bruce-Novoa 127). In trying to resolve these disputes and thereby lay down certain guidelines, a number of critics have suggested formal categories such as "chi-canesque writing" to designate works by "almost-Chicanos."[15] In addition, Raymund Paredes has argued for a notion of learned ethnicity, using the example of Chester Seltzer, who married a Chicana and settled in El Paso, hence making, in Paredes's opinion, a successful crossing of cultural boundaries (75). Such attempts to set boundaries have a distinct cultural legacy, being a distant extension of Spanish colonial legal practice wherein defendants were initially presented to the court with a verification of their racial/blood status; as in the current literary context, the interpretation of transgression and censure depended on racially coded parameters.

One can easily sympathize with Bruce-Novoa's ironic, if somewhat desperate, tone as he recounts this contemporary situation—a tone which is particularly evident at the close of his essay. The penultimate paragraph of the argument lists a collection of valuable authors, authors whom Bruce-Novoa asserts deserve critical attention; then a final statement quickly reasserts a division between "practicing canonization" and "criticizing the process," cutting off the rapid citing of appropriate works. While his sense of urgency is clearly situated in the political pressures which Chicano narrative must address within the academy, I would argue that Bruce-Novoa's relatively traditional assumption of a split between creating and interpreting the canon contributes to his predicament. This final dichotomy promotes a judicial vision of Bruce-Novoa criticizing the canonical process from a "disinterested," if latently ironic, position. However, the complexity of Bruce-Novoa's many implicit positions within his essay denies this vision. While it is true that at various points he refers to the consensus of critics and of the reading public in general, his clearly subjective attitudes regarding these opinions remain relatively clear. For example, looking back on the constraining and centralizing ideology of the Chicano movement during the 1960s and 1970s, Bruce-Novoa turns to the works of John Rechy and Oscar Zeta Acosta, noting the manner in which these novelists convey a subtle but clear subtext of criticism directed at the overly restrictive ideological criteria that often accompanied utopian notions of Chicano identity.

In the final lines of the essay, Bruce-Novoa's "corrective" project receives explicit treatment as he argues that "our rather incestuous focus has prevented us from looking beyond the circle of recognized or recognizable Chicano writers to find new and possibly important authors" (132). In the course of the essay, this "incestuous focus" is discussed in terms both of a particular, legitimated group of texts and of prevalent reading criteria or methods. Bruce-Novoa responds to the former by incorporating "new" works, yet at the same time— and this is the point I wish to underscore—he revises criteria, thereby exceeding his implicit division between "practicing" and "critiquing" canonization.

Before considering how this secondary, though very important, revision comes about, however, we would do well to define the dynamic which appears to affect the alternative critical project. For instance, the downplaying of the links between practice and critique has affected other "marginal" reworkings of canonization in a manner which leads me to believe that pressures within the separate emergent fields, and the academy at large, at best promote an indirect approach to discussing the criteria invoked and at worst silence the problem after it has been dutifully noted.[16] Given the opportunity for tokenization which confronts cultural critics if they do not address how Chicano narratives resist hegemonic assumptions about reading, future interpretations need to take up explicit discussion of how Chicano narratives challenge accepted criteria. As overworked as canonization arguments may seem, the paucity of critical material on the "new" works alluded to by Bruce-Novoa indicates that it would be most beneficial at this time to reevaluate reading methods in precisely this fashion. Considering the association Bruce-Novoa suggests between the perception of debilitating change and the perpetuation of incestuous conformity to "safe" texts legitimated by the Chicano nationalist project, it may be that the continual influence of Chicano narrative as a viable force depends on the sort of institutional rethinking which opposes canonical criteria at the service of monological or utopian ideology.

Returning to the specific question of Bruce-Novoa's implicit revision of reading techniques, the greatest value of his article lies in its indirect reevaluation of historically situated racial identity as a criterion. Bruce-Novoa grounds this reevaluation on an explicit censure of race when it is treated as a "monological absolute" (126).[17] Although Bruce-Novoa tends to defer to other critics, or to the anonymous pressures of the reading public—even while making the no-

tion of a *"prueba de sangre"* (blood test) an implicit object of satire—
it would appear that, given his endorsement of John Nichols's exclusion, he does continue to support Chicano heritage (both cultural
and genetic) as a criterion (128). His further elaboration of "an inner
circle" of "must read" authors also suggests that an "author who
deals directly with 'Chicano subjects' per se" should take precedence over others (130). These assumptions have predominated in
subsequent treatments of Chicano narrative, and, although specific
methodologies may vary, this overall consistency reflects a certain
"pragmatic essentialism" (i.e., an essentialism chosen as one strategy among others) that goes hand in hand with a desire not to lose
the historical specificity of a diverse community.[18]

It would initially appear, then, that Bruce-Novoa's stance, in
terms of the primacy of racial issues (the author's heritage and subject matter), remains consistent with the tenets of the larger Chicano
movement. However, two aspects of the essay significantly challenge the earlier canonical practices: (1) the turn toward historically
situated critical analysis that assumes more than a principally "cele-
bratory" role for the critic and (2) the assumption of a more dialogic
relationship between conceptions of race and issues of class, gender,
and sexuality. These aspects taken together call for more subtle elab-
orations of the politics engaged by the narratives and may in fact
demand that the canonical/noncanonical approach be reframed in
such a way that "inclusion" as a goal is supplanted by the imple-
mentation of reading strategies that better serve the elaboration of
Chicano perspectives and history (even while such strategies might
make use of non-Chicano texts). Such an approach is exactly what
we find in more recent studies of Chicano narratives like José Saldívar's *Dialectics of Our America* (1991). Identifying a global development of dependency stemming from the rise of capitalism, Saldívar
reads Chicano narratives beside Latin American works and "new
historicist" critical efforts in order to demonstrate a counterhegemonic historiography with a pan-American basis. Likewise, in *The
Mexican Corrido: A Feminist Analysis* (1991) María Herrera-Sobek significantly rethinks the inclusion/exclusion dynamic by rereading
the appearance of (and the historical basis for) women as subjects of
both Mexicano and Chicano *corridos* (ballads). Through archetypal
analysis she develops an alternative historiography, one which,
by virtue of its experimentation, opens doors to aggressive, self-

confident women throughout Mexicano and Chicano history and art. Both Saldívar's and Herrera-Sobek's works suggest a movement toward new critical practices which, by reevaluating and restructuring previously accepted historiographies, transcend the limitations noted by Bruce-Novoa.

As is the case with Herrera-Sobek's work, an important part of the cultural critique undertaken by much Chicana feminist analysis involves working through the implications of the colonial and postcolonial legacy of *prueba de sangre* for the Chicana community. Without question, the vexed issues that Chicana artists have raised have changed the face of Chicano studies, forcing more than inclusion-oriented amendments to syllabi and programs. In works like Gloria Anzaldúa's *Borderlands / La Frontera: The New Mestiza* (1987), readers find a crucial rethinking of Chicano history, one which reformulates content and structure to make gender and sexuality issues primary. Here, as in numerous other recent Chicana narratives, the legacy of *La Malinche*—the "traitorous" translator who aided Cortez and who became the "mother" of Mexico's mixed-blood race—is appropriated as a means of confronting the masculinist utopian desires of racial and political purity. With the specific context of Chicana activism in mind, we may see how this "blood-testing" legacy needs exactly this sort of displacement; it has repeatedly asserted an incestuous "monological absolute of race" in the face of growing demands for consideration of the unique position occupied by women of the community.[19]

Complex approaches to Chicano studies like Anzaldúa's, Herrera-Sobek's, and Saldívar's work from the premise that long-embedded cultural and psychological manipulations have informed structures of power in the New World, structures which have often stemmed from legal practice and have in turn affected historiography generally. Looking to the "origins" of such conflict, Ramón Gutiérrez has recently offered a study of marriage and sexuality in the colonial context that rethinks the play of desire and power, implicitly into the era after the Treaty of Guadalupe Hidalgo.[20] Attempting to address how Chicano artists and cultural critics have in turn reacted to such hegemonic manipulations, Ramón Saldívar elaborates a theoretical point of departure in *Chicano Narrative: The Dialectics of Difference* (1990). Saldívar uses contemporary Marxist criticism to delimit a semantic space for Chicano texts. According to Saldívar, a text does not simply reflect a society or express an ideology; rather, it may intervene and add its own individual voice as well, in some sense transforming the society out of which it has grown. I take this understanding of a narrative's interaction with its historical situation as fundamental. Foremost, it assumes that Chicano narratives carry out a cultural practice that has the potential to reformulate institutional issues, including the continued legalistic marginalization of Chicano communities.

While any number of institutions might be explored for the kinds of systematic discrimination I have associated with legal and literary practices, the question of how these alternative strategies might be "worked through" will no doubt depend in large part on the particular sociopolitical contexts they address. Even so, such cultural reforms, when linked to claims for Chicano narrative, need to challenge wherever possible the insulating vestiges of canon formation which continue to affect publishing and curriculum agendas even while the popularity of the "canonical debate" wanes.[21] As Bruce-Novoa demonstrates, this sort of insulation is exactly what may take over when Chicano cultural critics accept agendas in which the "celebration" of Chicano voices instills a potentially anti-intellectual stance. Such stances are particularly troubling since they seemingly feed off of the antipathy toward critical thinking promoted by recent conservative government administrations, bodies which would constitute the supposed political opposition. Below I take up the academy's larger participation in this antipathy, as evidenced by E. D. Hirsch's "cultural literacy" movement and his disavowal of "critically oriented" pedagogies; however, I turn first to the skeptical reception of theoretical projects in the Chicano academic community so that I might more clearly situate my own project.

The assumed political imperatives of Chicano communities have often been held up by critics who ask whether theoretical perspectives ultimately detract from the messages conveyed by the works under study. Perhaps one of the most explicit statements in this regard comes from Tey Diana Rebolledo, who finds that "we [Chicano critics] have talked so much about theory we never get to our conclusion nor focus on the [primary] texts" (131). Noting Bruce-Novoa's essay and the "desperate search for a theoretical/critical discourse in which to situate what is happening to us," Rebolledo surmises that our involvement in "intellectualizing" costs us "our

sense of our literature and therefore our vitality." While "intellectualizing" has many meanings as Rebolledo uses it, judging by her
conclusion, the project's most destructive aspect is the production
of critical labels, labels which deprive the literature of vitality and
passion while silencing Chicanas in particular. Although one of my
greatest concerns is that the study I have undertaken here reach
diverse audiences with similarly diverse expectations, my own experience of both Chicano and Chicana narratives has reinforced my
impression that they have themselves been consistently theoretical,
if by *theoretical* we understand a form of discourse which comments
on its own and other forms of discourse. Other critics, including
Rosa Linda Fregoso and Ramón Saldívar, have come to similar con-
clusions regarding Chicana efforts specifically, arguing that Chicana
work "is counter-hegemonic to the second power, serving as a critique of critiques of oppression that fail to take into account the full
range of domination."[22]

As I see the situation, then, the excitement of Chicano theoretical
activity lies exactly in its movement beyond encyclopedic categori-
zation and into an analysis of the various processes by which Chicano art has engaged in dialogue with and commented on the artistic and nonartistic languages circulating around it. In general, it may
in fact be much more problematic to take on the role of critic as
celebrator/ventriloquist than it has appeared in the past; as Abdul
R. JanMohamed and David Lloyd have suggested, cultural critics
now find themselves at a juncture where the choices between pursuing "archival" work and theoretical interpretation may no longer be
steadfastly maintained. JanMohamed and Lloyd sum these difficulties well in their introduction to *Cultural Critique: The Nature and
Context of Minority Discourse* (1987):

> One aspect of the struggle between hegemonic culture and minorities
> is the recovery and mediation of cultural practices which have been
> and continue to be subjected to institutional forgetting. Thus archival
> work is essential to the critical articulation of minority discourse. At
> the same time, if this archival work is not to be relegated by the force
> of the dominant culture to the mere marginal repetition of exotic eth-
> nicity, theoretical reflection cannot be dispensed with. Such theory
> would be obliged to provide a sustained critique of the historical con-
> ditions and formal qualities of those institutions which have con-
> tinued to legitimize exclusion and marginalization in the name of
> universality. (8)

At stake here is the justification for assertions of resistance, whether this resistance is located in particular works of art, in criticism, or in more general "practices." One familiar means of ascribing a resistance value to particular works involves recourse on the critic's part to a notion of cultural hegemony, a critical construction which offers an index of a work's political force by exposing its "target." The persuasive quality of notions of cultural hegemony varies greatly; the notion may, for instance, reduce the complexity of narratives and practices identified with a dominant culture, thereby ignoring aspects of internal contestation that could make such works and practices worthy of appropriation or manipulation within a resistant/minority agenda. As Rebolledo suggests, it too often appears as if such adoptions of weak conceptions of hegemony are an uncritical reaction—albeit conditioned by politically committed stances—to those limited rhetorical tools critics find, or do not find, at their disposal. (Literary scholars, for instance, may face such a problem when they react to the methods of their formalist predecessors.) In turn, awareness of such potential limitations fuels Lloyd and JanMohamed's call for a theoretically sensitive approach to the study of interactions between dominant and nondominant cultures. In addition to asserting the need for more subtle notions of how "historical conditions and formal qualities" interact, these calls have, like the CLS and CRS movements, accused institutions of reproducing modes of thought that reinforce cultural forgetfulness and denial. The two assertions, brought together, suggest that more theoretical work needs to be undertaken in determining how historiography legitimates certain rhetorical modes, thereby perpetuating the outlooks and interests of the dominant culture.

Like Kelman, JanMohamed and Lloyd project resistance as an ability to free nonlegitimated options—to challenge, if not escape, those aspects of rhetorical conditioning which perpetuate hegemonic institutional designs.[23] Such freedom is purchased by demystifying a system of legitimation and thereby cutting into the denial and justification it maintains. Inasmuch as such resistance-oriented study constantly finds itself dealing with issues of compromise—control through legitimacy continually asserts itself—cultural critics are compelled to fight their struggles from within contested territory; their tactics are not those of an opposition with its own proper space and history but rather those of the guerrilla insurgent, striking under cover, dissembling, relying on mobility.[24] Even with this imperative to maintain minimal visibility, open affiliation with institutions is sought in such accounts as the critic attempts to represent "minority" perspectives and thereby affect inescapable institutional contexts; thus, in JanMohamed and Lloyd's passage we note the insistence from the outset that the history of legitimation can be regained, that the denied practices and works may be recovered. With this desire for recovery (we may recall Williams's defense of rights discourse in this light), they solidify, however provisionally, a means of translating between the cultural designs of different groups.

The incentive to read Chicano narratives for how they might rethink historiography and the battle over rhetoric itself becomes all the more pressing as we consider the ways in which these narratives might easily be assimilated into an academic framework that is ideologically structured around notions of pluralism, notions that give priority to humanistic universalism and liberal-legal consensus rather than to historically situated cultural conflict. Of course, cultural criticism leveled at the history of this academic pluralism may be instructive in itself; however—as many minority authors seem to agree—other institutional realms may be equally or even more revealing. In particular, the legal realm has received extensive attention from minority artists; one thinks of the legal polemic embodied within the African-American slave narrative, the Japanese-American literature of internment, and the Chicano and Native American literatures of disenfranchisement, to name only the most obvious.

There is of course a significant reason why interactions with the legal realm receive this treatment by artists attempting to work through the historical designs of the dominant culture while recovering and reworking their own minority culture; the law, especially as it is played out in the courts, offers a detailed register of how "official" history functions within a society, revealing what evidence and rhetorics will be deemed admissible or functional in judging a contested event. As evidence of such historiographic and theoretical concern, one need only consider how often critical works by minority artists replace questions of guilt and innocence with queries about motivations and the production and reception of testimony. In such works, minority authors supplement projects aimed at di-

versifying culture or at recovering "lost" strands of history by demystifying not only the more obvious political agendas of institutions but also the rhetorical construction of modes of thought which
promote a denial of minority designs. Working from this perspective, I assume that by accepting a less "incestuous" and more
conflictual field for considering reading methods, Chicano studies
might institute critical practices more properly addressed to the
reading of narratives historically situated on the margin, narratives
which must contend with refashioning their positions from within
a field of Anglo institutional forces. To gain a full sense of how these
forces work in concert to consolidate cultural interpretive options
and of how they are in fact constructed in a dialectical response
to "marginal pressures," I will turn now to E. D. Hirsch's "cultural
literacy" project, a project which has had, without doubt, a tremendous impact on lay and professional notions of educational and
legal reform.

CONSTITUTING CULTURE: E. D. HIRSCH
AND THE NEOCONSERVATIVE STRATEGY

> There is, of course, a very good reason why the principle of
> cultural revision [in the United States] should parallel our
> principle of legal change and constitutional reinterpretation.
> They are fundamentally similar. The Constitution has bibli-
> cal status for the nation.
>
> E. D. Hirsch, *Cultural Literacy*

In the best-selling *Cultural Literacy: What Every American Needs to
Know* (1988), E. D. Hirsch, Jr., proposes to open access to culture by
giving it an encyclopedic conformity; at the same time, though, he
evades questions about his approach's possible complicity in maintaining institutional privileges for certain segments of society. In
particular, by focusing on the nature of data selection (accentuating
the role of the "founder") and its transparent reception (accentuating the passivity of the reader in all but the most schematic terms),
Hirsch presumes a problematic literacy scenario, one which does
not go beyond the sociological model of "learning to read." He
thereby avoids asking how the differential acquiring of literacy is
itself an aspect of the social reproduction of inequalities. While
these limitations in Hirsch's approach may be apparent in a general

sense to many readers, a fuller understanding may be gained by exploring the more subtle manipulations he must make to justify his efforts; here one should not lose sight of the fact that Hirsch is in some sense unique in that he attempts to justify his admittedly conservative defense of canonicity in historical terms. Limiting the broader history of literacy, including the concept's institutional implications, Hirsch's argument appeals to a circumscribed set of rhetorical gestures; these gestures repeat conflicts between reader-response and intentionalist interpretive paradigms, thus strategically limiting the boundaries of inquiry; in this manner the process of interpretation and adjudication is controlled a priori. By presuming to set social groups (for Hirsch the "reading public") into a democratizing process, yet effectively denying any real burden to the present function of educational institutions, Hirsch's "reformist" agenda fails to reconceive the problem of social inequality in any significant way.

One of the rhetorical strategies invoked by Hirsch to facilitate his conservative reform—Hirsch claims his method is "conservative" only in its technique, not in its politics—involves a conflation of functions located in diverse institutions. Ultimately Hirsch funnels institutional bodies as distinct as the schools and the courts into a particularly broad project, serving a grand principle: the achievement of "the fundamental goals" set out by "the founders at the birth of the republic" (145). For Hirsch, all U.S. institutions have legitimate purposes insofar as they reinforce "efficient communication" of the politically unifying cultural understandings which guarantee a secure nation-state (i.e., a communication whose efficiency relies on reducing difference). Inasmuch as Hirsch openly acknowledges the political efficacy of the cultural reform he supports, his argument, maintaining as it does the inclusion of the legal sphere in the cultural, offers a unique opportunity for studying the processes of denial by which contemporary neoconservative educational reformers have reconstructed a notion of cultural tradition.[25] His writings thus allow us to study a larger displacement of problems of method, particularly as these problems pertain to the reading of contested historical events.

In his preface, Hirsch proposes that political liberty requires educational conservatism. Assuming that only access to a common body of information will allow society's disadvantaged to better themselves, Hirsch suggests that a homology exists between cultural access and political engagement. This liberating homology is founded on Habermas's notion of consensual agreement, a scenario in which morality and truth reveal themselves in the "ideal speech situation." While Habermas recognizes that such ideal situations may be difficult to achieve in everyday contexts, he insists (as does Hirsch) that the possibility of proposing them, through counterfactual logic, indicates an ideal, consensual foundation for language. Reworking this approach, Hirsch's homology assumes that, in a nation-state where members gain access to the basic body of cultural material, social amelioration will follow. A concomitant supposition—that political reform will follow from the inclusion of texts "representing" socially marginalized peoples—marks a similar form of political sentimentalism, one which likewise projects changes without adequately theorizing how the variety of discursive and institutional practices involved might deter, or even co-opt, attempts at reform.

Critiquing the homology of cultural representation and political engagement as well as canon-reforming rhetorics of inclusion and exclusion, John Guillory has pointed out that such critically "weak" constructions rely on particularly problematic notions of literacy. The criticism is particularly apposite in Hirsch's case, inasmuch as his literacy is supposedly achieved simply by possessing shared symbols and the shared information the symbols represent (xiv–xv). Premised on a banking concept of understanding, Hirsch's notion of literacy assumes that a recipient passively appropriates "cultural capital," a term Pierre Bourdieu has suggested to describe the use of canonically designated works to create a self-sustaining intellectual economy within the academic institution (*La Distinction*).

Although Hirsch remains vague about the role of context and selection when discussing the transmission of cultural capital, a certain historically oriented rhetoric does make its way into his discourse and ultimately sets him apart from many fellow reformists inasmuch as he at least acknowledges some responsibility for explaining cultural legitimation as a historical process. In terms of addressing how early U.S. cultural texts were selected for canonization, Hirsch posits a point of cultural homogenization early in American history, a formation which Hirsch claims has remained largely unchallenged, although his normative warnings against present cultural fragmentation betray his confidence on this point (90). Anxious to posit the arbitrariness of the homogenization, Hirsch implies that politically invested selection of materials, as a historical factor, was absent from this apparently golden age, an age when—for Hirsch at least—class, gender, and race hierarchies were invisible.

A similar form of denial develops as Hirsch discusses appropriate reading contexts while situating the consumption of canonical materials. Describing the "young student's" absorption of a cultural base, Hirsch acknowledges the inability of the inexperienced receptor to orient a broad range of information in a meaningful manner, at least initially. According to Hirsch, the student will acquire a context through experience in, *and out of,* school. When, however, it becomes necessary to contend with the social factors affecting educational performance, Hirsch is quick to deny the importance of extracurricular experience (114–15); to grant this range of influences legitimacy would lead of course to questions about the larger, nonacademic hurdles restraining academic "success" in particular segments of the population. Hence, the larger historical context of education is schematized, but only in a global fashion which defuses questions about racially determined academic access and performance. Considering the educational impact on such social inequalities would disrupt Hirsch's ideal speech scenario, the very paradigm that supposedly guarantees the various qualities Hirsch associates with literacy: justice, liberty, and equality. Ultimately, social inequalities become recognizable only when we relinquish Hirsch's national security agenda, an agenda which institutionally legitimates the ideal scenario at the expense of minority-group perspectives.

Turning to research on verbal communication, Hirsch argues for the (re)homogenization of culture (and for the deemphasis of political differences) by claiming that "knowing about prototypes [also termed *stereotypes* or *schema* by Hirsch] is essential for understanding how we apply past knowledge to the *comprehension of speech*" (51; my italics). Rather hastily transferring this finding to the context of reading, Hirsch credits readers in general with a limited flexibility in selecting appropriate stereotyping models through which to compare and make sense of material in a text. However, Hirsch proceeds to defend his extensive cultural imperative (i.e., the need for acquaintance with a national set of stereotypes) by reasoning that the process of consuming information could become too halting (i.e., not sufficiently economic) if a strain on the reader's short-term memory made the search for a given stereotype less than automatic (53). The change in focus, from everyday, simple speech situations to supposedly reflective reading, allows Hirsch a very tenuous space for overstating the pitfalls of short-term memory (texts can be, and often are, reread). Further, this shift from speech to reading contexts encourages a notion of reading and understanding based on a particularly limited exchange of transparent information: readers become passive receptors seeking deposits, exercising choice only in a fleeting, virtually automatic realm of short-term cognition. While it is not difficult to see the advantages of Hirsch's program for employers seeking an easily trainable, politically dependent work force, it may be less obvious that the program is determined not by a concern for the intricate problems of literacy but rather by Hirsch's reverence for a concept of nationalism which he recognizes "is rooted in a certain kind of division of labor, one which is complex, and persistently, cumulatively changing" (73). For Hirsch, it appears that in the face of the difficulties posed by changing divisions of labor, the complexities of readers', consumers', and workers' interpretations must be sacrificed, inasmuch as they must yield to the model of transparent exchange (a model which, as Kelman notes, is fundamental to the law's utopian vision). Reduced interference between administrator and subordinate thus becomes the overarching goal in a "necessarily" hierarchized system of economic circulation.

In cultural terms, a collaboration with Hirsch's project takes place when it is assumed that canonical texts somehow relate "plain meanings," an assumption that masks the relationship of a text to the reading practices which perpetuate the canon. As Guillory has noted,

> canonicity is not a property of the work itself but of its transmission, its relation to other works in a collation of works. . . . Whatever the relation of the work to its initial audience, it must certainly have other relations as a canonical work, and these are the relations mediated by the form of the canon. The failure to make this distinction is the condition of every invocation of tradition, the supposed reproduction of cultural values by the monuments of culture. (494)

Keeping this point in mind while considering canonical practices, we should look skeptically on the logic of tradition, a logic which posits canonicity as some essential aspect of a text, if we hope to understand the very apparent dangers for Chicano narratives of co-optation and ghettoization; this is particularly true of attempts at canon creation for nonhegemonic traditions. There is perhaps no better example of such dangers than Hirsch's own defense of canonicity. By proposing to codify an extensive encyclopedia of cultural knowledge, and by emphasizing the transparent exchange model of communication, such defenses may well only consolidate already existing institutional practices while perpetuating a larger denial of minority worldviews.

Inasmuch as Hirsch's liberation scenario (cultural conservatism breeds political freedom) self-consciously defends the homology between cultural representation and political engagement by setting forth a particularly capacious anatomy of reading and understanding, it affords a unique opportunity to critique the rhetorical mechanics of a mode of interpretation which synthesizes both legal and literary practices. Through such a critique, we may begin to consider the ways in which dominant institutional discourses are re-created in Hirsch's text in new combinations that may reveal the long-standing complicities between these discourses.

TRANSPORTING THE LIBERAL FORCE/CONSENT DICHOTOMY TO CULTURAL HISTORIOGRAPHY

Hirsch's most explicit development of a coextensive literary and legal hermeneutics may be found in his essay "Counterfactuals in Interpretation." Anthologized in Sanford Levinson and Steven Mailloux's *Interpreting Law and Literature: A Hermeneutic Reader* (1988; hereafter *ILL*), the essay is situated among a variety of debates focusing on the interpretive relationship between the Constitution, its framers, and its present-day readers. Throughout this collection, contributions are united by an interest in the necessary translation which takes place between different historical contexts; whether the articles engage rhetorical politics, the lawmaker's intention, historically situated reading conventions implicit within texts, or arguments about the transcendent attainment of an objective perspective, all assume explicit positions with regard to historical understanding as such.

In Hirsch's essay the translation between temporal contexts takes two forms: (1) the "responsible communication" approach, identified with counterfactual logic, and (2) the "interpretation-as-exploitation" approach, identified with "unconstrained accommodation" of a text to concerns located in the interpreter's present. While both models emphasize the role of the reader, Hirsch distinguishes the latter as the form tending toward "intellectual simplicity," the form which "never has to submit to the uncertainties and complexities of historical speculation" because "[interpretive] decisions are based ultimately on nothing more stable or open to inquiry than the preferences of those readers who happen to be in power." Quite unlike the affirming approach Hirsch brings to bear on the "arbitrary" rise of American culture in *Cultural Literacy,* his assumptions here mark arbitrariness of choice as a chief intellectual defect; even so, Hirsch acknowledges that such "exploitation of what comes down from the past is a way of making something valuable out of the past" (*ILL* 57), a notion very much in keeping with the concept of cultural capital and the larger claim I have made that *Cultural Literacy* is more concerned with creating a malleable workforce than promoting literacy. Underlying Hirsch's distinction between his models is the notion that the complexities of counterfactual interpretation may significantly overcome the arbitrary interpretive impositions of those "who happen to be in power." While Hirsch's essay argues that "a context of intellectual freedom" makes the exploitation model "unacceptable," *Cultural Literacy* suggests that in actual historical circumstances both models tend to operate simultaneously, even in complicity; at least this would seem to be the message as the book becomes more explicit about the process of legitimation which grounded the consensual model quite literally on the arbitrary one.

Hirsch's codification of these particular models itself marks a crucial step in the process of limiting interpretive practices. What is at stake is not—as Hirsch would have us believe—discovering the more correct approach, the one which will more honestly approximate the character of a historical person or event. The sort of local truth either of the methods might claim remains secondary to the larger assertion of the methodological dichotomy. Inasmuch as this binary pairing re-creates the force/consent dichotomy (transposed to arbitrary power versus counterfactual reasoning and, assumedly, agreement), it fulfills the first objective of liberal institutions: legitimation both of coercion and of the hegemonic process itself.[26]

This institutional self-preservation drives Hirsch's argument inasmuch as it leads him to posit once again an ideal communicative scenario. However, in this instance Hirsch is much more explicit about the historical models which would ground the idealized exchange. The initial historical model offered by Hirsch assumes that, by appealing to an admittedly otherworldly transhistorical significance (grounded in the rather simplistic notion that "one has to have a lot of relevant knowledge" [*ILL* 63]), a reader may correctly translate a text into an unstable, present frame of significance. At the conclusion of the essay, Hirsch outlines his second, larger model of history, of which the first is but a part. In this larger model an explicitly religious notion of intellectual historical progress is premised on the Christian theory of biblical accommodation. Here Hirsch argues that both legal and literary canonical practices follow the same model of historical progress, in which "valid" advancement may be determined by the fidelity of particular interpretations to sacred "ur-texts," including the Constitution. By positing such unquestioned ur-texts, Hirsch fosters an approach which limits questions about how different argumentative starting points (points other than liberalism) might occasion different notions of historical change. Of course, cultural collaborations between literary and legal precedence play a crucial role in this regard.

The notions of continuity and transformation found in the essay, valid though they might seem in the majoritarian rhetorical context, are insufficiently sensitive to the legitimating institutional problematics we have been considering.[27] As Mark V. Tushnet has noted in a different context, such liberal-rhetorical mechanics drastically affect the construction of historical understanding itself, positing a self-negating enterprise. Concerning liberally grounded historiography, Tushnet argues that "interpretivism and neutral principles attempt to complete the world view of liberalism by explaining how individuals may form a society"; however, "the communication assumptions of conservative social thought" form "the only coherent basis for the requisite continuities of history and meaning" (*ILL* 195). As exemplified by Hirsch's liberal attempt to reform education, the notion that a consensus can always be reached about the plain meanings articulated in key texts relies on a reassertion of socially conservative notions, notions presuming "that we can understand what we think and do only with reference to the [dominant] social matrix within which we find ourselves" (*ILL* 195). Such an assertion posits a fundamentally reactive posture. While the turn to the social matrix, as Hirsch would construct it, necessarily and purposefully denies those interpretive pressures brought to bear by marginalized social groups, the rhetorical move nonetheless reveals an inevitable response to those pressures.

ALTERNATIVE RHETORICAL-LEGAL STRATEGIES, CHICANO NARRATIVE, AND CULTURAL RESISTANCE

As one might suspect, most of the essays collected in *Interpreting Law and Literature* describe historical understanding in a similarly binary manner: their models of interpretation either (1) suppose the possibility of consensual agreement about the advancement of certain traditions (based on the reader's access to transhistorical conventions, intentions, plain meaning, etc.) or (2) deny such a possibility, instead supporting visions of atavistic power struggles in which relativism invites a chaotic field of competing subjectivisms. Exceptions to this binary limitation may be found in the final section of the anthology, which is entirely devoted to revisionary methodologies instituting a more rhetorically sensitive approach to interpretation. These essays argue primarily for case-study analyses which would implicitly elaborate on Kelman's investigations of denial mechanics and of displaced counterhegemonic modes of thought. These approaches suggest a program of study that would reframe apparent critical impasses, inherent in liberalism, with different rhetorical options in order to reapproach problems of adjudication and interpretation.

In the case of James Boyd White's essay "Judicial Criticism," the primary critical impasse to be explored concerns the conflict between rights of privacy and government intervention, as it was raised in *Olmstead v. United States* (the 1928 case which initiated questions about wiretapping). Rather than asking questions about the "correctness" of the opinions handed down, White instead asks how the two primary opinions offered by Justices Taft and Brandeis constitute a "conversation" that defines "us." While "us" is coded variably—the term is associated with courtroom actors, individual citizens, the community, and the Constitution—two presuppositions stand out in White's development of the question. First, courtroom interpretation has a performative aspect which calls into being certain rhetorical roles which are often assumed uncritically; second, the implications of this performative aspect extend far beyond the boundaries of the court and in so doing present questions about the responsibility extending to all participants—but particularly the judges—to engage rhetorical practices that create opportunities for significant dialogical conflict. Celebrating Brandeis's opinion, White argues that one particular rhetorical practice initiated by the justice opened such doors: the incorporation of a vernacular voice. As a response to Brandeis's attack on Taft's literalist reading of the Constitution, this incorporation of the vernacular points, according to White, to a more democratic, dialogic engagement of society's voices. Inasmuch as such engagement is understood as unendingly conflictual, White poses it as a process of continual translation taking place through changing rhetorical presuppositions.

The judge and accepted legal procedure, of course, dictate to a great extent the rhetorical options of any given proceeding and thereby condition processes of translation or mock dialogue. However, as Crenshaw points out in "Race, Reform, and Retrenchment," beyond the results of particular decisions—even beyond the mass-media reproduction of legal thinking within society at large—there lies an arena where notions of social justice and social interaction are conditioned by powerful racial dynamics. While there is ample evidence of the existence of these racial dynamics (statistics treating education, poverty, incarceration, employment, institutional participation—just to name some of the most obvious), there is also ample evidence that these racial dynamics are maintained through processes of denial and legitimation, processes which are very much dependent on aspects of legal rhetoric. It is for this reason in particular that Chicano artists often focus on legal interactions with the dominant culture; while their goal in re-creating legal events is often received as a form of historical "correction" (with supposedly limited significance because of the topical nature of the subject matter), such an understanding misses the radical aspects of the engagements. As I will demonstrate, these aspects are manifold, yet clearly linked by a rhetorical manipulation of cultural translations and mock dialogues drawn from the official record of historical-legal performances. Hence, in works like Oscar Zeta Acosta's *Revolt of the Cockroach People* (1973), Luis Valdez's *Zoot Suit* (1981), and Robert Young's *Ballad of Gregorio Cortez* (1983), interpreters only begin to understand the more subtle aspects of the projects once they take into account the ways in which the works—via a focus on the production of testimony rather than on questions of guilt or innocence—offer their own dialogically attuned formal responses to the historical mock dialogue of the courtroom. What I am describing is far from a "trashing" of the law in the CLS sense, although the Chicano critical process certainly works from a finely tuned skepticism. However, as we will find throughout this study, the Chicano artists and critics considered here build on legal ideals in order both to critique the shortfalls of the legal process and to offer their own revised processes, often embedding them within the subtle formal structures of the works themselves.

Law may well serve as a tool of repression but it may also be used to project a radically new form of legality that cannot be achieved within present institutions.

Ramón Saldívar, *Chicano Narrative*

Treated as participants within the broader scope of cultural critique, Chicano narratives are frequently assumed to manifest resistant approaches to the discourses of institutions controlled by and for the dominant Anglo culture. Ramón Saldívar's recent study of Chicano literature, for instance, focuses on the narrative strategies employed by Chicano authors to demystify the relations between minority cultures and dominant culture; in doing so, he offers a conflictual notion of history which stresses an inevitably ideological "dialectics of difference." In this dialectics, "resistant" or "oppositional" aspects of culture gain significance inasmuch as Saldívar suggests an inversion of priority in which a society's dominant cultural center comes to be defined, even—to an extent—controlled by those marginalized cultural pressures to which it reacts (10–11). Saldívar, in turn, subtly describes such resistance as negotiations acted out in

narratives he has selected—narratives which constitute one historically organized trajectory of Chicano culture. As he notes with reference to Oscar Zeta Acosta's novel *Revolt of the Cockroach People*,
legal relations may become, among the variety of institutional dynamics studied by Chicano authors, a potentially liberating field
inasmuch as they may be manipulated to offer new conceptions of
social justice through a revision of historical understanding in general. Building on this notion, Saldívar takes up the more specific
question of how particular disenfranchised groups address the rhetorical continuum between translation and mock dialogue. Within
Chicano narratives devoted to legal questions (such as *Revolt of the
Cockroach People*), one would expect a more focused endeavor centered on questions of how liberalism refuses to recognize the perspective of marginal groups and victims of racism; this project
would oppose the manner in which the courts decide racial issues
by focusing on an individual perpetrator's explicit actions. However,
beyond such critiques an even more basic proposal surfaces; as Saldívar notes of Acosta's novel, this proposal takes the form of refiguring adjudication.

In this refiguring the objective quest for the truth (perpetuated
by the myth of the court's neutrality) is replaced by a conception of
the trial as a performance where success is gauged by a cultural
group's ability to gain a measure of control over the rhetorical options which will be deemed legitimate. Conceiving of resistance in
this way, these artists transcend more simplistic notions of resistance
as opposition to an autonomous "system." What is gained is a
clearer recognition of the rhetorical mechanisms functioning alongside more obvious ideological stances and of the more subtle options for engaging in negotiations with dominant culture; even as
these artists assert the potential for change, they counsel, as do the
CRS writers, a guarded approach, recognizing that resistance is often effectively restrained within the confines of the liberal-legal tradition with its tendency to look on historically marginalized social
groups as artificial constructions.

The critical demeanor toward liberalism, informing a wide range
of Chicano texts, subsequently extends to the most basic ideological
representations of the law's function. For instance, mainstream U.S.
legal thinking supposes that the public's consent to "the rule of law"
is essential if the system is to work successfully—if it is to achieve

justice. Such legal thinking assumes foremost that a choice exists between force and the solicitation of consent. Since the history of Anglo and Mexicano/Chicano interaction is one of territorial occupation through legal manipulation working in concert with violence, it comes as little surprise that consent, as framed in the mainstream manner, is significantly challenged by Chicano texts: consent cannot be the cornerstone of justice where choice has not played a significant role. This is doubly true of the representation of consent in Chicana narratives, where the critique of the force/consent dichotomy is embedded in a larger dismantling of patriarchal manipulations. In both Chicano and Chicana narratives, the consent/force dichotomy exists, from the nonlegitimate victim's perspective, as a rhetorical tool promoting discrimination at the very least, and most often outright disenfranchisement.

In terms of a tactical appropriation of legal discourse, an appropriation which elaborates both a general rhetorical approach to group power and specific consensual twists, Luis Valdez's *Zoot Suit* offers a particularly rich example as it reexamines the zoot suit riots which occurred in Los Angeles during the early 1940s. The play and its film adaptation focus on a trial in the 1942 death of a youth at a Los Angeles swimming hole (Sleepy Lagoon) popular with Chicanos who were essentially barred from public swimming facilities. What made the prosecution of the Sleepy Lagoon case unusual, and the aspect that Valdez focuses attention on, is the scapegoating of an entire "gang" by the courts and media; twenty-two youths in all were tried on conspiracy charges during courtroom proceedings that could at best be called biased.[28] Valdez's treatment of these proceedings is scathing, but, as Charles Ramírez Berg points out, Valdez's most innovative response may in fact be the creation of El Pachuco, a Chicano version of a trickster figure who also acts as a kind of "one man Greek chorus."[29] This cynical figure accompanies the audience through the crime, trial, and appeal, complementing the more earnest leader of the gang, Henry Reyna, in a way that suggests a mirroring of the antithetical relationship Chicanos feel toward the law: an ardent suspicion juxtaposed to a steadfast faith in civil liberties. The two characters carry on a bantering dialogue about the law throughout *Zoot Suit*; they thus act as cultural translators who expose for the audience the complex psychological turmoil that is finally placed in the audience's lap as Valdez, by offering multiple endings, forces the viewer to "join the action."

Both the dramatic and cinematic versions also shift the audience's focus away from the ostensibly central crime of a Pachuco gang, turning the audience's critical gaze instead on the variety of historical "crimes" which were perpetrated against the Chicano community by a xenophobic Anglo society caught up in wartime paranoia and primed for scapegoating. Although a conventional courtroom drama builds toward the revelation of the guilty party, in this work the audience's gradual recognition of a possible murderer is crucially displaced by Valdez's interrogation of the multitude of panoptic strategies exercised by the press and the courts; these strategies distort the cultural image of the Pachuco, purposefully misrepresenting it in order to exacerbate existing racial tensions (the historical criminalization of the zoot suit apparel is but one sign of this effort). Henry never deliberates about assuming the guilt of the implicit murderer (his brother Rudy) because the option would alter nothing in terms of the community, in terms of the power dynamic being played out between groups; Henry and the other gang members know that, whatever the moral implications of Rudy's act, the institutional process desires a scapegoat foremost.

The problem of Rudy's guilt remains irrelevant because the courts do not present a viable remedy; Valdez thus displaces Rudy's role in order to sustain one version of a Chicano community perspective. The move is, of course, crucial inasmuch as one of the larger efforts undertaken by the film includes turning a very cautious eye toward the interpretive process at play. Reading the "move" becomes more complex as we consider the particular rhetorical pressures which necessarily attend definitions of a Chicano community or its perspective. Such a "homogenizing" process (creating a Chicano worldview) may help crystallize certain perspectives and points for a non-Chicano audience whose primary work is making the cultural translation between their own cultural/historical contexts and the film's. In an analogous manner, the unification may be received by Chicanos as empowering in the sense defined by Crenshaw when she defends the civil rights movement as an era in which African Americans with great differences were able to form strong affiliations as they infused rights discourse with their own interpretive priorities. However, there also exists the possibility that such a uniting might re-create the problems identified with Hirsch's analysis. On this score, *Zoot Suit* and the community it creates are clearly open to question in terms of the representation of Chicana desires.

Perhaps the most interesting character with regard to the question of Chicana representation is Bertha, a raucous Pachuca who could well play a dangerously aggressive role in the narrative were it not for her virtual disappearance early on. Both Bertha and the traitorous "Marijuana" (a Malinche figure brought to life as the subject of one of the play's songs) are contained by Della, a Chicana, who, despite her claims for self-respect, plays a relatively submissive, even self-sacrificial role as she awaits her love, Henry Reyna. Such displacements of aggressive Chicana figures—certainly not limited to Valdez's work—systematically suppose that the most important conflicts for Chicanos are those engaged by men. As I will demonstrate in the final chapters of this study, such assumptions in fact reveal a form of male bonding that is fundamental to the maintenance of male social privilege; for now, though, my primary concern will be analyzing texts in terms of the power dynamics they engage while they favor often problematic notions of "the" Chicano community.

Throughout Valdez's film, the masculine-coded battle for power is associated with a struggle for recognition between the competing perspectives presented by the play. This struggle is quite literally played out in terms of winning control over an audience's gaze. Foucauldian readings of panoptic institutional strategies have taught us a great deal about how processes of hierarchical surveillance and normalizing judgments combine to produce the modern synthetic individual; Valdez's accomplishment includes a demystification as well as an appropriation of these strategies, strategies which the FBI and other agencies used widely and quite explicitly during both the Pachuco and Chicano nationalist periods.[30] In the play, the gazes controlled by the press and the courts take on an increasingly obvious, increasingly defensive role; the character of the reporter in particular becomes all the more desperate to win the attention of the various audiences (on the set and off), seemingly in response to Henry's growing refusal to accept the part of scapegoat. Strength here comes to be defined by how well characters resist the paranoia inspired by the apparently omnipresent observation.

In this manner, the judge—manipulating the power conferred by the gaze—forces the defendants to present themselves in a slovenly, unkempt manner, far from the image of sartorial care characteristic of Pachucismo. The court's revision represents a multifaceted strategy. While the mandatory filth carries a moral message contributing to the gang's "criminality," the revision also penalizes the Pachucos for expressing solidarity through a semiotic code of dress expressing cultural difference itself. The "rewriting" of the zoot suit apparel marks a systematic colonization of, in a broad sense, a community language. Far from irrational expressions of racism, such institutional manipulations aim to reconstruct the available rhetorical options of a given community in a homogenizing manner similar to that described by Kelman with reference to the effects of legal thought.

Propelled by the apparently all-powerful court and press, the attacks on Pachuco solidarity hope to destabilize by accentuating the sort of paranoia that the Pachucos must relive each time they remember being stripped in public by gangs of roving servicemen during the riots. (Paranoia is of course not paranoia if they really are out to get you, as Anglo gangs were out to get Pachucos at the time.) However, Valdez goes beyond the representation of the historical efforts of the institutions (however paranoia-inspiring they might have been), portraying machinations of an extended fantastic order. In the theatrical version of *Zoot Suit*, for instance, a collapse of identities exacerbates the sense of a totally connected system. One of the only hopes for differentiation in this system, at least in the first act of the play, exists in the contrast between Edwards and Smith, the two officers who initially interrogate Henry about the death. An anomaly, Edwards appears willing to entertain Henry's perspective; yet very shortly one finds that the actor playing Edwards has become Henry's official persecutor by assuming the role of the hanging judge. The change bears out El Pachuco's seemingly paranoid reading of the earlier interrogation scene, in which he advises Henry not to trust Edwards but rather to look to the latent significance of his assimilationist yet racist language. Although El Pachuco is apparently omniscient, his role as a paranoid reader has its limits as well, limits self-consciously explored in both versions of *Zoot Suit*; repeatedly, the existential isolationism El Pachuco advocates for Henry as a means of survival becomes a central source of conflict between the two. It is telling, however, that El Pachuco circumvents the height of this conflict by asserting his ability to manipulate the action of the play—by redirecting the audience's gaze toward a Chicano community's perspective on the riots.

In addition to his complex role as a paranoid reader, then, El Pachuco acts as a paranoia-inspiring panoptic force in his own right. The play and the film in fact begin with his transgression of the theater's traditional visual flow; he literally turns the gaze back on the audience, making it the object of his amusement. In both the cinematic and theatrical versions, the control suggested by this change in the dramatic gaze is then exercised by Pachuco through various extradiegetic manipulations of scenes.[31] Such acts culminate as El Pachuco interrogates the other primary manipulator of gazes in the film, the reporter. Chasing the reporter through the audience, rematerializing at various points in the crowd to circumvent his escape, El Pachuco turns the reporter's—and by extension the press's—power against itself by attacking its racism while it is exposed; here we find guerrilla mobility expressed in its most literal form.

This reversal of the gaze, premised as it is on Pachuco's fantastic mobility, intervenes to constitute a corrective framing for the paranoia which threatens, in Foucauldian fashion, to isolate Henry from his community. Denied the ability to alter significantly the institutions of the Anglo society, Valdez turns to a guerrilla strategy of social transformation, one that relies on the weakness of panoptic techniques: their dependency on anonymity. Reversing the gaze, turning it back on institutional designs, Valdez thus effects a reversal with a difference. The distraction created within the official panoptics, and the group appropriation of power, affords a precarious site for Chicano activism, for writing an alternative ending to the institutional script of synthetic individualism and its history. While a potentiality is written into *Zoot Suit* at its close with the collective rewriting of the play, a rewriting made possible by the critical space opened between the press (which attempts to gain the last word) and the various members of the Pachuco community who offer their own readings, the threat remains of not moving beyond the stage of reversal, of not significantly affecting the legal institution or the patriarchy that it helps maintain; the seeming power of the gaze may easily be turned into a means not of opposing hegemonic spaces and histories but of gaining a masculinist entitlement, a point we will explore further in chapters 4 and 5 as we take up the limited representation of Chicanas in male works and the critiques of "consensual" dynamics in Chicana narratives.

To the extent that individual, group, sexuality, and gender dynamics are affected by the legal thought addressed in Chicano narratives, an understanding of why particular artists might accept the consequent risks must begin with a more rigorous understanding of the diverse rhetorical mechanisms against which Chicano resistance is situated; only then can we fully appreciate the difficult process of cultural translation. This work begins when we reframe questions about resistance by recognizing the subtle rhetorical influences underlying more explicit ideological practices; as Kelman suggests, these influences place restraints on conceptions of change while they perpetuate particular institutional designs. Nowhere is this type of metadiscursive criticism more apparent than when we turn to consider the role of the law and legal rhetoric that dominates Chicano narratives; such a great variety of these narratives thematize legal interactions and injustices that, on reflection, one could be tempted to mark the legal-critical moment as a defining thematic of the art. The examples I develop in subsequent chapters are particularly rich in that their forms as well present subtle challenges to the paramount hegemonic voice of their settings. I emphasize this formal experimentation because I believe, as Ramón Saldívar has argued, that some of the most effective resistance set in motion by Chicano narratives derives from a challenging of hegemonic modes of thought which are subtly embedded in formal conventions.[32] As the narratives critique the historically dominant language of rights in U.S. society (with all its formal implications), they set in motion what may be translated as a Foucauldian approach to power and its disciplinary techniques, an approach which constitutes a truly radical literacy. Like Foucault's subtle reading of the interplay between the development of prisons and the rise of such techniques in *Discipline and Punish: The Birth of the Prison* (1977), these works often link more explicit institutional moments—for instance, trials—to latent sociopsychological forces that, along with material coercion, encourage both Chicanos and Chicanas to participate in their own disenfranchisement even while legitimating the process for those who gain privilege through it.[33] In the next two chapters, we will consider these latent forces in specific case studies that will provide a more subtle sense of the dialectical tension between the designs of the Anglo and Chicano communities.

2

Mission Denial

The Development of Historical Amnesia

THE STRUGGLE FOR A VOICE

As the first Mexicano to gain a public voice through radio—specifically through his 1928–1934 Spanish-language "Earlyrisers" variety show—Pedro González plays a crucial role in defining what is at stake in representations of politically active Chicanos and Mexicanos because his experience suggests the complex pressures which may come to bear as such personalities become symbolic figures in their own right for hundreds of thousands of listeners. The most extended and detailed account of González's life comes to us through the film documentary *Break of Dawn* (1988), directed by Isaac Artenstein.[1] As the film's three-way crosscutting indicates early on, González's life was most strongly determined by his commitment to improving the conditions of his community, by his resistance to the staunch repatriation-oriented racism in the 1930s that defined all Mexicanos as wetbacks, and by his survival of six years of confinement and torture in San Quentin—a period which was followed by thirty-two more years of legally imposed exile in Mexico.[2] In response to the repatriation drives (which affected approximately half a million Latinos), and in the face of intimidation by the Anglo political establishment of Los Angeles, González used his groundbreaking Spanish radio show to argue for intensified political response from the Mexicano community, a community which heretofore had remained essentially invisible as far as the city's politicos were concerned.[3]

Reacting to González's efforts, District Attorney Buron Fitts's office harassed González constantly, arresting him on misdemeanor charges that were consistently dropped for lack of evidence and similarly threatening on several occasions to revoke his broadcasting license (Parlee and Espinoza 37). Finally, these authorities fabricated a statutory rape case which garnered the radio personality a fifty-year prison sentence, a sentence which was amended by the presiding judge so that González might, by an admission of guilt, win his parole at the expense of his public voice. Although the principal collaborating witness in the case, Rosa Mazon, contradicted herself blatantly while on the stand, and although Dora Versus, the alleged rape victim, recanted her testimony shortly after the trial (claiming that she had been blackmailed into testifying by the police when she was caught in violation of a curfew), González won a parole only much later (without admission of guilt), thanks largely to the protest organized by Maria González, Pedro's wife, who helped build a combined defense committee membership of more than 100,000 people. This parole-in-exile lasted thirty-two years, finally rescinded only by virtue of a change in California's political leadership. As the film notes at its conclusion, to this day no official recognition of the legal travesty has been granted; González has yet to be fully pardoned although he has been allowed to return to the United States and continues his political activism.[4] As happens with so many of the Chicano narratives, we find here a study of the legal system, a study critically examining how the institution has managed to partially admit its error through its very own confusion but only after effecting disenfranchisement.

Break of Dawn suggests that González's only crime was the crime of transgressing public space, of seeking a public voice which could speak its own language.[5] When González gained this voice, the initial reaction of the opportunist Anglo establishment was to co-opt it. Such action promised the political control of the otherwise untilled, entirely dislocated community. Although the establishment represented in the film was at the same time busy scapegoating the Mexicano community in order to capitalize on the racist sentiments of the broader Anglo public, the promise of political gain clearly outweighed any moral considerations of this contradiction that these leaders might betray. However, when it became apparent that González saw through these machinations and that he would use the radio to expose them, these politicians, and particularly the film's district attorney—given the name Kyle Mitchell—attempt to put the genie back into the bottle by stuffing González into the insular, isolated space that he and the rest of his community initially occupied. The nature of this containing effort is in turn brilliantly captured throughout the documentary, as the viewer continually moves back and forth between González as a public actor and González as a prisoner in solitary confinement at San Quentin.

What remains most powerful about this film is the way in which it demonstrates how popular Anglo constructions of the Mexicano ultimately seek a systematic cultural and physical containment. This critique of containment is reflected in the stylization of the film itself, especially in the repetition of scenes one would associate with clichéd postcard representations of downtown Los Angeles; these scenes, developing a "staged" position for the viewer, suggest a symbolic or allegorical level of interpretation that undercuts southern California's cultural fantasy of Anglo (Spanish) purity. The stylization is just self-conscious enough to make viewers uncomfortable with the images of Los Angeles's tourist-oriented self-representation and thereby warns viewers to read mediums of communication with care—a warning very much in keeping with the film's larger goal of exposing the manipulations behind radio as a burgeoning political tool. This emphasis on the politics of style, in turn, helps call attention to the crucial implications of González's "invasion" of the radio waves. Specifically, the emphasis foregrounds the very effective manner in which González creates a new and powerful affiliation between Mexicano and Anglo cultural forms that is directed at an urban Mexicano population eager for greater enfranchisement.

To understand González's full impact on his chosen medium, it is worthwhile recalling that radio played an important role in refiguring the illusion of the "neutral" and monological information fashioned previously by newspapers. Hence, we find González explicitly framing his advertisements and endorsements as a way of "speaking for" others. His technique projects a self-conscious multivocality and a clear sense that transmissions are mediated. Information may thus be marked as passing through a Mexicano worldview. Were this not enough of a revolution, the film also emphasizes the manner by which radio creates a new, intimate contact with its audience. By watching González slip in and out of his roles as entertainer and product promoter, we thus become keenly aware of how advertising mixes with subject matter to affect desires, to entice buyers.

As a consequence, the film's viewers are sensitized to the great stakes that attended González's success. As a medium that was effective to the extent that it violated earlier barriers between the public and private domains, radio was made all the more potentially transgressive as Mexicano voices gained the power to "seduce" listeners. The technology's alteration of popular libidinal dynamics reinforced new cross-racial linkages like that portrayed in the movie between the Anglo district attorney and the Mexicano assistant district attorney. Hence, the homosocial elements evident in the relationship between these men are very much tied up with gaining control of the radio. As people like González and the assistant district attorney are "courted" by power brokers and then rejected, relationships develop that are given strong overtones of sexual infidelity. This larger suggestion of a libidinal dynamics thus becomes the context within which viewers may read the strategic "appropriateness" of the statutory rape allegations: these accusations manipulate this libidinal economy because the political struggle as a whole is informed by it.

Working with this notion of González's context, I take issue with apologists for the legal system (who too easily dismiss the scapegoating of Chicanos as an aberration, a localized fluke within an essentially just system of social interaction) and with neoconservatives (who see the Chicano narratives as the tainted testimony of discontents who would threaten the United States' political unity with subjective, even separatist criticism); instead, I argue that stories like those of Henry Reyna and Pedro González have everything to do with the threat posed by Chicano access to largely male-controlled public discourse. This chapter focuses in turn on two Anglo texts which have had a broad impact on the popular representation of Mexicanos/Chicanos, two works which might be said to have contributed significantly to a national amnesia with regard to Mexicano and Chicano worldviews: the novel *Ramona* (1884), written by Helen Hunt Jackson, and the film *Giant* (1956), directed by George Stevens.[6] As reformist works—works putatively committed to assimilationist stances that would bring the disenfranchised squarely into the mainstream—*Ramona* and *Giant* attempt to "work through" rather than repeat the scapegoating dynamics they single out for criticism.[7] Despite these reformist intentions, in both *Ramona* and *Giant* these public struggles are collapsed into private spaces. Such spaces, removed from the sphere of legal enfranchisement, thus become the only site where Mexicano political desire might be imagined, a fact that is intimately related to the overhasty priority given to assimilationist unity put into motion by Jackson and Stevens. Ultimately, these artists did not sufficiently think through dynamics of social interaction and therefore the larger institutional blocks to equality; hence, the retreat to private space, which these works posit as the only ground for political resolution, uncritically duplicates the message delivered by the Anglo establishment in *Break of Dawn*. As I will argue, the political implications of *Break of Dawn* which could be developed in *Ramona* and *Giant* are replaced in these reformist works by a legally inflected domestic romance that effectively sentences Mexicanos to a silent, withdrawn existence—to a "solitary confinement" that may well appease Anglo audiences who want to identify with, and thereby share, the experience of victimization in a manner that does not expose their complicity in the initial or ongoing disenfranchisement.

It follows that a study of Pedro González's attempt to win a public voice for his community, of the resistances which he calls forth, and of his filmic re-presentation points toward a critical approach to the specifically legalistic rhetoric that informs *Ramona* and *Giant*. In fleshing out this legal context, we may begin by noting that both *Ramona* and *Giant* are about rights to service, if service is taken to be respect for larger civil rights supposedly guaranteed to Mexicanos by the Treaty of Guadalupe Hidalgo. In a most basic sense, such rights begin with the protection of a public voice, something subtly yet effectively denied in the reformist Anglo texts studied here. Of course, *Break of Dawn* posits a similar loss of voice, but it does so critically, and inasmuch as the film is a product of a multifaceted Chicano collaborative effort, it becomes its own counterexample: its politics are not insulated in a romantic or sentimental way but rather remain irreversibly public. Any doubts about this fact are challenged immediately in the film. The opening scene—a confrontation between González and a prison official over González's use of Spanish in letters written for his fellow inmates—resonates deeply with current debates about English as an "official" language.[8] At issue in these debates, and in the prison scene, is the question of how our institutions will accommodate the process of cultural translation which must occur whenever Chicanos and Anglos interact, and perhaps more important how institutions will control the transmission of Chicano public discourse, especially in its Spanish medium. "English-only" proponents (the U.S. English organization in particular) often evade these issues of translation and control by falling back on arguments about the danger posed to national unity by a policy supporting multiculturalism, a strategy that clearly recalls the scapegoating tendencies illuminated in films like *Zoot Suit* and *Break of Dawn*.[9] Such English-only approaches fail to recognize that we need to examine dominant attitudes about biculturalism in the United States as historically and culturally specific moments always contending with ideological interests.[10] Viewed as such, these attitudes tell us much about the acceptance of Chicano/Mexicano public voicings and about the difficulties of representing or effecting such enfranchisement through cultural products like novels and film.

Although bilingual education saw a resurgence in the Southwest during the 1960s—largely a result of gains made by the civil rights movement (gains which were translated into law in the 1968 Bilingual Education Act and the 1974 Supreme Court decision in *Lau v. Nichols*), more recently the bilingual mandate has been open to erosion, particularly in the courts. As a response to the revitalized bilingualism of the 1960s and 1970s, and the rapid growth of Latino populations in the Southwest, the 1986 California English Language Amendment likewise erodes gains that would break through the U.S. historical amnesia that underdevelops Chicano voices. Unlike similar laws, the amendment specifies a process of enforcement that allows private individuals to sue the state. The function of this "process" is far from clear in the law's apparently contradictory statement of purpose: "English is the common language of the people of the United States and the State of California. This section is intended to preserve, protect and strengthen the English Language, *and not to supersede* any of the rights guaranteed to the people by this Constitution" (my italics). Perhaps the most ambiguous question raised by the law is how the institutional delegitimation of a social group's language can avoid impinging on that group's rights; to take the most obvious example, plans have already been made to terminate bilingual voting ballots, violating the United States Voting Rights Act (1965).

Various battles have of course been waged concerning the larger effects of such legislation.[11] But, as James Baldwin has suggested, haggling over statistics and policy details may become a means of avoiding more dangerous issues regarding race and culture, issues that are placed in relief in both Chicano and Anglo art.[12] Rather than recognizing the rights of various cultures within our national boundaries, a recognition which would in turn raise questions about mutual responsibility, the posture of national defense (preservation, protection) promotes nothing less than a scapegoating of Spanish public discourse. Where proponents of such legislation argue that this movement is about the promotion of political unity, most Chicanos know all too well that the stakes are much different, that they are about "rights to service" in the phrase's various senses, and that for many survival hangs in the balance. In broadly political terms, such amendments ensure the cultural insularity symbolized by *Break of Dawn's* prison scenes of solitary confinement; in addition, this sort of law—by guaranteeing the demise of essential programs—threatens the viability of public forums for the majority of Chicanos.

Hence, from the outset when González is portrayed confronting the legal system on this score, *Break of Dawn* throws light on the insulation of the Mexicano/Chicano voice, making the buried goals of the English-only movement and similar efforts an issue of public confrontation; like most Chicano narratives, this film announces itself as an intervention that stands in opposition to previous reformist undertakings and their "Mission" influences, influences which have come to shape the popular (mis)understanding of Chicano communities. But to fully appreciate this crucial aspect which informs so many Chicano projects, we must consider carefully those cultural precedents which have helped shape the interaction between Chicano and Anglo culture, including those which ask us to "step inside" Anglo fantasy, or, as I suggest in the final part of this chapter, inside the giant's castle.

THE MESTIZA WITHIN

Conceived by Helen Hunt Jackson as a complement to Stowe's *Uncle Tom's Cabin* (1852), the novel *Ramona* was intended to fuel a similar outrage which would likewise ignite political reform, this time in the name of the "Mission Indians" (Jackson's phrase). What actually took place was far from Jackson's intention. Instead of provoking an outcry over treatment of Native Americans, the novel won the affection of many faithful readers for its romantic plot, a plot which eventually reunites the title character, a cultural and biological mestiza, with her foster brother, the pure-blooded Spanish *hacendado* Felipe Moreno. Further, the novel frames its description of Native American life (caricatured as this representation may be) with a high-caste *Californio* environment befitting a courtly drama in any number of historical romances. This is not to say that the novel entirely fails in conveying the political message that Jackson intended. Her evaluation of the conditions faced by the Native Americans at the time are explicitly rendered through various reflections by her characters. Yet as the reception of the novel has demonstrated, readers may grant the romantic elements such importance that all other considerations become virtually invisible.

Packaged as a "romantic best-seller," the Avon edition of *Ramona* underscores the displacement of historical and reformist tendencies in the work by refusing to note the novel's original context; from the information provided on the cover and title page, a reader without previous knowledge would have no reason to doubt 1970—the only publishing date offered—as the novel's origin. This manipulation of historical context is, however, in line with an important aspect of the novel, one which dominated its original reception as well. As a result of its romantically oriented Spanish framing, *Ramona* ultimately became a lodestar for the re-creation of a historically distanced, and therefore both culturally insulated and politically secure, ethos, Spanish colonial California. With this new notion of "colonial" heritage, turn-of-the-century California—dependent on outside investment because of overzealous infrastructure development—constructed a base for tourism that would manifest itself in such institutional forms as Mission Revival architecture and festivals like the much-noted Fiesta Days held in Santa Barbara.[13]

While it is impossible to know for certain why Jackson left the novel so open for the romantic reading, particular facts are suggestive. Most obviously, Jackson wished to touch the United States's popular consciousness in a way that she had failed to do in her previous book-length invective against U.S. Native American policy, *A Century of Dishonor: A Sketch of the United States Government's Deal-*

ings with Some of the Indian Tribes (1881). This earlier reformist argument offers a series of case histories, differentiated by tribes. The collection is in turn framed by a carefully crafted legal polemic, claiming legitimacy for Indian nationhood on the basis of international law. Although Jackson's careful, rational style in *A Century of Dishonor* makes it clear that her rhetorical strategy will appeal to traditional legal and moral argument grounded in precedence—she explicitly rejects a sentimental stance toward the policies and their results—she nonetheless points out at the close of the work that her reform can be achieved only by touching popular sentiment. Readers may thus find Jackson writing herself into the romance intervention even as she attempts to convince the populace to exercise its influence on the legislature.

Reflecting on this desire and on the failure of the first book, which went largely unread, we may conjecture that Jackson might have been drawn too far toward the popular forms of her day in her desire to move her audience. But can we ultimately assume that this question of form was so completely miscalculated by Jackson, or is there some more complex relation between the romance's reception and the issues she wished to confront? Once finished with the novel, she certainly did not consider it a failure as a reformist effort; however, it was not until years after her death that the novel reached its zenith as an influence on neo-Spanish "revival." For Jackson, this project—as described in one of her letters—was wholly written for the "Mission Indian" cause, as distinct from her own desires. For a good portion of the time she was writing, the manuscript title was "In the Name of the Law," a title in keeping with this explicit desire to give fictional form to a legal argument for compensation already set forth in *A Century of Dishonor*.

Given that *Ramona*'s creation marks a translation from legal to literary realms, a translation that inevitably carries vestiges of the old into the new, we may consider why certain assumptions in Jackson's original legal argument lead her to the wholesale importation of a romanticism that ultimately denies the very issues Jackson hoped to enliven. Examining *A Century of Dishonor*, we find that Jackson cautiously aligns herself with those reformers who seek full enfranchisement and legal citizenship for Native Americans. While she warns that an overly hasty transition, especially in terms of citizenship, would jeopardize more than aid Native American living conditions, she nonetheless endorses a statement made by the Indian Affairs Office in 1857: "The utter absence of individual title to particular lands deprives every one among them of the chief incentive to labor and exertion—the very mainspring on which the prosperity of a people depends" (*Century of Dishonor* 341). This stance is complicated by the fact that government policy had long maintained a significant measure of control over the Native American population precisely by granting individuals ownership of properties on the condition that those who accepted sever their ties with their tribes; as Valerie Mathes points out, the provisions of the Homestead Act of 1862 were extended to Native Americans to weaken larger tribal claims.[14] Even for those reformers who could embrace an entirely assimilationist agenda, this method suggested little improvement once the effects of subsequent taxation were considered, taxation which virtually always ensured that Native Americans would be left landless and without other resources. To Jackson's credit, she recognized this impasse and did not attempt an oversimple solution. In effect, she counsels in *A Century of Dishonor* immediate responses to the most obvious outrages and a continued commitment thereafter to holistic reform. Of these immediate actions, she devotes her greatest energy to revivifying the treaty promises made by the U.S. government.

Employing a variety of classical legal statements, *A Century of Dishonor* presents a clear argument for the fundamentally salutary role of freely given consent in social interactions. Jackson thus attempts to make U.S. legal institutions live up to their ideological claims and therefore support the primacy of consent over force. However, Jackson perhaps inevitably uses the concept of volition in a very strained manner, inasmuch as she acknowledges that Native Americans were legally conceived of as wards of the state during her time. Such assumptions were very strong during this period and were often built on the encouragement given women reformers to pursue their activities, encouragement offered by male legal practitioners, among others, who understood Native Americans as children benefiting from women's "nurturing" proclivity. Given such assumptions about the inabilities of the Native American treaty subjects, we can begin to appreciate the primary cultural work that Jackson's argument neglects. This fundamentally necessary work would include attempting to transpose the treaty issues into a Native American perspective to gain some sense of "agency" and "volition" as those concepts might be conceived by the alternative culture. Instead, Jackson acts out a problematic assumption about social interaction, thereby limiting the reformist power in both her legal history and her novel. Ultimately, this failure set the stage for nothing less than a legacy of historical amnesia as entrepreneurs throughout the Southwest took advantage of the romantic elements of the novel to build a newly exoticized "Mission" culture.

Working from the assumption that "just" interaction between peoples is defined by the resolution of consensual agreements among autonomous individuals, Jackson grounds her legal polemic in *A Century of Dishonor* on the tenet that nations (tribes included) must respect one another as individual people would. With this approach, Jackson simply avoids confronting the racism and stereotypes which existed in the minds of her readers. An apparent victim of what Kelman defines as synthetic individualism, Jackson does not argue that the concerns of nations should supersede other interests. Instead, she explicitly conflates nationhood into personhood. Nations are therefore significant only insofar as they are models for, or are composed of, consenting individuals. In *Ramona* these assumptions lead to two principal failings. First, the Native Americans most central to the plot do not evidence any sustaining links to their community because from the outset they are portrayed as exceptions to their race and to the group logic which obliquely defines it as such. Second, the Mexicanos—who are thoroughly imbricated in a hierarchical caste system—become too much of a focal point for Jackson, indicating a shift in the narrative's overall designs. Led by the desire to present the Mission Indians as *potentially* full-fledged citizens, citizens capable of exercising respected contractual decisions, Jackson creates exceptional Native American characters who are described as standing apart from their race as much as representing it. In the Southwest, where oral and otherwise "informal" Mexican government contracts, especially concerning land, were consistently ceded by U.S. courts to Anglo challengers, written law and the ability to read and write English became a critical sign of transition for Native Americans; those who were literate could, in the eyes of reformers, not only act as intermediaries but also serve as symbols of "positive" potential assimilation. In particular, it appears likely that Jackson wished to exploit this latter aspect when she created Alessandro Assis, a Native American who gains entry into the principal locale of the novel, the Moreno hacienda, by virtue of his "European" musical talents (specifically, his skill with the violin), and who later steals away with Ramona, the mestiza ward of the household (a representative of the blending of Anglo, Native American, and Spanish colonial heritages).

Alessandro's initial success with the Morenos is premised on the exceptional training he received from his father, a training which his own people felt ambivalent about since they found him "a distant, cold boy." This problematic relationship to his village of Temecula "had come, they believed, of learning to read, which was always bad. Chief Pablo had not done his son any good by trying to make him like white men" (53). Ramona as well is repeatedly said to stand apart as a representative of her Native American race, a misnomer throughout the novel since she is undeniably a mestiza (biologically the product of Scottish and Native American blood, culturally a mix of Anglo, Mexicano, and Native American legacies). Her adopted family conceals her heritage from her until she threatens to marry Alessandro. Although Señora Moreno, the matriarch of the hacienda, hopes that the weight of Ramona's high-caste Mexicano upbringing will sway her thinking, the young woman ventures forth with her lover against the señora's commands, trusting instead to her unshakable Franciscan faith.

When Ramona and Alessandro resettle, their exceptional "training" continues to shape their lives in material as well as spiritual ways. For instance, their impoverished acquaintances marvel at Ramona's ability to decorate the poorest of hovels with a formal sitting-room arrangement. These acquaintances, poor Anglo neighbors named Jeff and Ri Hyer, represent an unsophisticated intelligence in the novel that nonetheless models the change in popular consciousness which Jackson would like to produce. As they come to know the exceptional Ramona and Alessandro, the Hyer family goes through a revolution in their thinking:

> Aunt Ri was excited. The experience was, to her, almost incredible. Her ideas of Indians had been drawn from newspapers, and from a book or two of narratives of massacres, and from an occasional sight of vagabond bands or families they had encountered in their journey across the plains. Here she found herself sitting side by side in friendly intercourse with an Indian man and Indian woman, whose

appearance and behavior was attractive; towards whom she felt herself singularly drawn. (277)

This change in the Hyer mentality, and especially in Aunt Ri,
reaches its zenith when she expresses the hope that all whites will
learn to care for their society's "displaced." As we will see, however,
such concern truncates any responsive political organization by
quickly transforming itself into a faith about natural law and the
justice that comes regardless of what people do.

The setting for Ri's "reformist" sentiment is the one context in
which Ramona gains unreserved support from her (anonymous)
Native American community: the aftermath of a tragedy in which
a local Anglo viciously guns down Alessandro after claiming that
he had stolen a horse. The occasion brings forth, as Ri describes, a
communal response:

> "The way the pore things hed jest stripped theirselves, to git things
> fur Ramony, beat all ever I see among white folks, 'n' I've ben raound
> more 'n most. 'N' they wa'n't lookin' fur no pay, nuther; fur they didn't
> know, till Feeleepy 'n' me cum, thet she hed any folks ennywhar, 'n'
> they'd ha' taken care on her till she died, jest the same. The sick allers
> ez took care on among them, they sed, 's long uz enny on em hez got
> a thing left. Thet's ther way they air raised; I allow white folks might
> take a lesson on 'em, in thet; 'n' in heaps uv other things tew. Oh, I'm
> done talkin' agin Injuns, naow, don't yeow furgit it! But I know, fur all
> thet, 't won't make any difference; 'pears like there cuddn't nobody
> b'leeve ennythin' 'n this world 'thout seein' 't theirselves. I wuz thet
> way tew; I allow I hain't got no call ter talk, but I jest wish the hull
> world could see what I've seen! Thet's all!" (336–37)

Perhaps nowhere is the reformist's motive more clearly (yet un-
clearly) enunciated in the novel than in this passage, with its rather
unfortunate attempt at dialect. Even so, had the novel concluded on
this note, it no doubt would have been more successful with regard
to its reform agenda because at the very least readers would have
been asked to imagine those alternate Native American social relations that are alluded to, if not explored, as Ri tries to describe the
group. In other words, readers would be asked to reintegrate the
exceptional character back into the community. Instead, the novel
pursues a forced attempt at individualistic romantic closure: Felipe
Moreno, Ramona's stepbrother, returns to carry Ramona away as his
new bride, thereby re-creating the context of the Moreno household.

As I would suggest by framing this approach to the novel with a reading of *Break of Dawn*, the forced reentry of the sentimental domestic conventions effectively models a form of cultural solitary confinement. The newly contained Ramona reclaims her hacienda legacy, including the family jewels, and what is Native American (or, more properly, racially "crossed") in her becomes safely contained in a closing vision of her passive young daughter (a literal infantilization) and in an occasional memory of Alessandro's voice lovingly calling Ramona by her Native American name, Majella or "Wood Dove." The process, and its assimilationist assumptions, concludes when Ramona agrees to raise her daughter severed from the ties of her race; as was the case with Ramona herself, this child will grow up not knowing her Indian mother.

Although the name Majella may signify Ramona's Native American identity, the novel's narrator uses "Ramona" in all but the most unusual circumstances—that is, when the character ventures angry criticism of U.S. policy. The final pages bear out this assumption about Ramona's unshifting identity; hence, the narrator's language marks Ramona's journey into the Native American community as a venture and little more. Ramona's options in the novel only gesture toward the possibility of accepting "Indian" status. As in Alessandro's case, her exceptional upbringing ironically sounds a death knell for her complex heritage, and especially for the recognition of her existence as a mestiza. This latter position is so forcefully written out of the novel that it becomes its missing symbolic center. Between the three idealized families which make up the world of this "historical novel," the Morenos, the Hyers, and the Assis, there exists a rapidly growing population of impoverished mestizos entirely displaced by Jackson. Jackson could not have avoided contact with this population during her visits to California, and she certainly learned of it from the high-caste Californios whom she interviewed; and these Californios were very much aware of the tremendous racially defined changes—inextricably linked to political, economic, and sexual conflicts—that had thoroughly devastated the once securely ensconced hacienda class. In fact, the essential demise of this caste was complete in all but a few enclaves during the period of Jackson's visits to the Southwest. Judging from Jackson's framing of the novel, her romanticization of the caste system is linked to the parallel legal treatment both the Californios and the Mission Indians received at the hands of colonizing immigrant Anglos. However, as the novel's structure suggests, separating as it does the different worlds of Native American and Mexicano experience, this mutual experience of discrimination fractures for Jackson onto radically different historical planes, inasmuch as the Californios' loss of land and power resided primarily in a distanced and therefore insulated epoch.

If Jackson provides readers with a character who exercises economic and social power to attain justice, a character who thereby threatens to speak to the reader's present, it is Felipe Moreno, who attempts to address Alessandro's murder. By contrast, the two potential sources of reform with Native American backgrounds—Alessandro and Ramona—are initiated into the Native American community by virtue of their growing awareness of their almost complete lack of legal status. It is crucial that, for both characters, their ultimate submersion in legal issues—Alessandro's "stealing" of a horse and Ramona's failure to testify about Alessandro's murder—is portrayed as a lapse of intentionality. Before Alessandro's theft, for instance, growing anger over the discrimination his community confronts leads him not to overt political acts of reprisal and protest but to increasingly severe mental lapses, fantasies of chase and flight (fantasies derived from Jackson's model for the character, a Native American similarly gunned down). It is in just such a confused state that Alessandro rides off with a horse belonging to a local Anglo. When this assailant guns him down, Alessandro is trying to explain his illness, his very lack of agency. Ironically, the attack, which concludes with two shots that remove Alessandro's face, inadvertently completes the process Jackson has initiated. This process includes the absenting of Alessandro as a group victim and the creation of a "faceless" though exotic victim, one deprived of agency who may be "inhabited" by Anglo readers without requiring of them a significant effort at cultural translation.

In an apparently rational moment, Ramona greets Alessandro's death as merciful, given his mental deterioration. Shortly thereafter Ramona herself falls into a fever that leaves her incoherent; it is for this reason that she fails to testify at the time of the investigation into the murder. While there is little doubt that her testimony would not have altered the case's outcome, it is important that Jackson has again premised disengagement on incapacity rather than volition.

Regardless of the outcome of the case, the public forum offered by the inquest would have yielded an opportunity to air a group-oriented critique and a group-oriented grieving.[15] Yet a danger underlies this narrative option: in such a forum Ramona could well attack the heart of the consensual-individualistic bias of the law, thereby undercutting Jackson's investment in the institution and offending her mainstream audience, which does need to mourn Alessandro but in a manner that conforms to the precepts encoded in the law; hence, he must remain an objectified, faceless loss. Inasmuch as the novel symptomatically repeats the synthetic individualism noted above, Jackson works toward enfranchising Native Americans legally while displacing them as culturally specific actors. That Ramona, as described by Ri, should find her closest link to her community in this critical moment of incapacity only reinforces the notion that tribal ties and group agency are roadblocks to reform as Jackson envisions it; in the novel these ties, as nurturing as they may be, seem to limit Ramona—as does the fever—to a state of preconscious, albeit saintly, victimization.

Insofar as the movement of the novel as a whole is concerned, an ironic passage to a more ideal/idealized past fulfills the reform project. Only the most blatant nostalgia can support the literal movement back into the colonial era and space (the return to Mexico City) that concludes the novel. Rather than attempting to address Jackson's contemporary issues and transformations in a significant fashion, *Ramona* puts these problems in motion only to circumvent them by leaving the most problematic rhetorical assumptions intact. Ultimately, the family romance may have overtaken Jackson's political intentions because her involvement in reform was continually subjected to patriarchal definitions of her project, definitions that always returned to the familial. However, in the end the most striking feature of *Ramona* is its ability both to claim itself reformist and to defer action, especially legal action.

While many characters in the novel understand the law to be almost uniformly unjust, this awareness never underwrites the sort of inversion of just versus criminal acts that takes place in other minority legal critiques—for example, African-American slave narratives like Frederick Douglass's.[16] Politically motivated retribution is the furthest thing from Jackson's mind, as she makes clear by her elisions of agency. The attenuated sense of justice that Jackson does

foster at the close of the novel traces a notion of natural justice originally announced at the conclusion of *A Century of Dishonor*. Essentially, this theory supposes that bad actions will bring bad consequences to their perpetrators; most obviously, guilty people—like
the judge who ignores Alessandro's murder—will be haunted by
memories and imaginings. Along with this supposition, however,
we may well assume that the law, imagined in this way, promotes
the various forms of denial that make possible such a return of the
repressed. Inasmuch as *Ramona* is a legal polemic, it seems only fair
to question whether Jackson has gone far enough in thinking
through the ways in which the legal machinations she criticizes
shape her own novel. As a text positioning itself between an essentially invisible Native American population (invisible inasmuch as
Jackson avoids representing it) and a thoroughly anachronistic hacienda caste, I would suggest that *Ramona*'s most fundamental object
of denial is the central character's mestiza identity, an identity that
has to be reconfigured in the narrative into different periods connot-
ing separate, secure racial natures.

Can it be any wonder that, as the Los Angeles history project
has argued, the "Hispanicization" wrought by California's tourist
industry traces in large part back to *Ramona*'s reception?[17] When,
for instance, Santa Barbara celebrates Fiesta Days each year at the
beginning of August, a pervasive yet virtually unrecognized leap
takes place in which a fantasized colonial past supersedes virtually
any links between itself and the present. First and foremost, the
Treaty of Guadalupe Hidalgo and its deterioration are eclipsed. Every effort is made to reconstruct the original myths of Spanish blood
purity because the process reinforces a security in the present, one
which attempts to institutionally manipulate political changes in the
Southwest, particularly in response to the demographic expansion
of the Latino population. Thus, the historical gap figured in these
ceremonies, and in their textual icon, ensures a denial of reformist
transformation by acting out a sentimentalized closure of the mission era and what was to come.

Although the novel's broad reception in this regard is entirely at
odds with Jackson's published intentions, it is likely that her assimilationist beliefs allowed little other choice. What Jackson asked was
that Ramona be permitted to emulate the Anglo-European conqueror. When denied this opportunity, Ramona, as a form of pro-

test,finds a home in exile. As is evident in *A Century of Dishonor*, Jackson does not significantly challenge the supremacy of the conqueror's cultural position, and although she offers several blanket condemnations of the law, no real threat to its power is envisioned in either work. If anything, the invocation of natural law suggests an acceptance of current institutions, as their wrongs will be righted by a higher source even while we live our lives in the "hit and miss" fashion conveyed through the metaphor of Aunt Ri's rug making:

> "Wall," she said, "it's called ther 'hit-er-miss' pattren; but it's 'hit' of-tener 'n 't is 'miss.' Thar ain't enny accountin' fur ther way ther breadths 'll come, sometimes; 'pears like 't wuz kind er magic, when they air sewed tergether; 'n' I allow thet's ther way it's gwine ter be with heaps er things in this life. It's jest a kind er 'hit-er-miss' pattren we air all on us livin' on; 't ain't much use tryin' ter reckon how 't 'll come aout. (337)

Thus, by the conclusion of the novel the deconstruction of Jackson's legal premises is complete. The "magic" which will suggest a cultural rallying point for the construction of alternative forms of agency in later Chicano texts, for instance *Zoot Suit* and *The Brick People*, is here a dislocated and universalized concept, essentially devoid of any power to unify a community around action or changes in perception. Instead, *Ramona's* focus on the family romance vitiates Jackson's declared political agenda. Like Stowe, Jackson hoped to motivate reform by demonstrating the deterioration of families suffering under racism. However, unlike Stowe, Jackson was unwittingly describing a mestizo class, a class like the mulatto, notable in mainstream anxieties not for its relative recognizability but rather for its ability to impersonate, and to a certain extent infect, Anglo (as well as Spanish) culture.

Arguing that American literature plays out obsessively the concomitant search for, and rejection of, father figures, Mary Dearborn has suggested that literature about mulattos—literature which frequently documents incestuous relations between slaveholders and their slaves, who were often half-brothers or half-sisters—constitutes a literal embodiment of larger cultural anxieties about self-definition.[18] As Dearborn's reading suggests, the incestuous nature of Ramona's final consummation of her stepbrother's love may be one crucial sign of the disruption produced when racial categories are thus threatened. Described elsewhere in the narrative as reminiscent of Lot's wife (267), Ramona finds herself caught at the novel's conclusion in a state of frozen somnambulism. She is essentially trapped between the Franciscan invective against grief, which would posit her angry remembrance of Alessandro's murder as a sin, and Felipe's (her stepbrother's) declaration of love. The incestuous overtones are supplanted only by the overtones of necrophilia one gains while considering Felipe's advances from the position of Ramona's "merciful oblivion." Ramona's sexuality thus comes to be equated with a saintly nature extolling the virtues of a family reunited. On another level, the retreat to the family romance also signals a switch from conventionally understood public spaces of political interaction to a "private" space defined by insularity. Taken together, these incestuous, necrophiliac, and insulating tendencies suggest the denial of an entire historical period representing *mestizaje* (the mixing of racial heritages) itself.

In all of this, there also lies a crucial manipulation of attitudes about mestiza sexuality, attitudes that are part and parcel of Anglo-American slanders of mestiza moral character premised on the failings that must come with racial impurity.[19] Jackson's novel is thus situated in a long history of political containment aided by the ideological suppositions of, and control over, sexuality. As Ramón Gutiérrez has demonstrated, this history reaches back to the Spanish colonial institution of marriage among indigenous Pueblo peoples.[20] Prior to colonization by the Spanish, Pueblo women "were empowered through their sexuality," which "was theirs to give and withhold" (17). Erotic behavior was pursued in "myriad forms (heterosexuality, homosexuality, bisexuality)" and did not recognize "boundaries of sex or age." As the colonization process gained ground, tribes like the Pueblos were more or less successfully convinced that sexuality must fall under the rubrics defined by the church, rubrics which conveyed a vehement distrust of love and sexuality as "subversive" sentiments that "glorified personal autonomy" and promoted "passion as an intrinsic desire of the species—natural, free and egalitarian" (227–28).

In more recent epochs, the general strategy has been carried over as stereotypes regarding mestiza sexuality have been mobilized by U.S. ideologues justifying aggression toward the inferior population of Mexico, which from the outset was damned by its racial mixing. In particular, Antonia Castañeda, in "The Political Economy of Nineteenth Century Stereotypes of Californianas," has followed the manner in which stereotypes of Mexicana sexuality ran seemingly contradictory courses as they altered to fit the specific political agendas that were part of the overall expansionist aggression and part of changing attitudes toward race and gender in the nineteenth-century United States. Highlighting the important justificatory role played by stereotypes denoting sexual immorality among Mexicanas prior to the U.S. invasion of 1846–1848, Castañeda surmises that the subsequent adoption of apparently antithetical romanticized stereotypes depicting "pure" high-caste Mexicanas fit a larger systematic subordination of Mexican society wherein certain limited "foreign" negotiations (Anglo marriages into Mexicano land-grant wealth) were valorized even while the majority of such marriages were not. A complex process, overall subordination thus allowed certain stereotypes obliquely representing cooperation between the cultures to take root—although, as Castañeda underscores, these stereotypes were entirely devoid of anything but the most censored acknowledgment of the Mexican social context. Hence, these high-caste Californianas become purely Spanish; such a Californiana would thus find herself divorced "from her racial, cultural and historical reality" (224).

Ramona is in fact the predictable extension of this historical trajectory. As the negotiation with the "other" within becomes even more intimate in the colonizing scenario at the end of the nineteenth century, so too does the denial of historical context that stems from the manipulation of sexuality, a manipulation that "succeeds" in Jackson's case by virtue of her exploitation of the romance form. In this manner, the mestiza population and all the potentially threatening sexuality that it represents becomes the symbolic center of the novel. Ultimately, the habitat for this missing center is situated between the lines of a systematic historical amnesia that would deny the rising mestizo class that Jackson must have walked among.

IN THE GIANT'S CASTLE

Film involves a kind of therapy with the audience and it must be handled delicately.

George Stevens

The retreat to family romance evident in Jackson's work is mobilized again years later in one of mainstream Hollywood's more explicit attempts to deal with mestizaje, George Stevens's *Giant* (1956). Adapted from Edna Ferber's highly popular potboiler novel by the same name (1952), Stevens's film seeks to convey the grandeur of a developing Texas by presenting, among other things, a feast for the eyes. Often remembered in film studies texts for its sheer visual scope, *Giant* is most frequently represented with stills that seem to take in the whole of the Texas countryside.[21] Nonetheless, Stevens wished to maintain a very focused line of narrative action in *Giant*, one in which the audience would become engrossed in "a story about the hazards of the marriage relationship."[22] With regard to the tension between the epic proportions and the film's specific themes, Stevens told another interviewer, "The title embarrassed us when shooting. It's not a big film, it's small. It closes up on things and on people."[23]

Stevens began his career as an actor, then worked as a cameraman before becoming a director; those early experiences are reflected in the mix of dramatic action and virtually sublime visual experience offered by *Giant*.[24] However, while *Giant* pleased critics particularly because it was able to convey an epic scope even while maintaining clear-cut character development and action, the filmmaking process itself was fraught with difficult decisions, as indicated by the 400,000 feet of film used over the course of the production.[25] Although Stevens was certainly not known for an economical use of footage, the tremendous editing task suggests that the film presented Stevens with one of his greatest challenges.

Certainly one issue that could not be divorced from the desire to make the film at least appear big had to do with new market pressures. From the beginning of the project, Warner Brothers was concerned about the new competition posed by the growing popularity of television.[26] Throughout the industry, this concern translated into a pressure to create films that would move significantly beyond the television viewing experience—hence the marketing impetus behind innovative, though often imperfect, techniques such as Cinemascope. Stevens met this challenge in *Giant* by masking the top and bottom of the lens to emphasize the width of his shots, a technique that avoided the distortion—especially in close-ups—inherent in Cinemascope and similar options. He was thereby able to convey as accurately as possible "the small." In addition to these photographic solutions, Stevens and the screenplay authors, Fred

Guiol and Ivan Moffat, substantially reworked Ferber's narrative, creating an entirely new conclusion to the story that could more effectively bring together the various themes of the film, particularly the familial, class, and racial matters. In essence, then, this film—most often remembered for its sweeping vistas—enacts a careful negotiation of wide-open spaces and crucial mid to close-up shots, a negotiation that allowed Stevens simultaneously to convey a Hollywood fantasy about the exotic grandeur of Texas and to funnel key dramatic conflicts into circumscribed spaces, as in the final episodes in the Benedicts' sitting room.

The story begins with an impromptu, whirlwind romance initiated during a brief horse-buying visit to Maryland, a visit in which the cattle-rich Texan Jordan "Bick" Benedict meets and marries the outspoken Leslie Lynnton over the course of a few days. In short order Leslie and the audience are introduced to the wide horizons of Bick's home state, horizons that are filled with cattle, at least at the start. One of the principal changes which will confront the political and economic establishment represented by Bick during the twenty-five years spanned by the film is the extensive exploitation of oil reserves, reserves which will later fill the horizons with endless oil derricks. Along with these economic and political jostlings come players like Jett Rink, members of a working class who gain through the discovery of oil a claim to power, thereby unleashing a virtually unbridled resentment between old and new money.

The enveloping scenes of cattle and oil derricks are juxtaposed with intimate shots of familial settings in which the central drama of the narrative is acted out: the ongoing travails of Bick and Leslie Benedict's marriage. The difficulties make themselves felt immediately on the couple's arrival at Reata, the Benedict family ranch. Leslie throws Bick into obvious discomfort as she discourses far too intimately with the Mexicano help as she greets them for the first time. The prophecy embedded in this early scene is borne out as Leslie takes a strong interest in the welfare of the Mexicano workers who are segregated into a nearby barrio.

Stevens exploits the sentimental appeal of Leslie's first visit to this barrio in a number of ways. In the first instance, the entire visit is crosscut with scenes from a savage ride in which Leslie's sister-in-law, Luz, takes out her frustrations with Bick's marriage on Leslie's horse, an episode that leaves both horse and rider mortally wounded. Through this all, there is a clear effort to build on the implied symbolic relationship between Leslie and the horse, both of which are explicitly and repeatedly linked in terms of beauty and independence. Hence, the horse's mistreatment becomes a foil for Leslie's "provocative" actions in the barrio, where her unconventional sympathies compel her to seek medical assistance from the white establishment for a sick Mexicano child, Angel Obregon. The particularly graphic close-ups which document Luz savagely spurring the horse and the ultimate—though unseen—consequences of these actions confer on Leslie a certain sentimental justification to pursue even more forcefully the improvement she would bring to the barrio, although these efforts lead her into a constant struggle against the racist norms supported by Bick. In this vein, the genteel, Eastern-bred woman is appalled throughout most of the film at the treatment meted out to the Mexicanos by her adopted family. Finally, her reactions to Bick's resistance as she seeks help become a partial barometer of their marital decline. Her dismay at his racism contributes to the mounting tensions in their marriage, tensions that culminate when Bick and Leslie's son, Jordy, secretly defies his father by eloping with Juana Villalobos, a Mexicana who, like Leslie, is committed to the betterment of the barrio.

Although throughout the film these racial issues are often distantly juxtaposed to the business wranglings that threaten the Benedicts' cattle-oriented lifestyle, events toward the end of the film suggest that in fact a common thread links the two spheres. This thread becomes apparent when Bick physically confronts his now-oil-rich economic rival, Jett Rink, at a "who's who in Texas" blowout thrown by Jett. The fight is instigated when Jett's Anglo workers refuse hairdressing service to Juana, now Bick's Mexicana daughter-in-law, and when Jett himself mauls Jordy in a less than fair fight over the same incident with Juana. While the spectacular ballroom fight between Bick and Jett (presumably the two giants of the film) is initiated by the racist treatment of Juana, multiple motivations affect Bick, not the least of which includes the battle over whether he or Jett will ultimately control the affections of Bick's daughter, Jett's most recent conquest.

The discrimination issue lives on as Bick and his son Jordy argue again back in their hotel room after the more public altercations. In this episode—where the son proclaims the father every bit the racist that Jett is—we find an unusual rhetorical display: the altercation is distinguished stylistically by the odd manner in which both participants repeatedly tell the other to just "forget it." The consequent dissolution of the racial theme is reinforced in two ways. First, the Juana of the film, unlike the Juana of the novel, remains largely silent throughout these scenes and is certainly not the angry force that she is in Ferber's novel. Second, moving the reaction to discrimination into the intimate sphere of the hotel room reinforces the sense that father and son are rehearsing a feud that does in fact all too easily forget the privilege they enjoy to choose or not to choose reformist action. Hence, the emotions tied up with the initial discriminatory act are funneled into a model of vicarious participation through this scene as well as others. As a result, audience members are more likely to come to terms with, for instance, Jordy's and Bick's anger than to situate themselves in the event of discrimination. Here, then, we find a therapy that would treat not the victim but rather the responsible, or tangentially responsible, perpetrators— the benefactors of the hacienda. Instead of exploring the consequences of the event for the victim, a kind of narrative deferral or dissolution takes place, one akin to that found in *Ramona* and one which likewise softens the experience of racism.

This tendency toward deferral at "moments of great emotion" is in fact a hallmark of Stevens's cinematic style, in which the "camera does tend not to look, or, at least, to back away" at critical junctures (Richie 43). Donald Richie pursues this point by noting that in Stevens's films, "Close-ups are used to make an emotional impact before the emotion-arousing event . . . and the results of the event are shown in a long shot" (43–44). Such is the case in *Giant* when the audience views an extreme close-up of Luz gouging Leslie's horse just prior to the mortal wounding of both. As Richie goes on to argue,

> The effect is that of making us emotionally involved before the fact. After the fact we are deliberately disinvolved. This is elegiac. We experience the emotion but not its consequences. We are not shown [Luz] dead, for example. Instead, an aesthetic appeal is instantly made. Those beautiful shots of the horse wandering off . . . suggest by both their nature and their context that emotion to be experienced

is suddenly over. We are invited to contemplate, to feel, and at the same time to refrain from action. (44)

This tendency to enact a "disinvolvement," described here by Richie in terms of style, appears to have influenced, or at least reinforced, Stevens's treatment of the racial themes in the movie as well. For instance, a similar process occurs in the closing episodes of the film, episodes which substantially alter the final events of the novel. Here again we find a process of narrative "softening" in which emotionally charged discrimination issues are developed only to be largely circumscribed in the privatized space of familial dynamics and contract law. In this case the legal discourse only implied by Juana's earlier question about right to service will become a primary topic.

Thus, we find Stevens interrupting the Benedicts' trip home from the Jett Rink "blowout" with yet another fight, this time pitting Bick against a diner owner who first complains vociferously about serving Juana and her son and immediately thereafter attempts to throw out of the diner another Mexicano family that has just arrived. In a moment that defines Bick's newfound commitment, he stands up and protests the treatment of the victimized family. The climax of the seemingly titanic fight that ensues between Bick and the owner is oddly comical and yet profound in its implications. Bick is thoroughly beaten by the cook, who proceeds to hang a "right to refuse service" sign around Bick's neck as he sits on the floor among the remains of a salad. In this scene one of the wealthiest men in Texas is knocked silly, virtually in his own backyard, and the cook's actions are framed as entirely consonant with the laws of the country, laws which define contractual negotiations as primarily private affairs.

As one would expect of a romantic director like Stevens, this turn of events is not without its silver lining. Retreating to the family space, Stevens plays out the vestiges of the racial issues as a grounds for the reconciliation of the marriage; Bick, in a dramatic comeback, has become Leslie's hero by defending the anonymous Mexicano family, a shift of fortune suggesting that although public action may be ineffective, even "indefensible," it still holds value in the private sphere, in the world of the "small." And to underscore the tentative sanctity of this sphere, Stevens leaves us with an image of the two grandchildren, mestizo by Jordy's marriage and Anglo by Luz's, playing together side by side in the near background.

The final turn to the children is worthy of some consideration since Stevens appears here to be building on the theme of "hope in the next generation" that Ferber exploits at the end of her novel. Although the novel never reaches Jett's blowout—at the beginning and end of the narrative, this event looms in the near future—Ferber does describe a diner incident in which service is denied. However, in the novel it is the women and children of the Benedict family on their own who find themselves confronting an owner who has taken exception to their mestizaje. Not only does no physical fight ensue, but it is the reformist Leslie who works desperately to avoid letting Bick know about the event at all. Leslie recognizes in her actions exactly the sort of seemingly passive racism she has despised in Bick, yet the best she can do at the end of the novel is to assume that Jordy and Luz represent "a real success at last," presumably because they continue to challenge the discriminatory status quo (447).

In Stevens's version, Leslie of course maintains a much higher level of integrity in terms of her reformist intentions. Unfortunately, the actions she helps Bick toward do not suggest the kind of political consciousness that bespeaks a profound change. As Bick and Leslie sit back at home to discuss both the incident in the diner and their relative successes in life, Bick can only look on his grandchildren in bewilderment, telling the young boy of Jordy and Juana's marriage that he will never be anything other than a "wetback." Defined by the status of "legal alien," mestizos in the film, even in the most private of spaces, maintain a conditional citizenship, a citizenship which asserts that their only security will be found in public silence and in the virtual invisibility represented by retiring characters like Juana.

Juana is nonetheless representative of a kind of activism which, if it is not given a proper voice, is at least liminally recognized by the film. The same may be said of the bit part of the Mexicano doctor who works with these reformists, a character based loosely in both novel and film on the very politically active head of the GI Forum, Dr. Hector García.[27] Yet it seems that the work of these reformists and their principal advocate in the family, Jordy, is actually devalued in the transformation from novel to film as the final focus on the hope offered by the "next generation" turns not to Jordy's work and Luz's anger, as Ferber would have it, but rather to the essentially mute grandchildren. This distinct shift and the dissolution it betrays are only exacerbated when Stevens adds to the final image of the grandchildren a background that includes a black calf and a white lamb. However secure the final familial sphere may seem, Stevens's visual equation of the children with a calf and a lamb suggests that, while the desegregation may have its "natural" side, it is also indebted to a commodity system that will ask for the children's sacrifice. Of particular note in this regard is an earlier episode in the film when a Thanksgiving dinner is entirely ruined as the children Luz and Jordy realize that their favorite pet turkey has been stuffed and baked for the occasion. Sentimentalized pet livestock do not fare well in this film, and the de facto legal rhetoric which intervenes in the Thanksgiving scene imbues the final images with the suggestion that these children have indeed not escaped racism and, further, that such escape may well be impossible.

As a work depicting various forms of discrimination against Mexicanos, *Giant* is certainly a Hollywood landmark; for this reason it can be appreciated for the step it took in promoting the discussion of racial issues as represented in popular culture. At the same time, however, it is crucial that we understand the ways in which the work perpetuates the legacy for Mexicanos of which *Ramona* is a crucial, if not foundational, part. At the close of *Giant*, racial issues are again afforded only the safe environment of private familial space. Recourse to public action appears largely stifled, especially because the final characters speaking to racism are the representatives of a wealth and power purchased through a discriminatory system. And if there were any doubt about this state of affairs, any doubt about the ability of the public to contain the private, it is erased when Bick reasserts the primacy of legal categories in the final reconciliation scene and therefore reinforces the lessons of the right-to-service issues.

In a sense, then, the racial themes that play such an important role in the marital dynamics of the film become encrypted, particularly after the intermission, when the film jumps fifteen years and leaves the viewer in a more retrospective context. This encrypting is acted out literally in one of the films more memorable scenes, the burial of Angel Obregon, killed in World War II. This scene calls forth a number of historically and politically sensitive valences that merit scrutiny. Bringing these valences together with the dynamics of the funeral, we may learn a good deal about the very deferred reform Stevens offers.

First, Bick and the Anglo establishment in the film recognize and attend the burial, thereby breaking with previous custom: Bick, for instance, has eschewed other contact, claiming that Mexicanos "have their own ways." At the funeral, though, Bick shares in the public grieving. Audience members viewing the film at the time of its initial release would no doubt recall the tremendous international scandal that evolved out of Texas in the aftermath of World War II, when segregated burial proceedings were fought by Mexicanos, including Dr. García and the GI Forum. The refusal of the Rice Funeral Home in Three Rivers, Texas, to accept the body of Félix Longoría in 1949 was perhaps the most famous of these incidents.[28] An argument may be made, then, that a certain distanced remembrance of these struggles is represented in the Obregon funeral; however, it appears as if this funeral becomes a rendition of how things should have gone, not how they did go. In this sense, the scene becomes a reformist fantasy strained by its own reference to how things actually evolved.

A kind of wish fulfillment in which the bigoted Bick tenderly hands the grieving Mexicano family a Texas flag, the burial gives way to one of the more striking visual constructions in the work. Here the camera moves away from the funeral and captures—again in a typically "disinvolved" wide-angle shot—a small Mexicano child playing in a field, his back to the ceremony. Offering the viewer an apparently disinterested and dislocated child, Stevens strives for a sublime effect in this scene by placing the emotional content of the funeral next to the seemingly untouchable power of life moving forward. Yet this child also embodies a kind of independence that is not explicitly written into the kinds of commodity and legal pressures that one finds, for instance, in the scene of the children at the film's close. Instead, a kind of possibility appears to be wrapped up in the image of this lone child, but a possibility that cannot amount to anything until the child turns and engages not only the funeral that escapes his private musings but also the latent political history that is only distantly recalled for the audience as Angel Obregon is laid to rest. In this sense, this boy may come to represent the sleeping giant of the film, the potential for active political involvement and for public voice; however, as he stands in the world Stevens creates, he is little more than another mute participant, an infinitely scriptable character waiting for sentimental investment.

These works reveal specific political issues, issues which pertain to gaining access to sites that might sustain public speaking voices—with all of the entitlements such sites confer in this society. However, as the title of *Break of Dawn* suggests, these sites remain on the horizon—a point reinforced when González leaves San Quentin in the film's final scene to be greeted by no one, although clearly the expectation of some bonding permeates the situation. Contemporary institutional histories confirm such deferred status for the Chicano public speaker by continuing to obscure the contexts within which Chicanos find themselves. Even in the much celebrated architectural study by Reyner Banham, *Los Angeles: The Architecture of Four Ecologies* (1971), the Mission Revival movement remains a ghostly presence, a treatment strangely at odds with the author's larger aims to clarify the heretofore apparently confused readings of architectural trends in Los Angeles (23). Gesturing toward the unique role played by Mission Revival, Banham notes that

> for the purposes of the present study, Spanish Colonial Revival will not be treated as an identifiable or conspicuously adopted style, but as something which is ever-present and can be taken for granted, like the weather—worth comment when outstandingly beautiful or conspicuously horrible, but otherwise simply part of the day-to-day climate from which ... much of modern California architecture derives. (61)

This diaphanous yet clearly fundamental presence masks, however obliquely, the historical pressures noted in the narratives and institutional strategies studied in this chapter, pressures that are both too apparent (a sense underscored by Banham's emphasis on the "conspicuous") and necessarily, though not entirely successfully, denied. It is precisely this haunting presence, embodied in Alejandro Morales's work, that the next chapter will exploit in an effort to counter a legacy of historical amnesia. Studying Morales's own alternative architectural history, we will thus explore the manner in which he critiques the systematic maintenance of Chicano dependency by turning the disciplinary tools of the dominant institutions back on themselves.

3

"Rancho Mexicana, USA" under Siege

As the title *The Brick People* (1988) suggests, Alejandro Morales's historical novel details the construction (or constructed nature) of a unique society—a workers' enclave that provided the labor to build one of the world's preeminent brick manufacturers. Documenting the importation of Mexican institutional and cultural forms by the Anglo Simons family with an eye for *lo real maravilloso*, Morales's novel offers a new form of historiography more sensitive to the manner in which specific groups are cultivated into dependent relationships vis-à-vis the dominant social classes and castes. Thus pursuing a version of the "dependency critique" associated with figures like Immanuel Wallerstein, Henrique Cardoso, and Enzo Faletto, Morales explores the manipulation of social pathologies and the political unconscious by southern California's entrepreneurial class as it builds what numerous Chicano historians have termed a "perpetual underclass" of Chicano laborers.[1]

Readers need only look to Morales's preceding novel, *Reto en el paraíso* (1983), to find such interests in hegemonic manipulation laid bare. As George Mariscal has noted with reference to *Reto en el paraíso*, Morales's notion of resistance should not be taken as "merely a question of repudiating the values and philosophies of [one's] class enemies, but rather of some much more complicated process of self-analysis whereby [critics] attempt to detect and eradicate the ideological infection inevitably present in [themselves] as well."[2] Through his principal character, the architect Dennis Berreyesa Coronel, who literally builds the Orange County paradise from which he must be excluded, Morales probes in *Reto en el paraíso* both the appeal and the impossibility of accommodation; as the architect discovers, "El chicano es una omisión." As Morales demonstrates in both *Reto* and *The Brick People*, Mexicanos and Chicanos are fundamental for the construction of Anglo utopias, paradises which are from beginning to end monuments of dependency.

As a means of expanding the historical dimensions of this critique in *The Brick People*, Morales focuses on the Anglo importation of the Mexican hacienda model of labor management. In large part the action of the novel evolves from the initial desire of Walter Simons, one of the brickyard owners, to discover what makes Mexicano workers tick. Walter craves insight into hacienda labor management not for humanitarian purposes but rather because he wants to harness—and profit from—the anger he reads on the faces of the workers who make it to the United States. To this end he travels through Mexico with another, more esteemed representative of U.S. capitalism and exploitation—William Hearst. What Walter sees on this trip is so incredible as to be fantastic. During one of the first nights of the trip, Walter wanders away from the main compound of Hearst's hacienda—a hacienda prophetically named "Rancho Mexicana, USA" in order to make it clear that Anglo economic prowess can rewrite national boundaries at will. While stumbling about, Walter comes across what appear to be large insects eating the putrid entrails of a dead horse. Before Walter can respond to this scene in any significant way, a band of Hearst's horsemen ride down on the "insects"—actually starving Mexicanos—and one of the novel's many massacres ensues. As we learn later, these Mexicanos—seen as insects by Walter—had not received permission to eat the rotting flesh and were therefore punished. Initially aghast at such inhuman treatment, Walter quickly defers his humanitarian concerns, succumbing instead to the pleasures acquired through the profits of this system of exploitation. It is not an accident that this sublimating seduction is also a literal seduction. Although a Malinche figure helps Walter strategically displace the "magical reality" of the situation, readers cannot fail to see how this woman, like the other women workers, is motivated by a desire for survival in a patriarchal economic system that gives her little that could be called choice.

If a process of betrayal through translation occurs (the archetypal crime attributed to La Malinche), it takes place when Walter returns to the United States equipped with his new management tools and ready to fashion his own "Rancho Mexicana, USA." Locked into competition with his brother Joseph, Walter applies his newfound knowledge to his own brickyard in the hopes that he might make it the most efficient in the world; the principle that will govern this new project is the creation of an indentured, dependent workforce. Operating firmly in the tradition of the patriarchal family, Walter provides the workers with various benefits, privileges which ultimately solidify the workers in their indentured status; he constructs homes, a school, and a store, meanwhile extending credit so that the workers may buy into the lifestyle of consumption. The stipulations that accompany these favors are simple: no one may purchase goods except at the company store, regardless of the prices one might find there; debts may come due at any time; and no questioning of the system, at any level, will be tolerated—a point reinforced by a constant show of potential, if not actual, force.

In this way *The Brick People* documents the adaptation of the hacienda system for the larger purposes of creating an enclave of dependency. A trained Latin Americanist, Morales depicts this translation of power with a twist, inasmuch as the Foucauldian disciplinary techniques initiated by the Anglo ownership—including panoptic strategies for "observing" the workers—are ultimately turned back on the bosses during subsequent magical realist moments of revenge. Morales thus depicts the Anglo translation of dependency in order to suggest a more complex strategy for reading and responding to border transactions.

TRANSLATING DEPENDENCY

Morales opens *The Brick People* with an epigraph drawn from Carlos Fuentes's *Terra nostra* (1975), an epigraph which reads, "The world dissolves when someone ceases to dream, to remember, to write." Fuentes's dictum is presented by Felipe, the Second's chronicler, a character loosely modeled on Cervantes. As you would expect, this character holds a privileged place in *Terra nostra*, a position built on the chronicler's ability to counteract the historical amnesia that defines the despotic project attributed to Felipe. Ultimately, this ethic of historical rethinking fuels *Terra nostra*'s wide-ranging mobilization of arcane and heretical memory arts drawn explicitly from Frances Yates's study *The Art of Memory* (1966), among others.[3] Morales, in turn, uses this epigraph to frame his novel's project because he wishes to emphasize the recovery of an alternative history: that of the Simons brickyards in Los Angeles during the first half of this century.

The inherently revisionary nature of Morales's project—a fundamental link with *Terra nostra*—and the quality of social realism have led the novel's best readers to gauge its success in terms of its accomplishments as a protest work. For example, Mario García has written the most thorough critical review along these lines, surmising finally that, although the novel does expose the horrors of race and class dynamics in the Southwest, it fails inasmuch as it conveys only the limitations of collective action.[4] Ultimately, García faults Morales for not having chosen to pursue a historical story of collective success. The point is important because García conveys a particularly resonant notion of political efficacy; according to this vision, protest novels should affirm collective struggle by holding out hope through positive examples.

García suggests that these are Morales's parameters for success as well, assuming that Morales is still situated within the strategies of the Chicano Movement. However, *The Brick People* is not, properly speaking, a product of the movement; it was published in 1988, well into a period of critical reevaluation. Hence, for Morales's principal brickyard worker, Octavio Revueltas, faith in conventional means of change is at best dubious, and this sense carries over to hopes placed in union reform as well. As we learn about Octavio, "He disliked the word hope. Hope, he believed, was a concept of oppression used by the dominant society to rule the mass of people . . . Hope was a void, a holding zone used to control" (188–89). Working in the frame of social realism, this passage could be read as a call to action, a call which is dealt a death blow with the subsequent failure of the unionization undertaken by the brickyard workers. Thereafter, Morales's protagonist moves into what appears to be an insulated space, a domestic space in keeping with the American Dream, according to García.

This movement into an apparent individualism mirrors what readers might assume about Ralph Ellison's protagonist, Invisible Man: that he too fails to fully engage Ellison's social realist political issues. The comparison between the works grows even more apposite if we stop to consider that readings of each of the novels have often overemphasized the role of social realism; though popular,

critical assertions of escapism into an insular space and into individualism make sense only as long as we forget the competing modes
of reading called forth by the novels themselves. These modes not
only supplement but also challenge the priority often given by critics to social realism. For Ellison, that competing mode is constituted
by the symbolic references he builds in throughout his novel to the
African-American trickster tradition as well as other "heretical" discourses or frames of reference.[5] While I cannot rehearse here the
resulting complications for Ellison's political dialogues produced by
this symbolic aspect, especially as he addresses interlocutors like
Richard Wright, let me simply suggest that "protest" becomes a
much more difficult process when understandings or projections of
reality become infected with overdetermined meanings, meanings
that must be taken into account if writers and readers are to deal
with the manipulation of desires described by theorists of institutional power, including Michel Foucault.[6]

Readers should have these difficulties in mind when considering
the role of lo real maravilloso in *The Brick People,* and especially the
role of the insects, which appear to wreak a kind of revenge on
Anglo capitalists throughout the novel. A similar preoccupation
with insects may be found in Oscar Zeta Acosta's works, giving
readers one context for understanding the apparent import of the
insects; in the cult novel *Revolt of the Cockroach People* (1973), Chicanos and disenfranchised peoples in general are affirmed as an
unstoppable natural force. Cockroaches, printed in the margins of
the text, further this sense of omnipotent power. However, this
power is significantly compromised at the end of the novel (as I shall
discuss later), when Acosta's protagonist reflects that his political
strategies may have been manipulated from the very start by the
likes of Los Angeles's Mayor Yorty, who privately counseled the protagonist to pursue violent action from the outset. The original episode with Mayor Yorty and its remembrance at the end of Acosta's
novel raise questions about the efficacy of Chicano political strategy
and its latent manipulation that are also taken up by Morales as he
builds his own symbolic "magical layer" into his text. This revision
of political literary strategies, similar to that produced by Ellison, is
grounded in presenting a collision of worldviews.[7]

In Morales's case, this collision takes part both in the cultural
tradition supported by the Cuban Casa de las Américas publishing

and research enterprise and in the critique of modes of dependency identified by scholars like José Saldívar (*Dialectics of Our America*).[8] Like Ellison, Morales develops a combination of social realism and specifically situated heretical symbolism. However, as long as the two worlds of meaning—the social realist and the magical—are resolved into separate spheres, it remains fairly easy to consider the symbolic a purely escapist, fantastic force. What happens in *The Brick People*, and at the end of Acosta's novel, is quite another matter—hence the importance of the phrase "When worlds dissolve." The "magical" in Morales's novel is not a textual effect to be categorized among others in whatever anatomy of literary techniques. This tendency to narrow the practice's implications in fact explains why many North American attempts to define "magical realism" have been unsuccessful.[9] As Saldívar notes, lo real maravilloso has a fundamentally extraliterary component that comes into view only when critics recognize the magical as a specifically situated response to institutional discourses in the New World, especially legal, scientific, and anthropological discourse.[10]

In the hands of authors like Carlos Fuentes, lo real maravilloso reveals institutional languages as perpetuators of particular worldviews, ontologies that appear inescapable only so long as their legitimacy remains a sheltered part of a political unconscious. The representation of ontological struggles in these works thus promotes a rethinking of historiography, and particularly the manipulation of desire within differing historical representations. *The Brick People* is written squarely in this "American" tradition, a fact underscored when readers consider the novel's embattled ontologies.

Morales opens *The Brick People* with an anecdote that defines an avenging force. Recalling the ghostly apparitions of a widow, Doña Eulalia, who had been terrorized by Anglo land grabbers, an anonymous waiter tells the brickyard developer, Joseph Simons, that the doña had thrown herself into a pit and turned herself into "indescribably large insects . . . millions of brown insects" after having discovered her murdered family (11); the doña had prophesied that this transformation would occur should harm come to her family. To further our sense that her pronouncements hold latent significance, the waiter adds that the doña "understood the earth in a special way and possessed powers of the earth" (11). Such powers are evident to those witnessing the transformation at her death:

"Horror choked the people as they watched the insects overtake them, spread out, and cover El Rincon" (11). This anecdote—based on an actual memoir dating from the period of U.S. colonization—sets a context for two important elements repeated throughout the novel: (1) images of workers falling—like the doña—into excavating pits and (2) images of Anglos literally choked with horror by a proliferation of "insects."[11] The novel uses this initial episode to write the manipulation of dependency, and the "magical" responses it receives, into the doña's prophecy. Although the prophecy is written into yet another mythology later, when the Mexicana El Eco attributes California's earthquakes to Quetzalcoatl's displacement of Anglo-European colonizers (55), the import remains essentially the same.

This "import" is not simply a fantastic wish for justice; however, to fully understand it, we must first consider what is at stake for the Anglo-controlled institutions in the novel. Walter Simons structures his brickyard to separate and observe the workers, thereby exercising a policing function that is ultimately meant to shackle any political action. Such panoptic manipulation is only confirmed by Walter's decision to collapse the functions of foreman and sheriff. As Foucault has suggested in *Discipline and Punish*, one purpose of panoptic techniques is to control a population by getting its members to internalize certain desires and self-imposed restrictions, a point mirrored in Mariscal's observations with regard to Morales's works. In fact, the novelist is keenly aware of this process; hence, he emphasizes moments like Octavio's payday dispute, when Octavio challenges his paymaster because his check has been manipulated without his knowledge. Responding to Octavio's raised voice, William Simons shoves Octavio out of the payline with a blow from his rifle butt. What follows is a subtle comment on the distribution of power:

> The tension subsided as Octavio walked away.... The men who were closest had observed the altercation. Some saw only the violent manner in which William had used his rifle.... The men had tensed up and no one knew where the battering of a fellow worker would lead. Their eyes followed Octavio, watching to see what he would do. [The paymasters] were sensitive to the unified energy of the workers. They could feel their power and their anger. A dangerous moment had passed and only the men in power had recognized it. The workers had simply lived it. (171–72)

Power here, as in Foucault's description of Bentham's Panopticon, is exercised through forms of recognition that are essentially specular. Thus, the administration's power, a disciplinary observation of workers in line, is disrupted by a retaking of the gaze as the workers focus on Octavio. Although various Mexicano steps toward collective action in the novel will attempt to harness the "unconscious power" suggested here, what wins out repeatedly, at least on the level of social realism, is meritocracy: some individuals self-consciously opt to "sell out"; others simply prepare defensively for their own isolated survival within the context of dependency.

However, the insects that populate the novel in plaguelike fashion offer, albeit on a symbolic level, their own form of disciplinary observation, their own form of panoptic control. Just as the doña escapes the surveillance of her pursuers, who "have been watching her for some time," the workers likewise threaten to transcend the cultural and economic dependency established by the management and the larger Anglo society. Doña Eulalia ruptures these supposed borders, creating an omnipresent force that asserts its own brand of justice. In a more conventional context, the workers threaten to violate the borders—both behavioral and geographical—that have been defined for them with the creation of the brickyard enclave that controls their "Americanization" and ensures a measure of harmony with xenophobic neighboring communities. In their case, the threat posed coincides with their desire to achieve full status as citizens. Those Mexicanos who would leave to work their own farms, or to buy their own homes, represent for most of the Anglos outside the brickyard an invading force analogous to the doña's insects.

Placing this central aspect of the novel in its contemporary context, it is likely that Morales is reacting to conservative political pressures, like those we have noted attending the English-only movement, not to mention recent attempts to limit immigration or to repatriate Latino immigrants. Never far beneath the surface of these arguments is the fear that shifts in political demography will stealthily disenfranchise Anglos. As I noted in the previous chapter, such a revelation was at the core of Linda Chavez's controversial resignation as president of the U.S. English (USE) organization, a move she made after a secret memo, written by a senior USE official, was leaked to the press; Chavez herself described this memo as "anti-Hispanic and anti-Catholic" (Califa 326). Keeping this context in mind, we may read the "otherworldly" forces in Morales's text as analogues for very significant demographic changes, especially in the Southwest.[12] It is, after all, the very fecundity of the insects, and the sterility of the Anglos, that portends the most basic change in the novel.

However, if my assertion is correct and Morales's "magical" practice is in part a response to institutional processes, what are the implications for institutional change in the wake of such demographic disruptions? May we read Morales's use of the magical as an empowering myth? As a means to think in terms of the potential group power coming with demographic shifts? If so, is the method of lo real maravilloso itself an attempt to circumvent institutional discourses that legitimate meritocratic values? Again, I think we must begin answering these questions by considering what is at stake in the political unconscious.

Consider, for instance, what happens when Walter Simon's wife, Edit, attempts to define the status of "her" Mexicanos for a sociologist interviewer. In a moment of distraction, Edit notes, "I must confess a strange thought that just came to me . . . Mexicans, like cockroaches, are extremely adaptable. They will survive anything. Many might perish but there will always be survivors to propagate the race. They're just like cockroaches" (126). The interview is instructive precisely because it reveals the basis for the latent fear encoded in the supposedly "altruistic" project of hacienda management that the Simons have conceived. Edit's own inadvertent prophecy appears to be supported by the unchecked gaze of the insects who pop up throughout the novel. This gaze, a reversal of the dominant culture's surveillance, acts as an intervention constituting a corrective framing for the paranoia which threatens to isolate Mexicano readers from their community. Unable to affect directly the panoptic institutions of the Anglo society, Morales, like Valdez, relies on the uncanny ability of panoptic structures to be turned back on the internalized desires engendered by those who control the strategies of the institutions.

Although *The Brick People*'s reversal of the gaze is explicitly communal and therefore a reversal with a difference, the threat remains of falling back into a simple reversal, of not making something of the institution's distraction. The seeming power of such omnipotent vision may easily be turned into a means not of opposing proper places and institutional omnipotence but of reimposing their inevitability. Morales writes this danger into the novel when he treats the diametrically opposed readings received by the company photograph of the workers. Repeatedly, the men who make up the workforce interpret the photo through the filter of company ideology: for them the photo is a monument, a symbol of their freely given participation in "a great working family" (119). Presumably by virtue of their unique position in the power hierarchy—the family within the family—the women whose husbands are represented in the photo see something much different: for them the images reflect only despondency and mistreatment. As Milagros Revueltas tells her husband, Damian: "It is a photograph filled with repression. The men are stiff, tense, as if they were dead. . . . It is a photograph of sad prisoners, of tired slaves. Of men angered for being where they are at. As if they are forced to do what they do, not want to do" (119). Pascuala Pedroza offers a similar interpretation to her husband, Gonzalo, adding, "You can have your photography; it is an exercise of another world. I'm afraid that someone, if they want to, could burn it and you too would burn" (120).

The critical interpretations offered by these women are almost immediately silenced, yet in their brief surfacings it is clear that an apparently ontological battle is being waged and that the power clearly rests with the hacienda management, which can literally remake and destroy worlds by virtue of controlling the workers' desires (consumerism, albeit indebted, being the ideal).[13] Assuming that such control is challenged by the novel as it poses its own manipulation of the gaze, how are we to understand this "resistance"? How, ultimately, can Morales's discursive experiments match up against both the discursive and nondiscursive barriers posed by the dialectical cooperation of hegemony and coercion? In considering this question, we might first review some current theories regarding the exercise of power in society.

TACTICS OF RESISTANCE

Like law (one of its models), culture articulates conflicts and alternately legitimizes, displaces, or controls the superior force. It develops in an atmosphere of tensions and often of violence, for which it provides symbolic balances, contracts of compatibility and compromises, all more or less temporary.

Michel de Certeau,
The Practice of Everyday Life

Michel Foucault's studies of institutional discourses have fueled important debates within the field of cultural studies on issues of representation. These debates may in turn be particularly important for Chicano critique as it gauges its potential for resistance in the context of seemingly omnipotent institutions, which, as in the architectural history noted at the close of the last chapter, provide virtually no grounds for positing an alternative collective agency. While Foucault's analysis of subtle hegemonic techniques has positively reinforced "the concrete analysis of particular ideological and discursive formations, and the sites of their elaboration," his extreme valuation of loosely contingent institutional forces has led a chorus of cultural critics to argue that Foucault underestimates everyday, and particularly consumer, practices.[14] In "The Discourse of Difference: Footnoting Inequality," Rosa Linda Fregoso defines succinctly one of the most fundamental problems in this regard when she argues that any representation of "social formation" experience must offer a more adequate account of inequality than is found in most Foucauldian projects. Citing the Mexican cultural critic Nestor García Canclini, Fregoso notes, "If all that we see is disseminated power, it is impossible to hierarchize the actions of different 'instances' or 'apparatuses': the power of the transnationals is not the same as that of the head of the family" (185).

Such recognition of hierarchies allows cultural critics to drive a wedge in the seeming omnipotence of Foucauldian institutional power and thereby achieve a more subtle conceptualization of the relations between critical categories and lived experience. The undervaluation of this problem, as Stuart Hall notes, may have dire effects, inasmuch as it implicitly forces Foucault into a notion of historical transformation that appears naïvely symptomatic.

> Foucault so resolutely suspends judgment, and adopts so thoroughgoing a scepticism about any determinacy or relationship between practices, other than the largely contingent, that we are entitled to see him, not as an agnostic on these questions, but as deeply committed to the necessary non-correspondence of all practices to one another. From such a position neither a social formation, nor the State, can be

adequately thought. And indeed Foucault is constantly falling into the pit which he has dug for himself. For when—against his well-defined epistemological positions—he stumbles across certain "correspondences" . . . , he lapses into a vulgar reductionism, which thoroughly belies the sophisticated positions he has elsewhere advanced. (71)

Absorbed into the shadows of institutional agency, everyday practices which might subvert such apparently omnipotent forces remain on a broad but essentially unrecognized level in Foucault's accounts. As Foucault's critical narrative records the desire for change, it assumes the necessity of radical historical breaks built on symptomatic reactions to historical forces which remain so general as to appear mythic.

In order to coax a less symptomatic, more subtle notion of the interaction between institutional forces and historical change, Michel de Certeau responds to Foucault by setting forth an understanding of the relationship conditioned by practices not wholly controlled by, though potentially inhabiting, institutions. Responding specifically to what he conceives as Foucault's overvaluation of the "privileged development" of panoptically informed social organizations, de Certeau argues that

a society is . . . composed of certain foregrounded practices organizing its normative institutions *and* of innumerable other practices that remain "minor," always there but not organizing discourses and preserving the beginnings or remains of different (institutional, scientific) hypotheses for that society or for others. (*Practice of Everyday Life* 48)

Implicitly attempting to balance the experiential and structural approaches to cultural studies identified by Stuart Hall in "Cultural Studies: Two Paradigms," de Certeau builds on the strengths of both projects, pursuing subtle forms of experientially oriented agency while remaining sensitive to the structures which latently condition the construction of agency. Historical transformation thus becomes not a cataclysmic event, not a utopian moment, but a subtle process of repetition and change in struggle. This pursuit is very much in line with Chicano rhetorical experiments which offer in their production and consumption alternate social "hypotheses" or worldviews in conflict.

One of the clearest examples of this sort of alternative practice is described by Gerald López as he recounts his and his community's everyday experiences of legal constitutions—Mexican and U.S.— during his youth in East Los Angeles. Locating constitutional texts in a material, political struggle rather than in a transcendent set of values, López focuses on the way in which Chicanos received such texts as rhetorically limiting:

> In our experience, constitutional interpretations and constitutional decisions reflect the provisional containment of fighting, not its tran-scendence. As Chicanos see it, through a constitution, we in this country publicly announce that "for the moment, there's no battle here," not always confident the words will create, much less reflect, the reality. ("Idea of a Constitution" 164)

As López points out, this alternative reception more than anything else defines the unique reading of constitutions performed by the many Chicanos who refuse to monumentalize the creation of such documents. The interpretation of constitutions involves from this perspective a recognition of the complex historical investments in inequality that are only obfuscated by either a sentimental faith in "the grand tradition" or a blanket overvaluation of institutional power.

Such recognitions often come with a normative desire that social life might find "a rhythm that may, to varying degrees in different areas of society and culture, be open to the interaction of norm and transgression, rule and exception, centrality and liminality, commit-ment and criticism" (LaCapra, *Soundings in Critical Theory* 181). Hall suggests that a critic might attempt to "work through" the extremes attending culture studies—the pressing needs to study both lived experience and conceptions of institutional power—by recognizing the common effort made by critics to expose and think the "latent."[15] Such projects would include seeking out undervalued practices, in-cluding rhetorical practices, and cutting "into the complexity of the real, in order precisely to reveal and bring to light relationships and structures which cannot be visible to the naïve naked eye, and which can neither present nor authenticate themselves" (Hall 67).

De Certeau locates such practices by distinguishing between "strategic" and "tactical" activity. The former is constituted by the calculation (or manipulation) of power relationships that become possible as soon as a subject with will or power (a business, an army, a city, a scientific institution) can be isolated. It postulates a place that can be delimited as its own and serve as a base from which relations with an exteriority composed of targets or threats (customers or competitors, enemies, the country surrounding the city, objectives and objects of research, etc.) can be managed. (*Practice of Everyday Life* 35–36)

In contrast, tactical actions are defined by their very lack of a "proper place." The advantage of this itinerant existence lies in the freedom it confers; the movements of the tactic act like guerrilla combat engagements. A tactic thus stands out as "a maneuver 'within the enemy's field of vision' . . . and within enemy territory. It does not, therefore, have the options of planning general strategy and viewing the adversary as a whole within a distinct, visible, and objectifiable space. It operates in isolated actions, blow by blow" (37). Within such a context mobility and survival, let alone success, become virtually synonymous. Inasmuch as the strategic depends on the panoptic structures analyzed by Foucault to maintain a mastery of sight over the terrain, tactics "must vigilantly make use of the cracks that particular conjunctions open in the surveillance of the proprietary powers" (37).

Chicanos work such strategies into their narratives by parodying the way they claim to expand vision, to "transform the uncertainties of history into readable spaces," thereby reinforcing the "power of knowledge." When, for instance, Luis Valdez dominates the opening set of *Zoot Suit* with a front-page newspaper reproduction, blown up to fill the stage, it is exactly this strategic manipulation of the visual that he parodies. The tactic turns the strategy's weakness against itself, in *Zoot Suit*'s case by demonstrating that "power is bound by its very visibility"; the redirection of the audience's gaze to bring the newspaper reporter under scrutiny could thus be taken as paradigmatic of the tactical approach.[16]

Although de Certeau's distinction between strategy and tactic may yet appear rough, the study contributes greatly to inquiries about rhetorical force and hegemony in general.[17] Numerous Chicano narratives and CRS efforts attempt to develop just such a tactical rhetorical approach (Williams's work stands out as a very successful example, as does Crenshaw's revision of rights discourse). Arguing that such projects begin to "work through" forces and structures promoting dependency, I read them as building on the tactical/strategic differentiation that de Certeau articulates in response to Foucault.[18] Without such a distinction, notions of historical transformation threaten to become their own parodies and, worse, to feed into a liberal sentimentalism which suggests that change will occur in some cataclysmic or utopian event regardless of resistant agency.

Focusing on the sociopolitical contexts and events which inform Chicano studies, we may thus ask what form the process of "working through" takes in Chicano narratives. While this question might be approached in a variety of ways (by analyzing narrative production and consumption, its dialogic appropriation of voices, etc.), I would suggest that a danger may attend the attempt to address seemingly omnipotent institutions with the psychoanalytic concept introduced by Hall. In a sociopolitical context in which Anglo/Mexicano interactions have been conditioned by a long history of inequality, the "working through" of dependence, resentment, and fear may require a significant rethinking of the psychological concept itself and of the reception of its larger context, psychoanalysis.[19] I would also emphasize that in some political contexts effective resistance may not be served by immediately attempting to move beyond the terms of a hierarchical binary relation (i.e., by "working through"); in certain cases a political agenda may in fact be best served by reversing a hierarchy. Contexts may exist in which reversal fills a crucial tactical function. Specifically, I think we can gain a greater critical understanding of complex tactical maneuvers undertaken by Chicano artists by examining how their narratives have appropriated the panoptic power of Anglo oppressors, at times conceiving of *la reconquista,* a symbolic retaking of the land, and at times reinforcing hegemonic assumptions.

Returning to the CLS scholar Mark Kelman, we may recall his argument that the rhetorical presuppositions of legal discourse displace "counter-hegemonic thoughts," making them simply "harder to think" (*ILL* 269). Of the presuppositions Kelman outlines, two are pertinent in relation to panoptic mechanisms: (1) synthetic individualism (including the limitation or displacement of specific forms of group agency) and (2) "the conflation of the potential legal solubility of a problem with the existence of a problem" (*ILL* 269). In both cases the crucial rhetorical operation may be considered in terms of the mechanics of sight; inasmuch as seeing serves as a metaphor for recognition—of groups, of specific problems—panoptic control is at stake. As a concrete way of spelling out what is involved in these two strategic forms of denial (of legal-rhetorical "disappearing"), an examination of Richard Rodriguez's *Hunger of Memory: The Education of Richard Rodriguez* (1982) will provide a best-selling example of their uncritical repetition by a Chicano writer. Before entering into a reading of Rodriguez—to date one of the most widely published Chicano authors—I will offer a more developed description of those modes defined by Kelman that predominate in *Hunger of Memory*.

In the mode of synthetic individualism, "social relations can be understood only as the sum of readily comprehensible individual relations" (Kelman 269). Liberalism is, in this regard, committed both epistemologically and politically "to the notion that groups are artificial, that they can be understood or analyzed only by reference to the individuals who compose them."[20] Such a presupposition has very significant consequences for potentially transformative legal arguments which recognize the interests of specific social groups— for instance, issues of affirmative action and institutional racism. The liberal orientation of U.S. legal discourse resists claims to recognize such group approaches and instead reasserts these claims as antagonisms between particular individuals. Hence, the Supreme Court, in its 1976 decision in *Washington v. Davis*, insists that relief pertaining to institutional racism will be granted only if individual intention may be aligned with a racist action. In cases like this one, a certain form of contractual protocol takes over in which legal actors are understood solely as transparent individuals working in a limited time frame. Such limitations effectively delegitimate considerations of long-term historical discrimination by one group against another (discrimination founded on identification with a group); thus, past and present social inequalities appear to be "natural," and the widely divergent, racially specific results on employment examinations at issue in the case become invisible.[21] The maintenance of social inequality through these limitations ends up being a way of guarding the status quo.

Such rhetorical constructions play an essentially anesthetizing role; they dull the pain of unresolved issues and contradictions in the law that would, if acknowledged, open radical perspectives on the law. Paraphrasing the CLS scholar Duncan Kennedy, Kelman goes even further, suggesting that the notion of "natural rights" itself defers a socio-existential conflict.

> What is too painful to face is that we both need and abhor others, for they both form and destroy us; give us all meaningful power and subject us to their domination. . . . What "rights consciousness" allows is for us to believe that we have *solved* this problem. We will fuse with people as long as they respect our rights. . . . That rights are in some deep sense so indeterminate as to be illusory—that the problems of fusion and separateness inevitably recur in *defining* rights, which may demand in an oscillating contradictory fashion more or less concern for others, more or less capacity to call on others to be concerned for us—never fully negates their fundamental mediating role. (*ILL* 289)

According to Kennedy's argument in "The Structure of Blackstone's Commentaries," rights—or, more properly, battles over interpretations of rights—rely on a critical blindness. However, in the critical vein suggested by Crenshaw, readers would do well to question the manner in which such rhetorical battles are reinscribed by Kennedy into an individualistic orientation, as happens when he defines the underlying conflict as existential. As Patricia Williams has noted in another context, members of marginalized social groups may take on a wholly different interpretation of battles over rights when those battles are seen historically as one of the few (however imperfect) vehicles to enfranchisement in U.S. society.[22]

The tendency to overvalue the individualistic is, however, quite strong, and it is only made stronger by the publishing industry's sponsoring of marginal writers who celebrate meritocracy and melting-pot philosophy at the expense of the historical analysis of inequality. For instance, Rodriguez's *Hunger of Memory*, a text engaged in exactly this sort of anesthetizing self-mutilation, is the quintessential example of an argument traversing cultural capital in the two senses (educational and legal) which I have emphasized. By situating a legal polemic in an educational context, Rodriguez's autobiography symptomatically combines parallel rhetorical drives aimed at reinforcing the limitations of agency inherent in U.S. liberalism. Asserting his, and everyone's, right to assimilate, to become a "public individual" (26), Rodriguez plays the discourses in such a manner as to make himself the ultimate receptor, a virtual *tabula de la raza*. By accepting this role and promoting it as a model, Rodriguez legitimates the great variety of institutional panoptic functions which would make us prisoners of anonymity. Ultimately, his scenario of the private, ethnic self being sacrificed to inevitable public acculturation dominates his view.

To those who would assert their difference through alternative, community-based notions of subjectivity, the seemingly inevitable response to the world Rodriguez describes is paranoia. As one might expect, the young Rodriguez, the child still somehow organically connected with his culture, conveys the experience of paranoia through concrete, if unanalyzed, reactions to his parents' marks of social difference. In particular, Rodriguez's reaction to his father's difficulties in communication reveals an extreme sensitivity to the public's gaze and to its (dis)approval. The problem is compounded by the anger Rodriguez exhibits toward his parents, anger provoked when they immerse him in English, thereby initiating a supposedly inevitable sacrifice of cultural and familial ties to educational success. In the beginning Rodriguez expresses this anger by attempting to make his parents feel intellectually inferior (a motivation supposedly overcome in Rodriguez's maturity, when he realizes that they are in fact intelligent, albeit in a "native" sense). Soon he recognizes a more subtle means of hurting his parents: instead of seeking direct confrontation, he cuts them off from his school life and successes (successes which mean so much to them) by imposing silence; he becomes, in his own words, "Mr. Secrets."

After announcing, in the confessional mode which permeates the text, his intention to hurt his parents, Rodriguez describes a conversation with his mother: "'Tell me all about your new courses.' I would barely respond, 'Just the usual things, nothing special.' (A half smile, then silence. Her head moving back in the silence. Silence! Instead of the flood of intimate sounds that had once flowed smoothly between us, there was this silence.)" (51). Although the master narrative of Rodriguez's text would explain this episode as part of an inevitable social change, what becomes more and more clear in the autobiography is that Rodriguez's resentment is fueled not by a "typical" process of assimilation but rather by an overreaction to immersion in the educational system; Rodriguez "overlooks" the fact that he lived in an Anglo community, attended a predominantly Anglo school, and therefore had no notion of what many Chicanos experience: Spanish as a public language and ethnicity as a social bond. Consequently, he becomes convinced of the inevitability of either/or choices regarding immersion. Reacting to the seeming rejection by his parents symbolized in their early blanket refusal to speak Spanish, and identifying with society's dominant rhetoric of synthetic individualism, Rodriguez attempts to carve out a new identity for himself, an identity which he achieves by symbolically sacrificing his parents who represent ties to a group situated beyond the liberal binary of individual versus public.[23]

This technique of imposing an aggressive silence finds a parallel in Rodriguez's larger argument about affirmative action, in which he criticizes the program for not being sufficiently radical; while the evaluation is conditioned by Rodriguez's failure to conceive of group interests, it is also informed by his tendency to conflate the existence of a problem with the ability to find a remedy for it within the assumed set of viable social interactions. Ramón Saldívar has noted that *Hunger of Memory*'s response to affirmative action is conditioned by Rodriguez's failure to "conceive of a form of subjectivity that would draw upon existing social practice, the life of the collective folk (of *la raza*)" ("Ideologies of the Self" 33). Saldívar appropriately concludes that the narrative significantly misconstrues the sociopolitical contexts it would engage by giving meaning to social events only insofar as they are connected to Rodriguez's private life and outlook. In repeated epiphanic passages, Rodriguez does in fact hope to build pathos, as well as justification, for the acculturation which accompanies his education. Each of the epiphanic instances is constructed around Rodriguez's ironic failure to discover a remedy for silence; in his repeated fatalistic confrontations with his own people, he takes *his* failure to speak, to engage the "other," as a sign of a determinate social force outside of his control. Failing to find remedy in speech, Rodriguez ignores the problem of creating meaningful dialogue between different segments of *la raza*, instead ascribing the problem the status of an impossibility. In this manner, the problem as well as the social group is pushed out of sight, made unrecognizable. As Saldívar notes, the issue is Rodriguez's failure to imagine a more critical manner of engaging his sociohistorical context; rather than developing more subtle interactions between his private self, his public self, *la raza,* and the dominant Anglo society, Rodriguez has created a portrayal of himself which enacts a symptomatic response to his legal context, unconsciously reproducing its dominant ideological strategies.

Duncan Kennedy's discussion of William Blackstone highlights one particular aspect of Western European legal ideology animated by Rodriguez, giving a historical perspective to the conflation of recognition and remedy.[24] According to Kennedy, an evolution has taken place in legal thinking, an evolution in which Blackstone's original, essentially descriptive, defense of a legal system of writs was reconceived by legal positivists in tautological terms. To assert the value of the writ system, Blackstone argued that each "pre-existing right" incorporated into the system found a remedy there as well. The consolidation of the legal positivist movement was then supported by a misreading which took Blackstone's understanding of the relation between rights and remedies to be totalizing. Thus, the recognition of a problem came to depend on the preexistence of a remedy. The power of such a reformulation lies in its ability to negate competing voices from outside the legal establishment, voices which might challenge the tautological approach, thereby opening the interpretation of both rights and remedies. Inasmuch as synthetic individualism dominates legal thinking, notions of rights and remedies are thus effectively limited, undercutting claims by groups who suffer discrimination. Focusing on the protection of individual rights at the expense of group action, the courts have indeed chosen to ignore long histories of racism because, in terms of legitimate remedies, the injuries of reverse racism are simply more easily corrected and more consistent with U.S. legal thinking.[25]

LO REAL MARAVILLOSO AND
DISPLACEMENTS OF THE STRATEGIC

With the rereading of social practices offered by de Certeau, we may claim that a radical revision of Foucault's understanding of social power has taken place in which a seemingly new ontological space opens, one latent with potential resistance in the form of everyday practices and tactical maneuvers. Likewise, it is crucial to understand that Rodriguez's uncritical repetition of legal ideology, despite his claims to representativeness, does not typify Chicano cultural texts; instead, such "tactical" texts tend to manifest far more resistant approaches to the discourses of institutions controlled by and for Anglos. This critical demeanor extends to the very basis of hegemonic notions about the function of the law. Again, Chicano history is the story of territorial occupation through legal manipulation working in concert with violence; hence, it comes as little surprise that "consenting social relations," as framed in the mainstream manner, are significantly challenged by Chicano narratives which underscore a system of dependency veiled by a larger ethic of historical amnesia.

As this "new" critical orientation opens, however, so does the opportunity for colonization. It is an unfortunate possibility that, by making such latent connections apparent, critics may extend the range and control of existing panoptic structures. To give the notion of Chicano tactical responses an aspect of resistance, and thereby to respond to this problem, we may recall that de Certeau poses tactics as "calculated actions" (*Practice of Everyday Life* 37). Rather than exploring the nature of this *tactical intention,* de Certeau comments instead on the more abstract reflections cast by tactics, including their temporal orientation (38–39) and their supernatural quality: tactical practices "circulate without being seen, discernible only through the objects that they move about and erode." They "are the ghosts of the society that carries their name. Like the spirits of former times, they constitute the multiform and occult postulate of productive activity" (35). Reminiscent of Patricia Williams's "ghost furniture" produced by elided race issues that mainstream legal practice must constantly fumble around, de Certeau's rhetorical displacement ultimately takes his argument to a metacritical level:

> The imaginary landscape of an inquiry is not without value, even if it is without rigor. It restores what was earlier called "popular culture," but it does so in order to transform what was represented as a matrix-force of history into a mobile infinity of tactics. It thus keeps before our eyes the structure of the social imagination in which the problem constantly takes different forms and begins anew. (41)

Countering Foucault's emphasis on institutional power, de Certeau claims a potential quite similar to that located in the Fuentes epigraph to *The Brick People.* Thus, de Certeau finds in Foucault an

"imaginary landscape of inquiry" that takes on "an overall corrective and therapeutic value in resisting . . . reduction" of the power
dynamics studied (41). Even if Foucault overemphasizes the omnipotence of institutions, his approach "at least assures" the presence
of alternative perspectives, albeit "as ghosts" somewhat less con-
sciously posed than those offered by Williams.

Pushing the claim even further with regard to Chicano narratives,
we may consider the omnipotence attributed to both Anglo institutions (the hacienda, the courts, the media) and the "magical realist"
responses (the revenging insects, El Pachuco) as homeopathic rhetorical manipulations whose value lies, in part, in their emphasis on
the constructed character of panoptic, disciplinary tools.[26] By thus
engaging a "magical" practice that has—as Saldívar has demonstrated—a particular cultural and historical trajectory, Morales
writes a novel that is balanced at that border site where Chicano
responses to institutional dependency may be played out, especially
with regard to current immigration policy and to the northern appropriation of the hacienda. Like the Rain God at the close of Arturo
Islas's novel of that title (1984), the suggestions of witchcraft in Ana
Castillo's *Sapogonia* (1990), and the cockroaches that infiltrate the
pages of Acosta's works, these ghosts play on the rhetorical organization of the dominant institutional apparatuses (especially, in these
cases, the legal) in order to gain at least the potential for *la reconquista*, for retaking control of the landscape.

To the extent that this reading applies to Morales's project, it confirms the position taken by George Mariscal when he argues that
the novelist reworks utopian elements embedded in the Chicano
nationalist movement. Hence, we may consider Morales as a postmovement writer who revises the utopian Aztlán—the goal of the
reconquest. As Mariscal points out, the implications of Morales's
work are such that "[i]f there is to be a Chicano utopia, it will not
be Aztlán. . . . On the contrary, instead of a place it will be a process,
a process founded on differences, a continual activity in which difference does not threaten the concept of paradise but instead serves
as its founding principle" (82). The impulse here recalls Bruce-
Novoa's desire for a less incestuous notion of reform in that for both
authors the object of censure is the utopian promise held out by the
Chicano movement, a promise which, according to their readings,
fueled a problematic collapsing of differences among Chicanos in

an effort to formulate an overriding concept of *the* community.[27] In this light, the drive to "monumentalize" the numerous political affiliations of the 1960s and 1970s may be read as an overreaction to the U.S. beliefs in individualism and meritocracy promoted in no small part by legal culture. As Mario García has suggested, the movement itself may be fully understood only when taking into account its critical-legal antecedents in the Chicano civil rights movement of the preceding "Mexican-American" generation.[28] From this historical perspective, we begin to see how the accommodationist demands for reform—for instance, LULAC's argument that "Americans of Mexican descent" be counted and therefore educated as "whites"—altered in the later, more radical movement to create an insulating separatism. Although this unifying vision did enable very important coalitions and reforms, its insufficient incorporation of bonds addressing the diversity of the community has led to a progressive erosion of collective action.[29]

For Morales and numerous other postmovement writers, then, one critical task has been representing a more successful means of coming to terms with nonhegemonic group thinking and identity, especially notions of groups not anchored in hierarchies. Utopian visions are thus not wholly discarded, nor are they wholly endorsed, at least not in their formerly dogmatic variations. Instead, as I have argued here, authors like Morales tend to complicate utopian promise by suggesting it be read as "a process founded on difference." What typifies a utopian *process*? Some of the most famous Western utopias—for instance, Thomas More's 1516 version—are foremost an opportunity to imagine a perfect state government and, perhaps most important, a perfect understanding of laws. If we combine this legal reform imperative with the critique (and manipulation) of panoptic techniques evident in Chicano narratives, we find a process analogous to that described by de Certeau when he demonstrates that critics of institutions may employ their own "counterpanoptic" techniques in order to screen what are actually tactical maneuvers, alternative interpretive practices promoting the worldviews of those who are not equal.[30]

4

Consensual Fictions

As suggested in the last chapter, Chicano utopian revisions have been the site of a complex battle with legal rhetoric. As early as the 1880s Mexicano authors like Mariano Vallejo were considering their disenfranchisement under the American regime in light of a projected utopian past, a time worthy of nostalgia when cherished values remained unthreatened and conflicts were avoided by recourse to an essentially benevolent patriarchal tradition. Not surprisingly, early texts like Vallejo's bolster their rhetorical authority to posit such utopian visions by turning to various legal documents and legal rhetoric, confirming both the authority of the Mexicano historian and the superiority of the lost society, of the imaginary landscape.[1]

The tendency lives on in the earliest academically sponsored Mexicano scholarship, which strategically posits a similar utopian past; hence, in Américo Paredes's *With His Pistol in His Hand: A Border Ballad and Its Hero* (1958), we read claims for the essentially utopian political life of Nuevo Santander—what is now the Mexico/Texas borderlands. According to Paredes, it is exactly this utopian governance that inspires the resistant corrido tradition, and perhaps its most famous example, "El Corrido de Gregorio Cortez" (1901). As with Vallejo's celebration of life before the Treaty of Guadalupe Hidalgo, the landscape portrayed by Paredes appears to remain pure by virtue of its insulated "patriarchal system," which "not only made the border community more cohesive, by emphasizing its clanlike characteristics, but also minimized outside interference, because it allowed the community to govern itself to a great extent" (12–13). As Renato Rosaldo notes in *Culture and Truth: The Remaking of Social Analysis* (1989), Paredes carefully builds on the Cortez legend, and the resistant force the ballad took on, to praise an ancient ideal of manhood associated with the lost "corrido century" (roughly 1830–1930). Summarizing this vision, Rosaldo recalls: "Descendants of the primordial patriarchs, these country men live in the old style. Unaided by microphones, their voices carry across the pasture and make their listeners feel *muy gallo*, literally very rooster, very male fighting cock, with rising hackles" (155).

Likewise, Cortez's "deeds as a warrior horseman confer the aura of medieval nobility," his shouts echoing with the "grandeur of the medieval epic" (155). Rosaldo acknowledges that these overtly masculine heroics have been significantly reworked by subsequent Chicano and particularly Chicana narratives; however, I will linger on Paredes's particular form of nostalgic remembrance because it is instructive in regard to Chicano representations of, and interactions with, consensual rhetoric.

For example, when Rosaldo takes up the question of resistance in Paredes's text, he emphasizes that Paredes "uses a nostalgic poetic mode to depict his Garden of Eden" in which "manhood" could be "endowed with the mythic capacity to combat Anglo-Texan anti-Mexican prejudice" (151). Here the utopian is implicitly posited as a reaction distinct from Anglo-Texan attitudes and, by implication, from Anglo-Texan legal rhetoric. It is precisely the potential complicities defined in this account—complicities between Mexicano resistance and Anglo-Texan racist ideology—that require further consideration. What subtly distinguishes Paredes's rendition of the pre-treaty era from Vallejo's is a fundamental emphasis on the consensual purity and egalitarian nature of Nuevo Santander. Thus, from the opening pages of *With His Pistol in His Hand*, readers are asked to measure the value of the earlier society on the basis of the minimal military presence, as if this absence of overt displays of force guaranteed a more democratic society (albeit one still nominally patriarchal).

This refinement or streamlining of the legal-rhetorical agenda—from Vallejo's citing of legal documents and language as a means of legitimating the previous society, to Paredes's positing of a consensual fantasy on a par with mainstream legal apologists—marks a crucial shift in what are distinct masculine-oriented notions of resistance. What readers find is a tendency to adopt increasingly specific Anglo legal assumptions while constructing "forms of resistance"; hence, we discover in Paredes's version of the pre-treaty era an amalgam of historical perspectives that nonetheless symptomatically emphasizes the ideals of the U.S. legal tradition. Taking this tendency into account and returning to Bruce-Novoa's claim about the entrenched "incestuous focus" of Chicano literary studies, we may now consider problematic nationalist notions of community in the light of this history of positing utopian forms of resistance that weld "benevolent" masculine rule to U.S. legal thought.

Building on this context, we may reread Chicana narratives and their strategies—which struggle against oppression both inside and outside Chicano culture—in terms of the growing tendency evidenced by Chicano authors to adopt the legal ideology of consent. In this manner, we may begin rethinking one important type of collaboration between the aims of the dominant society and the "Mexican-American generation" of political activists and their successors as well as the critique this collaboration has received from Chicana artists.[2]

THE POLITICS OF CONSENT

Attempting to conceive of a more perfect union, one which would circumvent the spheres of power left behind in Europe, the "framers" of the Constitution initiated what they felt to be a more participatory government in which the various forms of force experienced previously would be realigned in a new style of consensual interaction between free individuals. Numerous historians, including Sacvan Bercovitch and Michael Kammen, have noted the manner in which our earliest calls to consensus played out specific political ends, ends especially important at a time when an emphasis on liberty threatened to destroy burgeoning national unity.[3] Consensus as such has always had an important rhetorical function, a fact not lost on the British, who, during revolutionary times, were quick to point out the irony behind the colony's claims to a slavelike existence (as opposed to true citizenship) under British rule: slavery was obviously alive and well in America.

In the present context, a similar notion of consenting citizenry resurfaces in Archibald Cox's best-selling study *The Court and the Constitution* (1987). There is a certain irony in this, inasmuch as Cox is thought of by some as a constitutional Dirty Harry. Of course, it was Cox who, as appointed investigator, doggedly pursued the

Watergate tapes and finally helped force Richard Nixon to resign. As Cox himself notes, his zealous pursuit and ultimate success significantly challenged the power of the presidential office—both nationally and internationally. Committed to the notion of an objective legal system, if only as an ideal, Cox went ahead with his investigation of Nixon despite his awareness that such open confrontation between the judicial and legislative branches could potentially weaken the consensual foundations at all levels of U.S. society (15–16). As Cox presents himself, he was thus another rule breaker with the right intentions, a challenger of Winston Churchill's dictum: democracy must never show its weaknesses.

As Cox himself seems to fear, his investigative work contributed to a trend also exacerbated by protesters making their voices heard on the steps of the U.S. Supreme Court building; both he and the protesters appear to share, however tenuously, a legal-activist agenda in which they seek to influence decisions through public opinion. The dangerous result, in Cox's estimation: the public at large has come to see the Supreme Court justices more and more as a legislative body. He supports the claim by noting that recent polls have found that the majority of citizens favor choosing justices through an electoral process that would place justices on the bench for limited terms. As one might suspect, such polling results were met with horror by prominent legal leaders, including Cox, leaders who continue to believe that the judicial tenure system, and the principle of judicial restraint, are the fundamental reasons why people continue to respect and consent to the law. In one sense, then, we can read *The Court and the Constitution* as an attempt to rectify the damage done by the author's own role in the Nixon scandal. While I will not devote the time to a full analysis of the book, let me summarize by noting that it represents yet another attempt to put the genie back into the bottle, to "depoliticize" the law and thereby reinforce the Court's legitimacy as an objective body worthy of consensual support. From the beginning, the only other option offered by Cox is a government chained to its own use of force, a dilemma that derives from his liberal-legal outlook.

I would like to consider how this liberal-legal dynamic shapes the contradictions we find in Cox's work. Like all other institutions, the legal system in this country has as its primary goal self-replication. We may thus assume that various rhetorical mechanisms we identify with the law promote its own institutional survival. Inasmuch as U.S. law is founded on liberal-legal principles and the revolutionary context which reanimated those principles, its life—as Cox well recognizes—depends on the viability of the dichotomy of consent versus force; it is through this dichotomy that the law legitimizes its role in U.S. society by structuring a more perfect union. The law demands that we accept this dichotomy, but the mere fact of that demand by no means verifies that the dichotomy is actually determinant in events as we live them.

Approaching the law's masking effect from another perspective, we would do well to recall that rules often act as rhetorical devices put into play while people argue about and construct accounts of behavior; however, having lists of such rules does not necessarily throw much light, if any, on what people do. However, while the relation between rules and behavior may be complex, the rhetorical mechanisms of the law may enact politically efficacious modes of denial by giving the illusion of nonculpability. In other words, legal rules may throw up blinders that are reinforced by the weight of legal precedence and therefore appear to absolve individuals—and especially groups—of direct responsibility for political consequences that are attained by means that are often far more complex than the force/consent logic will allow. This tendency toward interpretive redirection is especially apparent in terms of what will and will not be allowed admissible for judgment—including evidence, but also directing principles—in particular situations. For now, I will note that only on rare occasions does mainstream legal thought inadvertently reveal the deeper rhetorical function of the consent/force dichotomy.

One such occasion takes place as Cox describes his understanding of the judge's role as passed down to him by the famous Judge Learned Hand. According to Cox (recalling Judge Hand), "A judge must preserve his authority by cloaking himself in the majesty of an overshadowing past, but he must discover some composition with the dominant needs of his time" (26). The figure here, authority cloaking itself in precedence, invites the male readers of this book—Cox seems to be focused solely upon male readers—to take up an apparently enlightening opportunity, to probe with Learned Hand beneath the robes. I offer my apologies to whoever might be offended by such puns, but they are apt. To risk offense even further,

I would suggest that the scene described here is, indeed, libidinally charged, for throughout the text Cox unselfconsciously describes the law as a male field, an approach that invites readings of homosocial desire.[4] For instance, Cox relies on crucial anecdotes that are made more personal by revealing the combination of dressing, undressing, and legal argument before the male gaze. Cox's masculinist notion of the law is made more explicit in his treatment of women and women's issues: he rarely mentions women as active participants in the law, and the only contemporary case that he openly criticizes is *Roe v. Wade.* While we will later pursue, as Eve Sedgwick has suggested, the homosocial desires embedded within the patriarchal exchange of women among men in the law, for now I will limit my point to the following: guarded revelations about the transgressability of authority, like the one offered by Cox through Judge Hand, both reveal naked power and disguise it in a sleight of hand that serves an ultimately symbolic function. Where Cox would play on consent and force as distinct sociosymbolic categories, the transgression that occurs when the boundary slides (as in the Learned Hand anecdote) carries an even greater charge, one which seems to destabilize the apparently settled contours of the categories throughout the rest of his text; ultimately these categories may exist in a dialectical relation that makes such tension, revealed in guarded moments, essential to the self-perpetuation of legal rhetoric.

While the claim might seem highly speculative, I would assert that a subtle erotics is at work within the descriptions of such transgressions between consent and force, an erotics which is intimately intertwined with all dominance/submission scenarios in a patriarchal and homosocially organized society. Peter Stallybrass and Allon White suggest such a possibility in their book *The Politics and Poetics of Transgression,* in which they propose that a psychological investment or dependence can develop when social phenomena are artificially dichotomized so that one part of the dichotomy may be symbolically excluded and subsequently eroticized (25). Despite the efforts of legal apologists like Cox, we move through society experiencing decisions made on a complex continuum between force and consent. We come to recognize a middle ground where the two categories may in fact break down, or at least become exceedingly complex; the notion of hegemonic power is informed by just such a recognition. The state, of course, has a considerable investment in the psychological manipulation of behavior. Its legal institutions have participated in such conditioning by reinforcing the force/consent dichotomy and by giving apparent priority to the latter term in order to build the liberal ideal of voluntary participation in "acceptable" behavior. Force thus becomes the excluded term. However, as Stallybrass and White suggest, such excluded spheres usually become "a primary eroticized constituent of [a culture's] fantasy life." It is in this sense that what is supposedly socially peripheral—here, the use of force—becomes symbolically central. Such arguments help us to understand why, in a society that prides itself on the democratic rule of law, the public spends much of its leisure time observing representations of murder, sexual assault, and cops crossing that fine line in order to do the right thing—in short, participating in a psychic economy which lives out in fantasy the violence that the illusion of consent masks in everyday life.

Granting Stallybrass and White's contention that there is an erotic content to such transgressions as those noted above, we find that the cases which reveal the most about this content include those delineating legal responses to issues involving sexuality. In this vein, Susan Brownmiller, Andrea Dworkin, and Catharine MacKinnon have all argued that the explicit dynamics of rape best explain the functioning of contemporary patriarchal society, including its legal structure. When we also consider Annette Kolodny's argument in *The Lay of the Land: Metaphor as Experience and History in American Life and Literature* (1975)—that the Western frontier has been almost universally figured in terms of masculine aggressive expansion seeking control of a resistant feminized object or property—we begin building a context for reading rape as it is represented in borderlands texts, a context that highlights the transgressive artistic shiftings that may take place between force and consent. However, no interpretation of such transgressive shifting could address the subtlety of the Chicana critiques without first considering the specific Mexicano iconography of rape and the politics of shame it mobilizes.

CRITIQUING CONSENSUAL PARADIGMS

As Norma Alarcón has noted, the terms *traitor* and *translator* collapse in Chicano cultural iconography inasmuch as La Malinche (Cortez's native interpreter) has traditionally been made the paradigmatic figure of feminine betrayal. While there is a great deal of supposition about La Malinche's history—ranging from claims that she was actively assisting a Christianization she herself believed in to claims that her sudden disappearance evidences a violent sexual violation—there is little doubt that she has acted as a principal reference point for the masculinist cultural production of Chicana shame. In turn, such shame has been used to reinforce Chicana gender roles, including passivity, by associating Chicana violation with an act of consent. In the Malinche context, the principal dynamic of rape in Chicano communities—which occurs predominantly between familiars within the same social group—is refracted through a cross-cultural lens, making the event but one moment in a larger history of betrayal. As Alarcón notes, the association between La Malinche and rape remains a Chicano and Mexican national male obsession, an obsession that in turn becomes one important context within which Chicana writers intervene (82–83).

In general, Chicana representations of rape have only recently gained recognition because editors and teachers alike—at times in the name of nationalist pride—have wished to avoid conveying the wrong image of "the" community. Chicanos and Chicanas are left to ask, however, how they might understand the use of gendered stereotypes without associating them with one of their most blatant expressions: rape. Certainly La Malinche becomes eroticized and calls forth a violent response because, within the economy of the masculinist myth, her "choices" demand it. The artists explored here repeatedly ask to what extent Mexicanas and Chicanas have "free" choices in either the colonial or contemporary contexts. Their approaches suggest that consent, as figured in the great wealth of legal-cultural material surrounding us, remains an essentially symbolic power denied in practice.

For instance, in Ana Castillo's poem "An Idyll" (*Women Are Not Roses* [1984]) consent is asserted as a meaningful option for women, but only within a darkly ironic context that explodes the pastoral mind-set that readers might expect from a poem with such a title. In "An Idyll" a woman protagonist rejects a physically godlike lover, who in turn becomes violent. Consent is not only reappropriated here but is also reinforced by police officers who, with the protagonist, kill the pathetically ineffectual yet pastoral god-man. On one level, this poem is about reclaiming the right to sexual access. However, sexual access, treated as a resource as it is here, leads us to fundamental questions about gender itself and the way it appears to be socially constructed through the actual or impending transgression of women's "supposed" consent. Inasmuch as this consent is supposed, I would read "An Idyll," like Castillo's poem "In My Country" (*My Father Was a Toltec* [1988]), as a utopian projection aimed at empowering women on an imaginative level, a fact reinforced by the highly improbable participation of the police, who have historically most often turned their backs on "domestic" assaults.[5] Such police inaction bears out what becomes painfully clear in studies of rape prosecutions, including Gary LaFree's *Rape and Criminal Justice: The Social Context of Sexual Assault* (1989): most courts cannot conceive of force being used against a woman by her male partner. This elision is potentially reinforced by those liberals who would promote the supposedly clear distinction between rape as violence and sex as sex. In fact, the relations between sex, gender, and rape inform one of the most radical Chicana feminist critiques, developed by Cherríe Moraga in *Giving Up the Ghost* (1986).

María Herrera-Sobek points out in her article "The Politics of Rape: Sexual Transgression in Chicana Fiction" (*Chicana Creativity and Criticism* [1988]) that Moraga presents rape to demonstrate "its function as a political signifier of women's inferior status with regards to men" (172). Herrera-Sobek in turn focuses on the way rape as a process engenders women as a group. Examining the metaphoric structuring of the rape scene, this reading notes how women are both made an absence—are literally "made a hole"—and transformed into silent, invisible objects. Emphasizing the collapse of father and rapist, of father's tool and rapist's screwdriver, Herrera-Sobek, following Moraga, initiates a radical rethinking of the dictum that rape is violence, not sex.

Moraga is very explicit on the conflation of gender construction and rape. Corky, Marisa's younger self, recollects slowly: "Got raped once. When I was a kid. Taken me a long time to say that was exactly what happened, but that was exactly what happened. Makes you more aware than ever that you are one hundred percent female, just in case you had any doubts, one hundred percent female whether you act like it or not" (36). The irony of the last line is perhaps one of the most resolute lessons for rape victims at trial. As Kristin Bumiller points out, legal rhetoric is such that most victims learn early on in their court cases that there is no room for their perspective in the court (101–2). To support an accusation in a rape trial, only one mode of self-presentation is acceptable—that of a stereotypical, traditional woman. Ultimately, a woman's capacity to be raped is never far from sight. The court's question almost always becomes: did she do enough to circumvent a man's response to her capacity to be raped? Corky understands this rhetorical situation well and describes her own attempts to think herself out of it: "I guess I never wanted to believe I was raped. If it could happen to me, I'd rather think it was something else like 'unprovoked' sex or something hell I dunno. But if someone took me that bad, I wouldn't want to think I was took . . . you follow me? But the truth is . . . I was took" (36). Corky's desire, considered in light of the legal institution's reaction to rape, suggests one context for reading the play's epigraph: "If I had wings like an angel / over these prison walls / I would fly." The law, in conjunction with the masculine mobilization of Malinche iconography, makes this "prison" inasmuch as it conditions Chicanas toward condemning themselves for having their ultimately illusory consent transgressed.

Although not developed at length, the link between the function of the law and the function of rape provides a central tenet for Herrera-Sobek's essay on the play. Her epigraph begins:

> Men rape because they own the law
> They rape because they are the law
> They rape because they make the law
> They rape because they are the
> guardians of the peace, of law and order . . .
> Bodily rape is merely the acting out
> of a daily ideological reality.
> (Herrera-Sobek, "Politics of Rape" 117)

"The law" here is understood broadly to encompass myriad social institutions. In fact, the culture industry constantly bombards us with a great spectrum of specifically legal rhetoric—rhetoric that in its various forms says a great deal about how we perceive ourselves as social and sexual actors. As I have tried to suggest throughout this study, this rhetoric emphasizes social interaction as a play of individual intentions limited in time and complexity. Inevitably, understandings of deeper group conflicts, along the lines of gender, race, and class, appear as insurmountable individual tragedies that in turn legitimate the status quo. Again, *Ramona* is the epitome, a fact confirmed by its reception.

These legal-cultural representations—which continue to eroticize "illicit" sexual assault and which continue to suggest to Chicanas, by denying their perspective, that they should remain passive with regard to rape—reinforce the larger engendering process that links aggression and passivity to gender, dominance and submission to heterosexual desire. Hence, rape is constructed by means of stereotypes emphasizing that violation happens to women who transgress culturally defined gender roles. Such representations argue that women bring rape on themselves by being outside of the home, by wearing provocative clothing, or by acting in "nontraditional" ways.

Throughout the various legal-cultural representations, but especially in those which critically acknowledge the prevalence of non-stereotypical experiences, a language is operating—a language essentially not far removed from the language of torture described by Elaine Scarry in *The Body in Pain* (1985). Torture, Scarry explains, often occurs in a confining cell complete with familiar, household objects, objects which are turned into instruments that become semiotic symbols of the torturer's power. Consent or confession in such scenarios plays only a masking role: what is crucial is that the perpetrator appear to confer power on himself by destroying the victim's world through pain. Inasmuch as familiar objects can evidence sustaining links for the victim to a world outside of the torturer's control, he must literally unmake these objects by forever giving them the taint of his uses. Is it coincidence that the domestic scene so often becomes the site of confinement and abuse when such torture is really an extension of the practice of rape?

This commonality between the languages of torture and rape and their representation becomes literal in Corky's recollection of the assault she suffered during her Catholic schooling. While this recollection is particularly loaded—including as it does strong suggestions that Corky is a survivor of incest—I wish to focus on the manner in which her assailant's props become a central concern.[6] When a stranger enters Corky's schoolroom after hours, she is initially reassured by the familiar tools he carries.

> *He had work clothes on 'n' all I remember but they*
> *wernt dirty*

> *or wrinkled or nutin like they shoulda been*
> *if he'd been working all day*
> *but he has this screwdriver in his hand*
> *so I figure he must be legit.*

(38)

Enlisting Corky's aid in "repairing" a broken drawer, the assailant soon has the young girl in an extremely vulnerable position in which he is literally working between her legs. Conscious of the threat he poses, but equally terrified, Corky grasps for ways to make sense of (or to escape) what is happening.

> *"Don't move," he tells me. In English. His accent is gone. 'n' I don'.*
> *From then on all I see in my mind's eye . . .*
> were my eyes shut?
> *is the screwdriver he's got in his sweaty palm*
> *yellow glass handle*
> *shiny metal*
> *the kind my father useta use to fix things around the house*
> *remembered how I'd help him*
> *how he'd take me on his jobs with him*

(40–41)

A highly overdetermined scene, one suggestive of traumas preceding or speaking through this recollection proper, the episode reveals a use of household objects by the assailant that—as Scarry argues— literally unmakes Corky's world. In turn, Corky interprets the violence directed toward her with an unquestioned assumption of the masculinist consensual paradigm: *"I knew I musta done something real wrong to get myself in this mess"* (41). Hence, even in Corky's world unmade, a logic yet remains, one delineated as a series of paternal figures (she also imagines her assailant as her older cousin, Enrique) evoke for her a sense that she is being punished for some transgression she has committed. The consequent "indoctrination" into gender ideology portrayed by Moraga, and identified explicitly as such, thus assumes that learning fear and vulnerability is part of a process that also includes the internalization of the consensual dynamic.

Perhaps the foremost requirement for the perpetrator of either rape or torture is that he not empathize with his victim; to do so would collapse the scenario of dominance and submission that supposedly grants him his power. Each time a Chicana describes her understanding of rape, translating her experience into words, pictures, or music, the act challenges the power as well as the process of gender construction and its goal of perpetuating silent acceptance. Returning to the works of Ana Castillo, we find an excellent example of just such a challenge in *The Mixquiahuala Letters* (1986). An epistolary novel that acts out many roles (including travelogue, love poem, and political critique), the work traces the frustrated desire for dialogue experienced by women—in this case Theresa the writer and Alicia the recipient—who try to keep an intimate relationship alive at a distance. Besides the limitations of their medium, however, Castillo defines a larger barrier for this relationship early on:

> When i say ours was a love affair, it is an expression of nostalgia and melancholy for the depth of our empathy.
> We weren't free of society's tenets to be convinced we could exist indefinitely without the demands and complications one aggregated with the supreme commitment to a man. (Letter eleven, 39)

The approval conferred by men drives Theresa and Alicia to sexual encounters, but these encounters are far from the fulfillment of the heterosexual romantic myth. In their least physically brutal form, such episodes become occasions for wry humor. As letter eleven itself continues, Theresa recalls observing Alicia's seduction by an unidentified suitor. While the language of this recollection is packed with erotic overtones, both in its poetic images and its play of sounds, the scene is crucially deflated as Theresa interrupts the action to continue with her nap, entirely undercutting the eroticism of the passage, an eroticism contrived by allusions to conventional heterosexual pornography and to voyeurism. Equating consent with somnambulism, the recollection both simulates one type of erotic contract and dismisses its tenet (the unquestionable power of heterosexual seduction to move women).

As Castillo has said of the novel, its goal is "to present the reality, the complexities of sexuality, and how that interplays in society and how at a given moment two people can come together and miss" (qtd. in Trujillo 121). Clearly the most important erotic register for this latter failure is not a heterosexual one but rather a lesbian one. To read the novel with this in mind, however, leads one to find that heterosexual imperatives constantly impose themselves, frustrating a fully erotic relation between the women. In the end the messages recalled in the letters, even the letters themselves, exist in a world that subverts them, makes them, as Theresa writes, "only the words of another woman" (letter fourteen, 46). Theresa is particularly clear on the captivity of her interlocutor:

Alicia,

of prophetic dreams, not a Pisces, sign of mysticism and premonitions, not one to assume power except that acquired by your curiosity of the laws that guide men.

(letter twelve, 40)

Understood in this light, the transgression that the two women enact by traveling alone is undercut by their persistent desire to connect with the men whom they meet (at the expense of their relationship).

In this regard, Theresa is absolutely on track when she compares Alicia to the girl in the fairy tale "The Red Shoes." Alicia's desire to dance freely with men results in a physical sanction akin to that visited on her fairy tale twin, whose feet are ultimately amputated when her desires and agency become too great. Theresa's letters tell us that twice in one night Alicia is sexually assaulted: once at gunpoint, once in a university hall as the target of a gang attack. Alicia survives such experiences, but it is Theresa who understands the systematic purpose the attacks encode. Alicia in fact resents Theresa's "edge on society's contradictions," an edge Theresa gains "by admitting their enforced power" over the pair and over women in general (letter twenty-five, 86). What is gained is not simply an acknowledgment of victimization but rather a new understanding of the subtle, economic manipulations engaged through these "contradictions."

Ultimately, it is Theresa who appears to grapple most openly with the breakdown between coercion and consent, the same categories which sustain the very definition of liberalism which she tries to defend to a would-be Mexicano seducer who reads "liberal" as sexually accessible. Theresa replies: "What you perceive as 'liberal' is my independence to choose what i do, with who, and when. Moreover, it also means that i may choose not to do it, with anyone, ever" (letter twenty-two, 73). The assertion of choice is qualified in each of the Cortazar-like reading options offered at the novel's beginning (patterns of letters set out by the author), inasmuch as each of these readings contains a pairing of letters twenty-two and

twenty-three. The latter, a response to the former, describes the attempted rapes and rethinks the viability of the choice defended in
letter twenty-two. Anticipating the gang attack, Theresa reflects on
Alicia's participation—her role as a "slave"—in a game located "in
the lion's den [where] one doesn't play by one's own rules" (78).
Theresa recalls,

> an invitation to dance
> in the auditorium
> with bored men fed up with poker
> who should have had to coerce you
> twist your arm threaten your life
> lead you bodily in had only to *ask* you to dance . . .
> Again, the self-appointed
> guardian, i follow
> knowing there is little in the end i can do. i
> have a vagina too.
>
> (letter twenty-three, 78)

Theresa's subsequent words—"Leave her be! Son of a Bitch!"—do
break "the spell," halting the rape. However, to the extent that the
"lion" is only kept at bay, that the process of gender construction
continues after an only momentary challenge—to that extent Theresa's ultimate sense of failure appears justified. At stake is the wom-
en's investment in categories of force and consent because the collapse that Theresa recognizes significantly challenges their "liberal"
self-definition. As happens elsewhere in the novel, resentment follows injury when Theresa fails to extend her understanding to Alicia, a refusal perhaps tied to her fear that her "edge" on society's
"contradictions" would only exacerbate Alicia's sense of betrayal.
While the novel itself may move beyond such self-imposed silences
experienced during the "events" it looks back on, its monological
epistolary form demonstrates Castillo's commitment to recognizing
the pervasiveness of the barriers women like Theresa and Alicia face
when they try to connect. (The letters all move in one direction,
from Theresa to Alicia, confirming this limitation.)

Manipulations of gender construction, like those created by Castillo, use passivity in a critical way to demonstrate the larger forces
acting on social interactions. In the past, as Maxine Baca Zinn points
out in "Chicanas: Power and Control in the Domestic Sphere," Chicanas may have too easily accepted academic descriptions of their

own passivity. The predominance of such stereotypical representations of Chicanas in texts by Chicano males only furthers such acculturation. By contrast, a great many Chicana texts are being created or retrieved, texts that not only demonstrate Chicana and Mexicana efforts as agents of change in the domestic sphere but also suggest a long-standing participation in institutions, including the legal.[7]

Yet even where Chicanas have avoided such participation, it may be a mistake to assume complete patriarchal control has succeeded. As Baca Zinn notes, "Deference to males, the 'giving in' whereby women temporarily relinquish their control of domestic sphere matters, when males exercise their generalized authority, has not been submissiveness, but a mechanism for safeguarding the internal solidarity of the family" (29). Although such an analysis may seem somewhat dated in terms of more recent radical critiques of Chicano familial patriarchy, the problem of translating between academic spheres and different, more traditional segments of Chicano society suggests that at the very least, such claims to agency deserve attention. It is this sort of problem that Alarcón appears to have in mind when she notes that the Chicana feminist turn to La Malinche as a critical model opens problems which go beyond the specific appropriation or reappropriation. At stake is a "Chicana's own cultural self-exploration, self-definition and self-invention through and beyond the community's socio-symbolic system and contract" (72). The possibility of "anglicizing" the culture also accompanies such attempts to exceed this "contract," a term that reinforces just how extensively legal culture has permeated the language of social interaction.

If traditional roles have appeared silent, but may not necessarily be so, writers may ask how critical work is to understand its own participation in the problems identified by Alarcón. Assuming as I do that Chicanas and Chicanos operate within spheres of cultural conflict that may be described as borderlands, then an appropriate model of interpretation might well build on the theory and practice of translation—with all the productive betrayal implied by La Malinche as a Chicana feminist cultural force. Such an interpretive mode of translation, enacting a switching of codes and worldviews, is very much in evidence in some of the most innovative Chicana feminist work to date, including Gloria Anzaldúa's *Borderlands / La*

Frontera: The New Mestiza (1987). Drawing on such "innovations" is particularly appealing for many critics who feel that the legitimation of certain Chicano male "safe" texts has harmed Chicano studies. Yet for all the subtlety and complexity that might be offered by such new efforts at translation, there are clearly whole new horizons for co-optation, both intra- and intercultural. After a history of active underdevelopment of Mexicana and Chicana voices, what role if any exists for non-Chicanas to participate in current discussions? Is it in fact too soon even to ask questions about participation? Have the various ways Chicanas are forced into silence been addressed— opening anything like a mutually consenting partnership—or is consent in this scenario like much of the consent I have alluded to: a manipulative elision perpetuated in part through legal rhetoric in the hands of publishers, university bureaucrats, and many others irrespective of their position vis-à-vis Chicana history and the displacements it experiences? In my own thinking about these questions I have found a particular story by María Helena Viramontes, entitled "Cariboo Cafe" (included in *The Moths and Other Stories* [1985]), to be very helpful. Because this story offers a subtle rethinking of positioning—of what it means as a writer to treat historically silenced others—I believe it has much to say to readers and writers who find themselves in analogous situations.

"Cariboo Cafe" focuses on displaced persons, their voices ostensibly silenced by their marginality within society. The story is told primarily from the perspectives of three characters: the lost child Sonya; a cook in the run-down cafe; and a refugee from Central America, burdened with grief for her "disappeared" son. Each of these characters must confront representatives of legal authority in the course of the story. The nearly omniscient narrative voice which opens the story shadows Sonya's own, reciting a list of rules that include the necessity of avoiding the police, who are also "La Migra in disguise." Sonya's narrative, which immediately follows, seems to bear out this particular rule, as Sonya and her brother Mackey stumble on a neighbor being taken away by the police, presumably for deportation. Escaping the scene, the two soon find themselves in unfamiliar territory. When the two lost children seek refuge at the Cariboo Cafe, they are "appropriated" before they can enter by a nameless Central American woman who has likewise come to a stark understanding of "society's contradictions." Her narrative

presents the painful recounting of a mother in search of her ab-
ducted son. Her previous interview with the legal representative of
her government, the young señor, stands out as a mockery of dialogue; the señor's deferrals and accusations are practiced, even
clichéd, and after he has rationalized virtually everyone's guilt, he
proceeds to displace the child's name, sending a clear message to
his mother: your language, even the simple name of your child, will
not penetrate this rhetorical machine. This same mother subsequently finds herself a refugee in the United States, a refugee so
overcome by grief that she would "illicitly" substitute the lost children she finds outside the cafe for her own disappeared.

The third perspective developed in the story, that of the diner's
cook and owner, again tells us a great deal about the interaction
between these displaced citizens of the barrio and their legal over-
seers. His story, like the refugee mother's, is replete with displacements, in his case of his estranged wife and his son lost in Vietnam.
Driven to action by a frustration similar to the Central American
mother's, the cook finally turns the "kidnapper" in to the police, in
some sense reuniting his own family by reuniting another's. Yet the
cook's actions earlier in his story, when he turns in three illegal
aliens who had been regulars at the cafe, also indicate a submissiveness to the police which betrays other seemingly autonomous reso-
lutions not to consent. Hence, his recourses to the police are undercut by a general lack of commitment and a recognition of the law's
hegemonic control over his decisions. But in fact his cafe is the place
of displacement, of marginality: in the cafe's sign, only the "oo" of
the name remains, a symbol of the evacuated semantic field that the
cafe's population must contend with, a symbol of "an empty space,
the unrecuperable locus of the discourse on silence, and on the
silenced" (Debra Castillo, "Double Zero Place" 13).

Given such a situation, the critic's role within a legitimate societal
institution may well be complicit with the police's role. Taking this
complicity further, Debra Castillo has argued that the critic symbolically participates in "a police action: separating out the voices,
bringing law and order, soliciting confessions" ("Double Zero
Place" 4). Castillo in turn notes that, along with questioning the
semantic space woven by the author for the displaced, we must ask,
as does Michel de Certeau, from where do we speak? "This makes
the problem directly political, because it makes an issue of the

social—in other words, primarily repressive—function of learned culture" (4).

Both the question and the response posed by this story may significantly engage the problem posed by positioning, and specifically the problem of how a non-Chicana might speak about issues such as rape. By providing a series of testimonies, the story invites different interpretive constructions for the final event of the story: the killing of the Central American mother-kidnapper by a police officer who refuses to engage in a process of translation. Resisting the monological authority of the law, the story presents multiple distinct voices, which are significantly *not* resolved into a judgmental closure by either an omniscient narrator or a reflective character. The problem of reading the events recounted and the desires expressed is thus placed in a frame which recognizes differing criteria calling out for translation, a frame whose thematic lack of a "key" is supported by a structure which is oriented toward process, not product.

This dialogic quality stands in stark contrast to "Cariboo Cafe's" legal discourse, particularly as it is enunciated by the señor, with his clichéd manipulations of patriarchal rhetoric. While the story is essentially built on a series of monologues, the critical irony of the work is that these monologues are far more dialogic than the one ostensible representation of dialogue, the interview with the señor. Castillo suggests a similar point when she notes that Viramontes's style "obeys an unrecorded wish: the parallel monologues are projected into a single space, creating the effect of dialogue, a dialogue between the characters, a dialogue between the characters and the readers, and between the characters and the writer" ("Double Zero Place" 11–12). Another qualitative difference which distinguishes the story's form from that of the law rests in the story's willingness to improvise in the face of authoritarian repetition.[8] Built to convey a committed political stance, "Cariboo Cafe" strategically positions its interlocutors in a manner which allows the separate stories to convey a sense of the semantic invisibility of peoples historically omitted from society and its realms of cultural regulation, including the literary. Hence, the story highlights translation not simply in principle but also in a historically and politically rigorous manner.

Emphasizing the function of the desired—if not fully realized— dialogue in this story, I would suggest that non-Chicana scholars may approach Chicana representations of figurative and literal rape only in this bracketed manner. Like the separate voices within "Cariboo Cafe," the gendered voices "outside" these brackets may register their desire for a dialogue yet to be realized while at the same time recognizing that scenarios of consent understood in conventional ways remain, at least in part, coercive and illusory, particularly because they obscure a whole realm of homosocial manipulation—a realm to be explored at length in the next chapter. For now, let me note that the illusory quality of such consensual participation may be especially pertinent in the context of embedded legal issues where Chicano (male) readings have often implicitly associated the acquisition of culturally resistant power with the stereotyping of Chicanas. It is with this particular problem in mind that we now turn to Chicano nationalist discourse and its attempts to deal with lost voices, and loss generally.

5

A Social Context for Mourning and Mourning's Sublimation

HOMOSOCIAL CONFRONTATION
IN OSCAR ZETA ACOSTA'S
REVOLT OF THE COCKROACH PEOPLE

In the previous chapter, I suggested one means of understanding the Chicana critique of "consensual" social relations—relations intimately linked to the legal culture of American society. Because this Chicana critique is very much at the forefront of the overall legal criticism we have been following, and because the excitement about Chicana works in general has convinced many that a new chapter is being written in Chicano cultural historiography, I might reasonably conclude this study at this point. Were I to do so, however, an important intellectual opportunity would be missed. While it is certainly true that Chicana artists have been excluded in myriad ways, it is not sufficient simply to reinclude them, even if doing so would lend their works preference on classroom syllabi, publishers' lists, and so on. Instead, one activity that is called for at this time is an extension of the critiques embodied in Chicana texts. Following this trajectory, we will partake in these final pages in a critical practice not unlike that outlined by my introduction. However, here I suggest that we disrupt the dominant inclusion/exclusion criteria in order to reapproach conflicting reading practices primarily *within* differing strains of Chicano cultural narratives.

In what follows, we will consider two male-produced, masculine-oriented narratives which are particularly explicit about the interrelation of gender, sexuality, and group affiliation. Although, as I will argue, these works differ in the degree of critical reflection they bring to questions of "consensual" relations and their violation, both reveal a form of masculine bonding that is best understood not

as a "natural" or inevitable cultural factor unifying Chicano communities but rather as a replication, albeit culturally influenced, of
social conventions embedded in, and perpetuated by, the law. My
point is not that the legal actors somehow conspired to "create" all
of the varied attitudes which have been taken to constitute machismo. However, what is apparent—especially in terms of the narratives and historical contexts under study in this chapter—is that
the patriarchal imperatives of both U.S. legal culture and Chicano
culture have collaborated in the codification of machismo as a concept around which to ground cultural affiliation. Further, the courts
and prisons act as crucial sites for this codification, a process which
reached new heights in the late 1960s and early 1970s as new rhetorics of empowerment found patriarchal privilege both inside and
outside Chicano communities scrambling to win or secure "entitlements" for males. I have chosen to focus first on *Revolt of the Cockroach People* (1973) and *American Me* (1992) because each offers
important insights regarding two definitive legal experiences—adjudication and "correction"—and because both narratives represent
the struggle to define a language of empowerment for Chicanos that
is nevertheless severely compromised by its assumptions about consent and sexuality. Once we have examined the co-optive use of consensual dynamics by Chicano masculinist texts, we will then explore
the possibility of an alternative Chicana social reform, a reform that
significantly rethinks what it means to work through historical displacement and loss in general.

Oscar Zeta Acosta's autobiographical novel *Revolt of the Cockroach
People* documents an insider's view of the legal system—a view not
often afforded Chicanos, and a view even more rarely represented
in Chicano art. The second of two works focusing on Acosta's experiences (particularly his attempts to come to terms with various cri-
ses of identity during the tumultuous 1960s and 1970s), *Revolt*
refigures the "on the road," gonzo journalism of Acosta's *Autobiography of a Brown Buffalo* (1972). Perhaps the greatest pressure to change
which Zeta (the narrator) faces through the course of the books is
brought to bear by the Chicano militants that he hooks up with
early in *Revolt* as he attempts to write the magisterial journalistic

story which will propel him toward his initial, individualistic goal: writing "THE BOOK so that I could split to the lands of peace and quiet where people played volleyball, sucked smoke and chased after cool blondes" (22). Although the contact with the militants does significantly alter the narrator's outlook—Zeta finds in his early encounters an almost unconscious affinity for the nationalist project—the novel documents throughout the narrator's embattled search for the appropriate balance between group ties and an "apolitical" self-exploration of the type celebrated by Jack Kerouac. As I will argue, it is hardly a coincidence that *Revolt* recreates *On the Road's* (1959) supposedly epiphanic visit to Mexico, complete with its whorehouse scene. While the revision does bring to the fore the Mexican political strife that Kerouac romantically ignored, thereby highlighting Kerouac's problematic description of Mexicans as "noble savages," Acosta's own purchase (both figurative and literal) of a nostalgic connection to Mexico through prostitution reinscribes other problems, which will be explored later. Hence, Acosta exposes presuppositions which divide politics and pleasure, a division which is revealingly undermined, although in ways that appear largely uncritical in the novel.

The narrative lives out these complicated negotiations between sexuality and group affiliation as Zeta finds himself drawn (the sense of being passively swept along is quite strong) into the Brown Berets and the Católicos por la Raza (CPLR), militant groups which confronted racism at the institutional level with notable success (Acuña 335–51). In turn, we follow in fictional form the author's actual role as an organizer and lawyer for these groups. Historically grounded in the author's political and legal wranglings, the novel thus depicts the strategies by which Acosta was able to defend with relative success the Chicano participants in the 1968 public school protests ("the blowouts"); the 1969 Saint Basil protest against race and class segregation in Los Angeles's Catholic church; and the 1969 Chicano Moratorium, primarily denouncing the disproportionate number of Chicanos being killed in Vietnam.

Experimenting with legal strategies that would significantly influence the litigation of Chicano civil rights groups (especially the Mexican American Legal Defense and Education Fund [MALDEF]) for years to come, Acosta sought in the cases that followed these protests to demonstrate a radical discrimination against Chicanos in the legal system as a whole.[1] Focusing on the construction of the grand juries which initially indicted his defendants, Acosta argued, as does Zeta in the novel, that a systematic exclusion had taken place during the grand jury selection process, a misrepresentation clearly borne out in the statistical evidence.[2] His attack was two-pronged: while he attempted to show that the selection process was flawed (the judges who nominated potential jurors were insufficiently aware of or manipulated representation issues), he also attempted to establish Chicanos as a distinct racial group and therefore as a people capable of being targeted for systematic exclusion. (Until this time, civil rights activists, in particular the League of United Latin American Citizens [LULAC], had pursued an assimilationist strategy, arguing that Mexican Americans, as fully entitled individuals, should be treated as whites and should therefore receive similar institutional benefits.)[3]

Given that *Revolt* follows this litigation, raising the issue of Chicano definition itself, it is understandable that Acosta's fiction has been read by prominent Chicano cultural critics as a lodestar for some of the most basic Chicano problematics. Genaro Padilla, for instance, argues that Acosta's approach to the genre of autobiography shows him to be entirely in line with similar ethnic revisionists. Acosta's texts thus reveal that "it is in moving away from the 'I,' away from the isolation and sickly self-consciousness, that the Chicano shapes a personal identity, an 'I' capable not only of living with a troubled historical legacy, but also of acting to redirect that legacy" ("Self as Cultural Metaphor" 243). While Padilla's generic, autobiographical approach goes a long way in demarcating the struggles between individual and group identity in the novels, what it does not do is situate the specifically legalistic context of the "I," an "I" that comes across as particularly rhetorically aware, even manipulative, while it delves into outright confession.[4] Such a reading would, in turn, take up the question of why the "I" is socially constructed in a particular fashion and the issue of what sort of cultural work the construct enables. To understand this legal valence, it will be useful to situate the literary precedents for lawyer figures.

As we learn from Richard Weisberg's study of "procedural novels" (spanning authors from Dostoevski to Malamud), a distinct novelistic form has flourished in the modern age, one which exploits the introversion and rhetoric of lawyer figures. In such works, this figure bears the task of interpreting some anterior reality presented in the novel. In turn, such novels are calculated to undercut ironically the lawyer figure's use of language by demonstrating the failure of this discourse to account adequately for the prior, contested event. According to Weisberg, these authors develop the problem of the lawyer figures in terms both of psychology (aspects of *ressentiment*) and of a specific failure with language (Hamlet enthralled with his own words). Ultimately, Weisberg sees these authors, if not their characters, as standing in opposition to the skepticism and nihilism which strongly influenced the aesthetic practices of their times; in this sense, their development of a critique of legal discourse was an attempt to reinstate the primacy of a historical reality "obtainable" through a sufficiently cautious use of language, a use which guarded against the biases of the individual and the rhetorical obfuscation of the courtroom.

As a narrator who is both author and subject, Buffalo Zeta Brown, the "lawyer hero" of Acosta's *Revolt of the Cockroach People*, offers a rich opportunity to test Weisberg's assumptions while applying them to an inevitably complex context. As Ramón Saldívar has noted, Zeta apparently gives up his legally guided search for reality and its significance when he concludes that American law is "an arbitrary weaving of semantic threads" created to displace the failure to defend justice and natural rights: "Whereas we would expect law, at least in its ideal form, to permit us an approximation of the state of transcendental right, Buffalo Zeta Brown shows us, in a series of increasingly allegorical trial scenes, that the truth of justice is intimately tied to its differential opposite, the lie of justice" ("Dialectic of Difference" 23). In the climactic trial scene Brown decides that "every single witness both prosecution and defense . . . is lying. . . . The bastards know exactly what we have done and what we have not done . . . but they have all told their own version of things as they would like them to be" (272). During this particular scene Zeta gives up the notion that "an objective truth, sufficient unto itself and available for all to see" can be made present ("Dialectic of Difference" 23). Not necessarily throwing away the notions of truth and falsity, he comes to see them as social constructs. The novel itself may thus be read as an answer to this discovery, inasmuch as it constitutes "THE BOOK" which Zeta announces will present his life. Acosta's "answer," in turn, explicitly rejects the monologic dis-

course of the courtroom while creating a "historical," albeit conflictual, record of Zeta's development away from a personality dominated by, but unable to fulfill, his own schizophrenic desire both to
merge with Chicano nationalism and to secure himself the insulation he feels he needs to write. Above all, *Revolt* establishes from
the outset an opposition between legal discourse and novelistic
discourse, an opposition whose purpose finally is to reveal the
constructed quality of laws and rights and to question the deeper,
perhaps more sinister functioning of these constructs.

Both of Weisberg's principal elements of the procedural novel—
the criticism of the disparity between legal discourse and events
(making the renewed interpretation of the latter a priority) and the
use of a central lawyer figure—are present in Acosta's work. However, Acosta's lawyer figure has taken on a new role, inasmuch as
his more complex position as lawyer figure, "author," and courtroom subject matter allows him a unique critical distance and a recognition of himself in the other actors within the legal world. Considering the cultural translation involved, it seems fairly clear that
this diversion from Weisberg's norm (a norm which assumes the
autonomous focus of the lawyer) more accurately reflects the concerns of Chicano legal narratives. In other words, the multiple roles
assumed by Zeta, even the sense of multiple sliding positions,
should not be surprising since Chicano community experience with
the legal institutions has been, by and large, from the position of
the spoken for, not of the speaking (i.e., from the position of those
who must necessarily *imagine* their full participation).

Returning to Padilla's point in "Self as Cultural Metaphor"—that
Acosta uses the autobiographical form to present basic Chicano
problematics—we may now start to rethink such claims for the representative power of the novel by considering how the apparently
pathological isolation and ressentiment associated with the invariably male lawyer figure plays itself out as a tool within the larger
scheme of Chicano activism. Can readers assume with Padilla, for
instance, that the psychological processes of ethnic self and group
discovery are uniform across the range of the community? After all,
the great farce uncovered by Zeta is in many ways defined by the
cynical manner in which "all" the participants of the court *consent*
to a performance that welds them together in denial: "they have all
told their version of things as they would like them to be." When

the rhetoric of the law can be so pervasive as to unify both Chicano militants and their ostensible enemies in this manner, what are we to surmise about the ties that link groups of Chicanos in particular? At issue is the homogenizing aspect of the consensual paradigm. Given that consent plays a determining role in this set of issues, can any attempt to work through these difficulties afford not to address the Chicana critiques previously discussed? Specifically, is it possible to continue positing anything like a uniform developmental process for Chicanos and Chicanas when Chicana narratives like *Giving Up the Ghost* make readers painfully aware of the systematic manner in which Chicanas are indoctrinated into the community by virtue of their growing awareness of their unique relationship to consent through shame? And, by extension, how has the power of shame exercised by Chicano males against Chicanas been itself turned against those males?

These questions impose themselves with some force when we consider that a good part of the "sickly self-consciousness" that Padilla describes works itself out in Acosta's novel as overt, even reactionary sexism—sexism which spills over into this innovative approach to Chicano litigation when Acosta cites machismo as one of the principal bonds uniting "the" Chicano community: "MACHISMO, that instinctual and mystical source of manhood, honor and pride that alone justifies all behavior."[5] Acosta gives us one means of understanding this situation when he details early on in *Revolt* his burgeoning political consciousness, his burgeoning "Chicano-ness." Lying in his sordid hotel room, Acosta interrogates himself about his apparently self-imposed isolation from other Chicanos. He hears again the voice of his mother, admonishing him in his childhood for rejecting his Mexicana classmates when he refused to go along with a last-minute reorganization of a graduation march that paired the boys and girls of the school according to their race.

The memory challenges his relations with "the feminine" on a number of counts; of course, the opinions of both his mother and his Mexicana peers are at stake, but this moment also defines his relationship to shame itself. As he asks, "Had my mother hit it on the head? *Am* I ashamed of my race?" (31). The sliding that takes place here, between the Chicana collective and a "larger" Chicano community, suggests an important conflation early on in Acosta's life narrative. This conflation, which joins the desire for partners and the quest of revolutionary righteousness, acceptance by Chicanas and participation in Chicano nationalism, is most often figured in the narrative as a willingness to step into the incipient heterosexist designs implied initially by the school march that had the boys and girls locked into symbolically loaded pairings. Thus, in the logic of this narrative, to be a Chicano (male) means to sleep with Chicanas. As this conflation works itself out in the novel, participation equals group acceptance, and acceptance equals the "granting" of sexual relations. Hence, it is quite appropriate that Acosta should open *Revolt* in the midst of one of the CPLR's most controversial actions—the Saint Basil protest—and describe the militants' most strategic decisions as being motivated by the question "Will we get laid tonight if we cop out now?" (13). Certainly such statements have overtones of satire, but the diversity and weight of the many other aggressions toward women in the novel—aggressions typified by the reduction of women to sexual capital—make it impossible to defend such instances as programmatically satiric.

At least one critic has suggested that such extremes evidence the broader alienation experienced by Chicanos in the U.S. context.[6] The problem with such notions of alienation, whether Marxist or psychoanalytic, is that they are often highly abstract and thus limited in their ability to explain specific cultural contexts. What is needed is a more accurate account of the interplay of shame, sexuality, and race in the dynamic described by Acosta. We know from the work of Norma Alarcón that shame plays a crucial role in the formation of resistance to Chicana activism; the mobilization of La Malinche in this regard is without question a powerful cultural tool applied to those who refuse to conform. Yet if shame is a dominant force in Zeta's political and social participation, what role does this situation prescribe for Chicana/Chicano interactions in the world Acosta creates? Can Chicanas be seen as anything but a mirror of his own internal divisions?[7]

In the course of the novel, the only sexual relation with Chicanas established by Zeta takes on a complex, apparently symbolic form. The relation is constructed not with one partner but with three, simultaneously, and these three "have grown up together as sisters" (86). Far from obliquely representing anything like his own internal strife, these sisters appear to function as mechanically reproduced, mechanically exchangeable objects, sexual capital in all but name.

Although they adopt many of the chores associated with mothering—their skill in this regard is designated an essential qualification prior to the relationship—they are also quite young, even underaged, ranging from fifteen to eighteen years. The suggestions of incest (with mother, with daughter) become all the more pronounced as Zeta describes himself as an uncle attending to his visiting nieces.

While these avuncular relations might be said to expose a kind of alienation in which Zeta is revealing a continued obsession with the problem of defining himself over and literally against his Chicana familiars, what seems more immediately apparent in the sexual relations I have described is the tendency to transform women into a commodity exchanged among men. Consider, for instance, two representative scenes. Having returned from the successful bombing of a Safeway store, Zeta and his male accomplices settle down for a celebration which soon becomes its own "orgy of nationalism" (175). After Zeta has begun "making out" with one of the sisters/nieces, the scene takes a tense turn as the two remaining sisters are parceled out, each ultimately joining one of the other male accomplices. First the Chicanas look to Zeta for permission; his response, again suggestive of the incest theme, is a halfhearted denial of the role of father. While the remaining two sisters act out the male fantasy in which "no" means "yes," one, at least initially, puts up more resistance. Although the familial revolt is shortly deferred (when the suitor complies with her request to remove his establishment-oriented tie), the scene is reminiscent of other sexual encounters in the novel that verge on rape.[8] Another resonant example occurs during a combination party and trial preparation, when a crowd of Zeta supporters sneaks off to an isolated lake to drop acid and discuss political strategy. Here again the prospect of rape—more explicitly gang rape—develops, only to be narrowly averted, in this case by intoxication with chemicals and utopian ideals. The exchange begins when the one woman participant's enthusiasm is reinterpreted as a sexual gesture:

> "All right, you guys, let's get the party going," Lady says.
> "Jesus, Armida, are you going to gang-bang us?" Black Eagle says. (66)

After the misreading of her intentions is corrected—"I thought we were going to have a meeting. Aren't we here to prepare for the goddamn trial?"—the immediate tension gives way to yet another sliding between supposedly distinct political and sexual objectives:

> "I call this orgy to order," Mangas says.
> "Hear, hear!"
> "The first meeting of the, uh, Brown Buffalo Party will hereby come to erection," the tall Indian says in his actor's voice.
> "Can we all vote?" Gilbert asks, leering.
> "Just don't get any funny ideas, ese," Lady Feathers says. (67)

Such suggestions of gang rape which attend Acosta's political "orgies" need to be distinguished from traditional theories about alienation. These scenes document, more than anything else, the construction of a group mentality that is premised on men sharing their desires; although the object of desire remains female, what supersedes her "acquisition" is the voyeuristic collaboration in the desire itself.

Another way to think of the "sharing of desire" represented in this scene, and many others in the novel, is to pose it as a form of homosocial activity. The concept of homosocial bonding has been the mainstay of Eve Sedgwick's readings in *Between Men: English Literature and Male Homosocial Desire* (1985) and *Epistemology of the Closet* (1990). In these studies Sedgwick argues that sexuality as a concept has altered dramatically in recent centuries as once "incidental" sexual acts have shifted in import, becoming definitive moments in a person's identity. According to Sedgwick, such changes— including the provocative vilification of homosexuality which began in the late nineteenth and early twentieth centuries—mark crucial moments in the patriarchal reorganization and distribution of male entitlements. Assumptions about sexuality and, at certain historical junctures, sexual identity are thus mobilized in ways that best benefit the historically specific needs of the patriarchal moment. What may be mistakenly considered in the contemporary context as "sexual givens"—primarily the distinction between heterosexuality and homosexuality—in turn need to be recognized as provisional sociocultural negotiations that guarantee particular privileges and rights to particular males.

One basic tenet of this approach is that certain rhetorical options, maintained in large part by institutions such as the courts, attempt to coerce sexual desire into accepted political and economic patterns. This effort, of course, meets constant resistance since desire is far more complex and ambiguous than the legitimated conventions allow. To claim, then, that homosocial bonding significantly informs a particular group's relations—for instance, Chicano nationalist relations described in Acosta's novel—is not the same as to argue that such a group is latently homosexual. Instead, Sedgwick leads us beyond the artificial binary between homosexual and heterosexual orientations, demonstrating how they give way to a more complex continuum of desires—a whole range of tones—that is fundamentally important even while it is denied by the legitimated binary between homosexuality and heterosexuality. In fact, as Sedgwick argues, how a man succeeds in the patriarchal environment, in the world of men granting entitlements to men, depends fundamentally on how well he manipulates this gray area. Homosocial bonds thus ground a great variety of partially covert relations, all the while remaining a subtext to the overt sexual economy that posits homosexuality as the step too far.[9]

Recognition of such sexual economies may in turn have a profound impact on our understanding of the sexual dynamics in Acosta's novel, not just in terms of the overt examples of sexism but also in terms of the sharing of that sexism among Chicano males. In response to the claim that *Revolt* is most troubling for its rejection of the law, we may now suggest that Acosta presents a much more subtle, more disturbing vision in which the law promulgates homosocial bonds in such a way as to limit revolutionary actions by setting marginalized groups into patterns of self-inflicted violence. While it appears that Acosta (as well as Olmos, as we shall see in the next section) considers the more general patterns of self-inflicted violence a central problem for Chicanos, one linked to the manipulations of hegemony, I believe that both artists demonstrate a tendency to deflect such gender and sexuality issues when the homosocial register could be approached more critically.

Instead, self-victimization becomes a point of anxious focus for Acosta as he tries throughout his novel to atone for the deaths and mutilations of Chicanos caused by his participation in the movement. While there is ample cause for delving into such a confessional mode, the psychological work that is left undone—the examination of sexism and its sharing—leaves the larger mechanics of shame and homosocial bonding in relief.

"AN ORGY OF NATIONALISM"

As we learn in *Epistemology of the Closet*, reorganizations of the homosocial economy can, in times of political upheaval, lead to particularly tenuous renegotiations of the gray areas of desire and consequently to outbreaks of what Sedgwick terms "homosexual panic."[10] Even without detailing the various social and cultural factors at work during the historical period described by *Revolt*, it is not difficult to conjecture that the activism typifying much of the political scene of the 1960s and 1970s significantly disrupted the mechanisms of male entitlement within Chicano communities, including the militant vanguard. To carry this notion a step further, I would propose that new homosocial strategies were required to maintain patriarchal privilege as new rhetorics of empowerment threatened to dismantle the accepted coercion which kept Chicanas subordinate.

Of the strategies undertaken, one of the more volatile yet "effective" included defining the Chicano community as a social group consensually unified around a reverence for machismo. Acosta was of course a primary force in this regard, using as he did his highly publicized cases and statements to define this reverence (with the eager collaboration of Anglo sociologists). Hence, we find in one of his most important legal victories (*Montez v. Superior Court*, 1970) an argument which establishes the Chicano community as a social group demonstrating "a commonality of ideals and COSTUMBRES with respect to masculinity (MACHISMO), family roles, child discipline, religious values," and so on (legal brief, p. 19). Going further in a legal position paper, Acosta made machismo the fundamental motor behind Chicano interaction, claiming (as I have already noted) that this "instinctual and mystical source of manhood, honor and pride . . . alone justifies all behavior" ("Challenging Racial Exclusion" 7–9). While Alfredo Mirandé has pointed out the problematic allure of the machismo stereotype for both Chicanos and non-Chicanos (*Chicano Experience* 148–50), little has yet been done to situate the complex role of machismo in the larger economy of homosocial bonding as described by Sedgwick. Clearly, despite the notable absence of treatments of Acosta in Chicano histories describing this period, his role of confirming and codifying machismo warrants careful study.[11]

If machismo gains currency as it attempts to contain potential

Chicana empowerment, it may also be the case that the consequent reification of gender roles, built as it is on an extreme heterosexist ideology, leads to a "panic" much like that described by Sedgwick. In Acosta's reliance on machismo, readers may discover a trend that limited sexual roles—as was the case with the rise of the oedipal family in general.[12] As a result, the all-important gray areas of desire turn pale in the glare of the new radicalism; dominant sexual assumptions are in turn threatened by transgressive association with the heterosexual antithesis, homosexuality, and thus a homosexual panic arises. As behaviors become associated with one extreme pole of sexuality or the other, the crucial middle ground, particularly as it is shared by men, threatens to collapse into homosexuality. This potential for homosexual panic may tell us a good deal about the links between rape culture, allusions to homosexuality, and nationalism as developed in Acosta's novel.

Studies of group rapes in institutional settings (fraternities are a key example) have demonstrated that the desire expressed in such acts, from the aggressors' point of view, has little if anything to do with the victim's intentions or reactions. Rather, such attacks present an opportunity for the attackers to codify their relationships among themselves, even their desire for each other.[13] Working with this understanding, we can in turn reread the near rapes described in Acosta's novel with regard to his definition of Chicano nationalism. Such an assertion is not intended as a stock condemnation of the Chicano Movement. The movement was obviously far more complex, in intentions and effects, than Acosta's treatment allows. However, if the goal is to understand better some of the more important mechanisms contributing to Chicana oppression (as was the case in the previous chapter), critics must consider how those mechanics have been and still are perpetuated. Interpreters can thus no longer afford to treat Acosta's critiques of Anglo U.S. culture and its legal system without specifically addressing the relationship between the critiques and the more problematic sexual politics of the novel.

How, then, does Acosta figure the political work of the movement? The following scene depicts a crucial moment in Chicano political activism: the first public collaboration between Mexican Americans established in the Anglo community (movie stars, politicians, etc.) and Chicano nationalists. In this "orgy of nationalism . . . the crowd melts into one consciousness and no man is alone in that madness any longer" (175). Zeta is himself the focus of much of the audience's attentions, but, as is so obvious throughout the novel, the symbolic value of his actions and his presence are the key to his "power":

> The stomping of feet, the clattering—clambering—deafening roar of the crowd giving up its excess of exultation, not to me but to the idea of a cockroach-man sticking his thumb up the white man's ass—and getting away with it.
> "Chicano Power!"
> "Viva La Raza!" (172)

The point of highlighting such figures of anal rape is to suggest that any resistance attributed to Acosta must first contend with those rhetorical forces—especially those consensual assumptions explored by the Chicana artists and critics—within which the movement and the author specifically worked. Although Acosta's campaign for sheriff—the focus of the rally described here—is in itself considered an assault on larger Anglo authority, what becomes more and more clear as we move through this novel is that a symbolic subtext exists which projects such transgressions as rape of and between males. Hence, while virtually every antagonist Zeta faces in court is coded by the narrator as effeminate, Chicano resistance, from graffiti to courtroom argument, is appended with the phrase *"con safos"* ("c/s") or, as the narrator translates, "Up yours if you don't like it, ese." Even the Chicano handshake, symbol of partnership in revolution, is turned into an overt symbol of sodomy as Acosta interrupts the reading of a critical court verdict in order to describe an encounter between Zeta and Liberace:

> I look into the man's face. Sonofabitch! It is the world-famous fag. The white hair and the big grin. He is wearing a pink suit, a pin-striped pink suit!
> "Mr. Brown? This man tells me that you're running for Sheriff."
> "Yeah, I sure am."
> "Well . . . I hope you win."
> He reaches for my hand. I clasp his thumb. "This is the Chicano Handshake," I say. He blushes and squeezes.
> "Hey, Mr. Liberace, will you vote for Zeta?"
> The man looks at Victor and twinkles his green eyes.
> "Why of course." (163)

Given the valence of thumbs, sodomy, and political-resistance-as-rape patterned in the novel, this episode stands out as more than a suggestion of Zeta's diverse constituency. First, any acceptance of homosexuality that readers might attribute to Zeta at this point needs to be contextualized by the way homosexual association is consistently used as a sign of derision in the novel, even to the point of revealing panic. Second, we need to consider the manner in which the significance of the episode transcends antithetical homosexual/heterosexual definitions and instead opens a window on the continuum of homosocial relations that support political affiliations among males.

Maintaining the economy of desire described by Sedgwick, Zeta remains committed to heterosexual designs, although with a feverish anxiety that ultimately contains the moments of intense male bonding like that shared with Liberace. The tendency toward almost defensive gestures of heterosexuality consolidates when Zeta flees militant Los Angeles for a vacation in Acapulco, where his twin brother, Jesus, resides. While Zeta apparently spends a good part of his time attempting to justify his revolutionary activities in Los Angeles to his brother, the stories tend to elicit only muted amusement as Jesus would rather initiate Zeta in the ways of the local brothels. From Jesus's perspective, Zeta's actions may well be permitted by the Anglo establishment, which, he tells Zeta, is "just letting you guys get your rocks off" (189). The specter of such manipulation is perhaps the crucial problem explicitly set up by the novel; hence, early in the narrative Mayor Yorty tells Zeta that a repetition of the Watts riots will be the only way to effect change—a call to violence which is in fact acted out in the moratorium, although not as chosen by the militants. Instead, it appears that the police have sought to take advantage of the atmosphere—for instance, by using the generally chaotic situation as a cover for the "accidental" death of one of the foremost Chicano media personalities, a character based on Rubén Salazar.[14]

At the close of the novel, then, we find Zeta pondering the highly ambivalent gains such violence has wrought as well as reconsidering the ways he himself may have been manipulated:

No they didn't catch me for any of the shit I've pulled. But the fact of the matter is, they know exactly what I've done. That is the frightening thing. Those bastards know every single act of violence I ever pulled off with the lunatics from Tooner Flats. But why don't they arrest me? Why don't they haul me in? That's the nut. That's the old apple. If you can figure that one out, you'll be as smart as me. And just as paranoid. (257)

The "paranoid" awareness of the ultimately homosocial observation and control that applies to Zeta's political activities pervades the supposedly private escape to the Mexican brothel as well. Here the primary sexual encounter is framed by references to an anonymous male voyeur, a previous customer who was left unsatisfied. As a trace of previous transactions, this passive though significant participant shares with Zeta—who after all invites him to remain— a link that reinforces the larger homosocial economy. The interruption of the heterosexual escape is in fact fully in keeping with the larger revolutionary ethic of the narrative, an ethic encapsulated when Zeta refers to the movie *Viva Zapata* (1952). For Zeta, Zapata's legendary refusal to consummate his marriage so that he might begin learning to read is the key to the film and Zapata's heroism (233).[15] Inasmuch as Acosta himself elides his marriage in the autobiographical fiction, choosing instead to give one of the ultimately rejected prostitutes his wife's name, we may only speculate on Acosta's replication of Zapata's supposed sacrifice for the revolutionary project. What is clear is that the objectification of women, and the desire for yet denial of them as "objects," is part of a larger system of sexuality in the novel, one which Zeta vaguely glimpses at the story's close when he considers how his revolutionary desires have been disciplined by people like Mayor Yorty, who seems to be motivated by inexplicable desires to expose the collaboration itself.

Zeta recalls this comment at the end of the novel in the context of explaining the murder of an innocent Latino who is killed by a bomb Zeta and his fellows intended for a judge. This symbolic aggression toward the law is set up when Zeta is "pushed over the edge" during an earlier incident in which the courts steadfastly ignored another Chicano's murder by the police. Part of what makes this failure to prosecute so painful to Zeta is his own participation in an autopsy that leaves the Chicano victim's body horribly violated. Zeta's musings during the autopsy—he wonders whether or not the body had actually been raped—suggest great anxiety about the collaborative dissection that the lawyer is taking part in at the time. Throughout the descriptions of the situation, Zeta walks in a cloud of guilt and confusion brewed from his transgression of the respect that he feels should be granted the corpse. This anxiety is only furthered by the sense that Zeta has abetted the conspiracy originally suggested by Mayor Yorty. More than an attempt at self-expiation, the highly confessional tone and the recounting of his part in the autopsy mark an attempt to correct what has transpired, especially in the sense that Zeta has contributed to an abuse of proper mourning.

The fixation on the two Chicano victims taken together (and in particular Zeta's participation in their fates) creates a larger context for understanding the central role played by grieving in the novel. With respect to this issue, it seems that Acosta at first tries to use the law to mourn successfully, forcing it and himself into a confessional mode. When this attempt meets insurmountable resistance, he then strikes out at the law's almost inevitable failure, a turn of events that constitutes what could be taken as yet another layer of mourning as he comes to terms with his own illusions about the law. Acosta thereby creates his own form of "sublimation" in which the proper grieving, initially blocked by the injustice in the courts, finds itself derailed once again, this time by a negative fixation on the law.[16] Hence, this novel suggests that such truncated grieving may be thoroughly dominated by the rhetorical dictates of the law. Specifically, the novel suggests, however uncritically, that the sublimation of mourning occurs in a combative field of homosocial bonding where the struggle for male entitlement from the start supplants the successful coming to terms with loss. The literal battle in Acosta's courtrooms between the different male actors for the allegiance of female audience and jury members, as well as the notion of history according to machismo, may be taken as appropriate figures for the larger homosocial economy whose formal structure includes all those aspects of legal rhetoric we have noted.[17] In order to elaborate the nexus of relations among mourning, its sublimation, and the homosocial economy of desire, we will now turn to one of the most explicit Chicano treatments to date, Edward James Olmos's *American Me*.

AMERICAN ME(LANCHOLIA)

For one screening [of *American Me*], the studio recruited about 100 young people of various ethnic groups off the streets of South Pasadena.... "When they got there, there was so much verbalizing between the groups that [studio] people were afraid to turn off the lights," Olmos recalled. "But when the lights went up [as the film ended], nobody moved, not one person was talking. It was as though they had just gone to the funeral of a close relative or homeboy."

Los Angeles Times

Edward James Olmos's debut as a director, *American Me,* is a relentless film which details the rise of the Mexican Mafia (La Eme) and the often brutal strategies it employs. The central character, narrator, and founding member of La Eme as it is represented in the film is Santana, a homeboy who seeks from his youth onward an alternative to his father's hatred of him—an alternative of kinship and self-esteem that evolves first in a street gang and later in a prison gang. Although viewers may guess at the source of the father's anger almost immediately—the film opens with a depiction of the zoot suit (more properly servicemen's) riots and the group rapes which were a part of the attack on Chicanos—it is not until the end of Santana's life that he becomes aware of his conception through rape. The revelation occurs as father and son attempt to come to terms with the loss of the wife/mother after Santana's parole (in his mid-thirties, he has spent nearly twenty years of his life incarcerated). Standing over the grave, the father and son find quite literally their first common ground on which to communicate, a common ground of speech ironically premised on the mother's eternal silence.

The changes initiated by his new understanding of his parents' past in turn work with and on the new ideas Santana gains from his first heterosexual relationship with Julie, a member of the barrio whom he meets shortly after being paroled. Although Santana's "crime partners" claim that his relationship with Julie leads him to his subsequent rejection of La Eme, much more than a simple romantic change of heart is depicted. The relationship with Julie greatly affects Santana's outlook because he gains with Julie, as he does with his father, a person to share the process of mourning. Hence, one of the most crucial moments in the film, Julie's analysis of Santana's apparently split personality, is prefaced by a sharing of grief over the brother Julie has lost to an overdose, an overdose brought on by Santana's gang-related activities in the barrio. Olmos's intention, as suggested in my epigraph, reinforces the notion that this film is much more than a condemnation of gang violence, although it certainly is that. As I will argue here, the film's goal is to subvert a cycle of despair perpetuated by the forces which block proper mourning, a goal roughly analogous to that pursued by Octavio Paz with regard to Mexican culture.[18]

Of the early criticisms leveled against the film, perhaps the most prevalent is typified by the East Los Angeles activist Father Gregory Boyle. His concern, simply put, is that the film's vision is too dark. According to Father Boyle, "[P]art of the epidemic problem out here is despair. . . . Certain kids, if you rub their face in more hopelessness, I'm not sure they won't come out even more despondent" (*Los Angeles Times,* 24 February 1992). Olmos's narrative is in fact very bleak, depicting as it does very little in the way of successful collaboration among Chicanos to improve their situation. Early on in the film, the disaffection between Santana and his father undercuts what strength we might expect to find in the family. In turn, Santana heads to the streets for the sense of belonging that his gang, La Primera, may provide. Even this aspect of community, however, is permeated by an aura of displaced loss; we are first introduced to the gang during an initiation in which the new member—the same who will kill Santana at the film's end—is welcomed into La Primera, which has met inside a mausoleum. Notions of alternative social affiliations become even more circumscribed as the gang confronts the legal system. Once Santana's early gang activities lead him to juvenile hall, he finds himself in an escalating economy of violence. As he learns after killing an inmate who has just raped him, Santana can assure his own safety only by being more brutal than any of his potential challengers, thereby winning their respect. Translating the bonds built by this newfound esteem into a community of Mexicano prisoners, Santana is thus credited with giving rise to La Eme.

Becoming an economic force in its own right, La Eme establishes a crucial accountability among prisoners by organizing both inside and outside the prison, thereby keeping dealings on either side of the prison wall "fair," that is, respectful of the obligations accepted while "inside."[19] As we know from various studies of prison gangs, groups like La Eme do not work in a vacuum; other gangs—the Black Guerrilla Family and the Aryan Brotherhood, for example— also flex their entrepreneurial muscle. In the film, the competition

among these rival organizations leads to an even more horrific theater of violence.[20]

Olmos successfully captures this sense of the theatrical, allowing
viewers to enter the symbolic understandings attached to the "performance" of acts of violence: killings of rival leaders or even members of one's own gang as a sacrificial message to rivals. As shocking
as the brutality of the film is, the audience cannot help but see that
such violence has a language of its own, especially given Olmos's
concentration almost solely on the symbolic struggle between the
gangs (as opposed, for instance, to a focus on guard/prisoner relations). Perhaps one of the most disturbing uses of this semiotic coding takes place as Olmos depicts the gang rape and murder of a
competitor's naïve son, a recent internee at the prison. Using the
son's vulnerability as a lever (he is a newcomer without the protection of a gang), La Eme tries to break into the rival's Italian Mafia
drug trade. After the Italian Mafia refuses to be blackmailed, La
Eme carries out its action.

To gain the full impact of the scenario, viewers must decode what
they see by recalling that, as the film emphasizes repeatedly, "showing weakness" is the greatest threat the symbolic economy of respect can sustain—an economy thoroughly invested in homosocial
bonding. The rape and subsequent murder of the new internee—
he is sodomized with a saw—"feminize" the victim to send out
a broader challenge that will resonate with gang competitors who
likewise depend on a manipulation of the desires among men. As
we learn in the film, the sexual coding of violence—a kind of
buffer—serves a crucial role as the various gangs attempt to avoid
outright race wars which could ultimately harm the covert, necessarily interracial prison business on which each group depends.[21]
Hence, the symbolic manipulation of sexual dynamics, and particularly of "consensual" violation scenarios, plays a central role in the
winning and losing of prisoner respect for gangs that are organized
along racial lines.

The suggestion that prison rape culture is homosocially oriented
needs to be carefully situated, inasmuch as this kind of approach
can appear to offer an overarching explanation for rape, an especially problematic gesture when linked to *American Me* since the
film offers a clearly limited perspective that could seemingly leave
women as victims of violence out of the analysis altogether. As with

all of the discussion of rape culture undertaken here, the analyses brought to bear are intended to suggest alternative means of reading the social construction of sexual assault. Throughout this study I have focused primarily on the rhetorical forces perpetuated by, and in reaction to, the legal system—including adjudication, enforcement, and "correction"; this approach is therefore limited, although in ways that I hope are productive.[22]

Olmos's best attempt to address this larger culture of rape develops as his representation of the rape/murder plays on the prison's sexually coded dynamics; here Olmos carefully juxtaposes the assault on the rival's son with Santana's first act of heterosexual intercourse. Through carefully orchestrated crosscutting, Olmos parallels the seduction and betrayal of the male victim with the growing intimacy between Santana and Julie. It thus becomes apparent as the latter two begin intercourse that Santana cannot escape the coding of sexual experience being simultaneously manipulated by the gang inside the prison; he becomes increasingly aggressive, first by binding Julie's limbs and finally by forcing her into the same position assumed by the sodomized and then murdered inmate. This collapse of heterosexual intimacy into violence against Julie is one of the most obvious signs of Santana's inability to escape from the worldview he has helped create, a worldview which inextricably links sexuality and domination.

From this moment on, the film documents Santana's failure to intervene effectively in a spiraling escalation of violence that not only pits rival gangs against each other but also pits brother against brother in order to punish those who would defect. In fact, Olmos juxtaposes Santana's own disaffection and subsequent murder with the story of a member who is forced by La Eme to kill his rebellious brother. In one of the film's more horrific scenes, viewers watch from below as Santana falls several stories to his death after having received dozens of stab wounds. Carrying his condemnation beyond the prison walls and back into the barrio, Olmos ultimately leaves the audience with an even more dire indicator of this cycle of violence. Hence, the film ends with yet another gang initiation, one that is consummated by a random drive-by shooting—a scene powerfully filmed from both the victims' and the shooter's perspective so as to leave the audience trapped in the exchange.

Taking up concerns like those expressed by Father Boyle, Olmos has admitted that for Santana's family there is in fact no hope.[23] If there is any escape from the cycle of violence described by the film—and the possibility of escape appears tentative at best—it rests on the promise of education and on the symbolic value of Santana's repentance and salvation, which become invested with attributes of martyrdom. The educational investment is overtly, even stereotypically illustrated by Julie's return to school at the film's conclusion, a return which would suggest a newfound confidence and desire on her part. Earlier Santana tries to persuade Julie to return to her studies so that she might take part in the larger empowerment of Chicanos, an empowerment that he sees, at least at this time, reflected in his gang's attempts to improve the conditions for inmates through group affiliation.

In a final letter to Julie, a letter which mourns the opportunities Santana has lost even while it frames her return to school, he contextualizes the symbolic meaning of the death he must suffer for his rebellion against La Eme. What becomes crucial in the economy that Olmos establishes is how survivors both recover loss and recover from loss; although the film emphasizes the former process (the best Santana can do is attempt to portray his death as a martyrdom), the film is in fact very much about the latter as well. *American Me* may depict despair-filled histories, but it does so to offer, in the grieving which is represented, an alternative to the sublimation of grieving perpetuated by the institutions of Anglo society. There can be no doubt after seeing this film that the California Department of Corrections has virtually nothing to do with reform and that the environment it creates has a great deal to do with the perpetuation of violence. The question remains, though, just how much of an alternative is the audience offered? Does Olmos envision a new, more critical approach to loss, or does he codify a particularly masculinist agenda, one that simply replaces Acosta's earlier grieving process for an updated version? We might also ask if there exists something fundamentally similar in the mythification of La Malinche carried out by Octavio Paz and Olmos, both of whom clearly intend their studies to play on the anxieties of a male audience.[24]

To understand the nature of Olmos's "alternative," we must consider the historical manipulation of mourning by U.S. institutions, particularly the legal institution with which Chicanos necessarily interact as they treat loss. As Robert Breitwieser demonstrates in *American Puritanism and the Defense of Mourning* (1990), a great deal of the initial institutional efforts in America's Puritan colonies focused exactly on sublimating mourning in such a way as to reinforce politically unifying ideologies (7, 53, 65). Examining the tremendous pressures which the early Puritan political bodies faced—primarily as a result of their poor handling of relations with native populations (leading to King Philip's War, 1675–1676)—Breitwieser argues that the political-religious establishment contained discontent by funneling divisive emotions about individual losses into a larger religious typology that made it a sin to interpret death in ways contrary to the church's precepts. The "approved" mourning method depended in turn on reading one's own experience into a larger transcendental script and ultimately into a master narrative that would free the leadership from a more worldly accountability even while it continued to exercise social control.

Because Breitwieser's theory about religious sublimation is crucial to understanding how the law (in a sense, religion's substitute) works in the contemporary context, it will be useful to consider his argument in greater depth. According to Breitwieser, the "brilliance" of the strategy behind events like the Protestant funeral sermon lies in the successful *simulation* of

> what mourning would eventually arrive at: an ability to survey the chaos of grieving emotion, rather than being governed by it, . . . a sensation of a measure of control, . . . and a disengagement from fixation on the past and a receptivity to hope. Theology is a *bargain* because these things can be had without having "to lye tumbling in deformitye, to wast and consume thy selfe with sorrow." But the semblance of bargain depends upon hiding a cost: the stark freedom that would be eventually achievèd by the minute memorial solicitudes of mourning is here sought through a cultivated derision—for the singularity of what was loved, for the love itself, and for the emotions that broke out when the love was broken; . . . the derisive self that is constructed above the corpse of mourning is not a freed self, but one carefully bound to imposed specifications. . . . If such phantasmal gratification leaves the work of mourning undone, even unbegun, this is perhaps the desired end, because the deranged and subterraneanized misery of grief is now constituted as a *perpetual reservoir* continually provoking the phantasmal typic self to renewed derision and renewed acceptance of the introjected value system. (64–65)

Breitwieser goes on to claim that this "perpetual reservoir" of blocked mourning itself becomes a larger social pathology best described as *melancholia* (65). Taking the implications of the Puritan practice further, he suggests that the specific subject of his study, Mary Rowlandson's captivity narrative, reveals a kind of masochistic self-loathing in which the ideal of Puritan theology "meets with its grotesque and nearly perfect realization" (112). Here, sublimated mourning works so well to control the populace that the congregation becomes frozen in conflictual reflection, a reflection so detrimental that it is only by virtue of "an external and unrationalized mandate to live appended to the system" that the group avoids extinction (112).

The pathological melancholia Breitwieser describes is certainly not limited to the early Puritan context, and its continued resonance is at least peripherally suggested when he notes the relevance of the Puritan typology to writers such as Thomas Pynchon and William Gaddis (53). In fact, Breitwieser extends his reading of sublimation across centuries, seeing in the collaborations between war-making and religious institutions (Protestant and Catholic) a fundamental rhetorical effort to trade in mourning (43). To carry this reading of sublimation to the contemporary legal context may at first seem a large step, yet it has almost become a truism in the post–World War II period that "[r]emedies for personal wrongs that once were considered the responsibility of institutions other than the courts are now boldly asserted as legal 'entitlements' [with the result that] the courts have been expected to fill the void created by the decline of the church, family and neighborhood unit."[25] Chief Justice Warren Burger's comments reflect exactly that tendency I am trying to describe. In cases like that presented by the 1925 Scopes "Monkey" trial, we find a transfer of explanatory power in which the courts come to dictate what was, during the lifetime of Mary Rowlandson, the domain of Puritan typology. Hence, I suggest that the rhetorical modes highlighted throughout my study take on a role analogous to that fulfilled by Puritan typology. These rhetorical modes sublimate mourning by offering a system of interpretive gestures that likewise offer a "phantasmal gratification" while creating a perpetual reserve of unsatisfied mourning. (All the while, U.S. culture becomes more and more fixated on litigation in general.) Although more study needs to be undertaken, it may at least be conjectured that (1) sublimation continues to play a fundamental role in American institutional designs and (2) the fairly recent penchant to seek litigation to problems previously addressed through religious constraints has made the legal institution a primary site of sublimation if in fact it was not one previously.[26]

If, as I am suggesting, the law perpetuates the melancholia Breitwieser describes, this process may well give us important insight into Olmos's complex approach to despair in *American Me*. To examine this notion more thoroughly, we first need to define the contours of melancholia more specifically. According to psychoanalysis, pathological mourning may take a number of forms, of which melancholia is one. In Freud's now classic study "Mourning and Melancholia" (1917), it is suggested that melancholia takes the work of mourning in a distinct direction by virtue of the fact that the debilitating ambivalences directed toward, or inspired by, a lost object radically affect the ego itself. Unlike other forms of pathological mourning, the psychic disturbance stems not from the retained presence of the lost object—a refusal to let go of something yet distinct—but rather from an incorporation of the very split into the ego, a process which allows the ego to turn on itself, so to speak, and to do so with surprising force, even to the extent that the instinct to live may be overcome (167–70). Although Freud himself suggested at the close of *Civilization and Its Discontents* (1930) that groups of people, even whole societies, might develop their own forms of psychosocial pathologies, including melancholia, it has been left to those coming after Freud, including Breitwieser, to study this possibility more thoroughly. Given that a reading of melancholia, as it may affect Chicano communities, could be a book in itself (especially as we try to understand the complex negotiations between Protestant and Catholic assumptions), I will limit my application to these immediate points pertaining to *American Me*: (1) the inward turn of the prisoners' violence—a group action analogous to suicide—may be better understood if we take into account what Freud defined as melancholia's "attitude of revolt, a mental constellation which by a certain process has become transformed into melancholic contrition" (170); (2) the nature of the revolt or "splitting" turned inward may well leave its trace in the movie's title, which combines a sense of declaration, even demand, with a form of self-referential dividing that suggests both an allure and an animosity directed toward assimilation or Americanization; and (3) the moral self-condemnation associated with melancholia may well be reflected in *American Me*'s own unrelenting criticism of La Eme's mechanics, at times at the expense of criticism that could, and most likely should, be directed more explicitly at the legal institution.[27]

Going at the film in a less piecemeal fashion, we may recall that Olmos looks back to Luis Valdez's *Zoot Suit* and Beatrice Griffith's *American Me* (1947), giving an explanatory role to the first events of the film, the servicemen's riots, by showing them to be wounds that were never allowed to heal. Although the audience sees this blockage and melancholia played out in large part on an individual level, Chicano (male) viewers in particular—the audience at which Olmos aimed the film—will connect the failure to work through the initial riots to the broader history of social injustice, a history which virtually denied any access to the riot victims' perspectives. Even while these viewers take part in this reading between the lines, however, another critical tack is being taken, one which comments on the "understood" history I am describing. This line of inquiry contextualizes the experience of living with a displaced history and thereby posits a genealogy of shame, shame which is fostered in Chicano communities from both without and within, but always with the assistance of legal-rhetorical manipulations.[28] The synthetic individualism identified by Critical Legal Studies, in particular, plays a crucial role in the manifestation of such shame, telling Chicanos, as the assumption does, that group affiliation set above a celebration of individualistic meritocracy amounts to a fundamental social betrayal of exactly what it means to be American.

In a complex manner, then, the institutions (including the media, the military, and especially the courts) which sanctioned the riots and the denial of the victimization they wrought become sources for the ultimately self-destructive gang tendencies on which Olmos's *American Me* fixes. La Eme adopts an extreme version of group logic, as evidenced in the killing of its own as an act of purification; indeed, the gang appears to repeat rhetorical techniques analogous to those employed by the invading sailors during the riots. Specifically, we find in the actions of La Eme a similar mobilization of shame, through rapes or other claims of effeminate weakness, a mobilization that likewise establishes a hierarchy of male entitlement, in this case a hierarchy defined by who will control the exchange of sexual capital, whether women or their substitutes among men. Santana's principal claim for the rise of gang organization is that, with the protection afforded by group affiliation, Chicanos in prison need no longer remain vulnerable, a vulnerability associated in the film with the rape experienced by an isolated Santana in juvenile hall at the age of sixteen. Yet what replaces the "individualized" rape/shame dynamic appears to be an "institutionalized" rape culture which trades on an economic continuum between respect and shame, a form of negotiation prophesied by the quiet endorsement of Santana's retaliatory murder of the rapist by the other juvenile hall rape victims.

American Me may thus be read as a narrative about coming to terms with the grieving which attends the mythic "original" consensual violation and with the subsequent incorporation by certain groups of Chicanos of yet another homosocial economy built on the fallacy of the shamed and guilty victim. Creating a film primarily about men's prison life, Olmos perhaps necessarily leaves the viewer trapped within masculinist ideologies and the melancholic context (or as Father Boyle would say, despair) they carry with them. Yet this Chicano history, like all others, makes a choice about what will constitute its "originary events," a choice that is far from inevitable and so remains open to critical review. On the one hand, any historian interested in the mechanics of sublimation and homosocial bonding will quite likely be drawn to a period of war—the context of the zoot suit riots—as Olmos was, because it is in such times of loss that these mechanics are put into high gear, revealing in their extreme manifestations functions which are normally only implicit. On the other hand, Olmos's decision to make this history the tale of a bastard conceived through rape may reflect an ultimately patriarchal orientation, a position once again aimed at the anxieties of a male audience intent on confirming patrilineal descent and male entitlement in general. Here in particular we have to be concerned with Alarcón's critique of Octavio Paz and the generation of Mexican writers who turned the history of the colonization and its aftermath into a melancholia best defined by its masculine focus. Finally, Olmos appears uncomfortably close to this interpretive trajectory, leading to the suggestion that *American Me* has been relatively successful in large part because it has revitalized this Mexican melancholia in almost stereotypical fashion for Anglo audiences.[29] The film may also exacerbate the problem through its emphasis on the rape anxieties of young Chicano males: the film's power dynamics suggest so little in the way of alternatives that this audience could well come away with the message that one rapes or gets raped. Given the homosocial context explored in the film, the rhetorical manipulation of rape also raises a particularly vexed set of questions about the activation of outright homophobia.

As critical as the film tries to be with regard to gang violence, it does finally use a version of the Malinche myth in such a way as to reinforce potentially the larger economy of Chicana shame detailed by Alarcón and the other Chicana writers we have considered. Such criticism gains support as we analyze the song with which Olmos concludes the film, a rap version of Bill Withers's "Ain't No Sunshine" performed by Kid Frost (and entitled "No Sunshine"). This version takes the original longing for a female partner and rewrites it, framing it from the perspective of an inmate who is being betrayed by his lover while he is "doing time." Hence, the song's proposition that one should "Take time to read between the lines / 'cause there ain't no sunshine / Ain't no sunshine, anytime" asks the listener to fill in the original refrain, "when she's gone." While the emphasis is on loss, or at least prospective loss, the song's rhetorical approach—the inmate is being counseled by a male third party—again suggests that the relations among men, including those that negotiate shame, are at least as important as the specter of the dying love.

Even while the film suffers from these fundamental limitations, its narrative—unlike that of *Revolt of the Cockroach People*—carries a submerged yet countervailing line of interpretation that details a legacy of homosocial rape as a phenomenon of the present. Having noted this fact, we are forced to return to the point that, as a larger reading of the dynamics of rape, the approach is finally inadequate even though it does reveal important aspects of the negotiations between U.S. legal assumptions and Chicano culture. Ultimately, Olmos's somewhat romanticized depiction of Santana's "conversion" and subsequent martyrdom appears to have truncated the director's ability to present alternative visions. What one loses with the director's final sense of hope—Julie's stereotypic educational and familial orientation—is a developed recognition of the long Chicana history of wresting the dictates of institutionalized mourning for their own often activist purposes, for a means of dealing with inevitable loss in something other than a wholly masculine register. With respect to *American Me*, the point is that, as hard-hitting as Olmos's demonstration of masculinist ideologies is, it does not create a sufficient space for examining the ways Chicanas have been actively pursuing alternative visions. In this sense it seems that however much Olmos struggled against the mandates of sublimated mourning, they continued to impose themselves inasmuch as the turn to the Catholic metanarrative and the Malinche myth becomes a too conventional grounding for the historical problems that the film sets in motion.

TOWARD A GENEALOGY OF CHICANA
ACTIVIST MOURNING

Sandwiched between Santana's ritual murder and the drive-by shooting at the conclusion, *American Me* presents one potentially positive option to viewers, the only alternative vision which appears to recognize the most important historical forces shaping the community. This option is reified in Julie's woman-headed household. The sense of empowerment which Julie supposedly represents at the end of the film is crucial inasmuch as Olmos uses his final scenes to set up a contrasting vision between the families of the barrio. What Olmos's contrast conveys is that some families may be able to keep their kids off the streets and away from gang activity like the drive-by shooting. We thus see Julie leaving her son in the care of her mother while she goes on to the night school courses she has desired, not for her own personal gain, but as part of a revolution through education.

The difficulty with this scene is that, even though it avoids the fatalism of the martyr and Malinche metanarratives, the promise it would convey lacks historical depth. The audience knows that Julie has dreams; it does not know how Chicanas in her position go about realizing their goals against such overwhelming social, political, and economic barriers. The problem is a crucial one because the film so effectively details a melancholia which would condemn the Chicano community to a repetitive sublimation of festering wounds. And we cannot ignore that Olmos's representation of this sublimation has a particular homosocial foundation which places Chicanas in a unique situation "outside the loop" of entitlements reserved for men. With such an economic manipulation of desires, we are forced to ask how a character like Julie can be taken as a potentially reformist force. There simply is not enough of a sense about how she would manipulate her historical situation, nor how she would build on a communal legacy of activism by other Chicanas and Mexicanas. Despite Olmos's response to critics like Father Boyle, films like *Stand and Deliver* and *The Ballad of Gregorio Cortez* will not act as correctives for the dynamic of despair revealed at the conclusion of *American Me*.[30] Only works which focus on the interaction among legal rhetoric, the sublimation of mourning, and the roles of gender and sexuality will offer that type of intervention.

The materials which could support a genealogy of Chicana activist mourning have recently been working their way into academic circles—a result of important archival efforts carried out principally by Chicana historians and similar explorations by Chicana artists. To suggest what such a genealogy might look like, we will consider evidence from three critical periods: (1) the post-treaty U.S. colonization; (2) the post–World War II consolidation of Mexican-American civil rights efforts; and (3) the contemporary post–Chicano nationalist context. In each of the historical contexts explored here, Mexicanas and later Chicanas have worked together to effect a social process of mourning during a time of critical political transformation. In this manner, they have thus created their own gendered "subtext" to the United States' official legal record, its Mexicano/Chicano male collaborations, and the sublimation it promulgates. This point deserves highlighting because it suggests why I choose to reapproach these Chicana materials in terms of mourning, a focus not often pursued by Chicana cultural critics who have worked hard to write themselves out of the stereotypes that can be associated with mourning as a Chicana's gender-bound work.[31] In this vein, mourning may be framed as a largely private affair, usually situated in the home, an understanding reinforced by larger cultural icons, like La Llorona, icons that perpetuate the notion that a Mexicana's or Chicana's purpose is wholly bound to her offspring, even to the point of irrational and dangerous attachment, as is played out in popular versions of the Llorona legend.

Recognizing these difficulties, I have chosen to pursue the study of Mexicana and Chicana mourning because it appears that there are crucial ways in which social conventions are violated in these grieving practices, yielding very important acts of resistance and coalition building. In what follows, I undertake the process of working through the complex negotiations between U.S. legal discourse and these aspects of Chicano culture because I find that the project of historical recovery and interpretation—dealing with what has been lost to the present—involves reading how U.S. institutions have consistently functioned in opposition to Mexicana and Chicana mourning practices. In fact, a full understanding of U.S. history is, as Breitwieser suggests, quite likely dependent on a better conception of how such alternative means of dealing with loss have been accommodated as institutions have taken new reactive stances. It is in this spirit that I will shortly turn to an examination of wills, testaments, funerals, and artistic representations of the same in order to consider what is at stake in the Mexicana and Chicana pursuit of a socially and politically situated grieving.

Although, as I have suggested, Chicana scholars (and Chicano scholars generally) have tended not to frame their analyses in terms of the La Llorona motif or in terms of mourning conflicts generally, examples of these types of inquiry do exist. For instance, the Viramontes short story discussed in the last chapter, "Cariboo Cafe," may be read as a quite insightful study of the politics of mourning, a study which brings specific allusion to La Llorona together with an assertion that barrio police tactics mirror the use of "disappearance" in Central America. Other contributors, including José Limón and Monica Palacios, have added both academic calls to reevaluate La Llorona's political potential and humorous reworkings of the legend in a Chicana lesbian context.[32] In addition to these efforts, we may also note works like *Replies of the Night,* Sandra Hahn's tribute to both her grandfather and to the Days of the Dead, a tribute rendered "using computer graphics and digital voice-reproduction" in order to parallel "the cognitive process of revivifying him in her own mind."[33]

Such practices approach the politics of mourning in ways that do not rely on the cultural iconography associated with La Llorona. Instead, the examples considered here often have a more pragmatic bent inasmuch as institutional tools—actual wills, testaments, or their simulacra—become the chosen means of contestation. In this sense, these Mexicanas and Chicanas are, like their Argentine counterparts, Mothers of the Plaza de Mayo, holding up representations of loss, or grieving material, so that they may coalesce around the process itself, as maimed as that process might be by institutional forces.[34]

Recently published material supports the contention that Mexicanas and Chicanas in the Southwest have a long history of manipulating their circumstances through the use of legal documents, especially wills and testaments. Hence, critics like Angelina F. Veyna have demonstrated the crucial roles played by official records, records often initiated at the request of interested women parties.[35] Likewise, Deena F. González documents first the dire poverty and political disenfranchisement experienced by Spanish-speaking women in a burgeoning Anglo capitalist system and second the resistant strategies adopted by these women as they built on a Mexican tradition wherein women often held property in their maiden names—property which could be disposed of without a husband's signature ("Widowed Women of Santa Fe," esp. 35). Among other things, such research points to an important history of politicized mourning in which these women used Anglo institutional practices to define both their dealing with loss and their resistance to post-treaty Anglo rule.

As González notes, many Spanish-Mexican unmarried women found themselves forced into accommodations with relatively wealthy Anglo men who radically devalued the labor provided by these women even as general prosperity and inflation hit record rates. Hence, "by the 1870s intermarriage had become a custom with important ramifications for a community experiencing a Euro-American onslaught. It offered Spanish-Mexican women—women with few choices and limited means—a degree of stability" (43). Even though many women did choose interracial marriage as a means of coming to terms with the post-treaty shifts in power, this was certainly not the only option. As González argues,

> The unmarried woman who wrote wills pointed to another solution. The majority did not marry the immigrants; these women displayed minimal interest in easing men's transition to life in a new society. Instead, they sought stability in their own worlds; they sought to impose order on a world increasingly changed by easterners and their ways. For more and more of these women, the act of writing a will offered a measure of control over their circumstances. Spanish-Mexican women had followed the custom for generations; worldly

possessions, however meager, required proper care. The custom took on added significance in the postwar period. Its assumption of stability contrasted sharply with an enveloping sense of disorder; it promised children a continuity, a certainty, their parents lacked. (44)

Although the language of the wills suggests that these women were using the documents to order "their lives around people first, institutions second," what becomes apparent from González's revisionist history is that the women were growing increasingly aware of the collusion between church and state in the newly colonized lands.

In response, the wills gained a clearly political valence, solidifying an important collaboration between the women's private and public lives. The wills were therefore a means of using the forum provided by the courts both to dispose of one's possessions and to officially mark the significance of one's life. The process itself had crucial ramifications:

> The witnesses brought into the courtroom were almost always other women, relatives or friends, and reliable. Altogether, a minimum of five people knew what a will contained. If the judges were suspect, at least the community knew a person's final wishes. Never much of a secret, the written document now conveyed a strong public message to residents and newcomers alike; it was an act of faith, but it had its practical side as well. (46)

While there is an obvious economic context for understanding this resistant practice, one that addresses the essential coercion such women faced, the will making may also be read as part of a key transition in a larger social worldview. Here I depart from González's project to recall the emphasis that psychoanalysis places on the necessary rebuilding of reality that occurs as people mourn.

By effectively controlling their wills and the public legitimation of the wills, these women were in an important sense gaining power over the process of mourning and the remaking of reality that mourning entails. While González avoids such larger and potentially abstract explanatory metanarratives, she does suggest this power when she notes, "Irrespective of religious meaning or other symbolism, the document laid a life to rest, giving a dying woman (the majority said they were gravely ill) a sense of order and perhaps revivifying her" (46). Such revitalization may best be recognized as we acknowledge the meaning gained by will making as an essentially social practice, one built on the strength of family and cultural community. With this social context in mind, we may assume that will making was a useful subsistence strategy for women facing coercive, hegemonic manipulation, especially where this manipulation worked through legal rhetoric by forcing the widows to purchase their salvation with appropriate monetary sacrifices to clergy and lawyers alike.[36]

The textual mourning encoded in wills is of course complemented by the sociosymbolic language which animates our experiences of funerals. I emphasize this sociosymbolic aspect because funerals may, and often do, transcend their putatively metaphysical focus, thereby suggesting how survivors should read their historical circumstances—the Chicano Moratorium might, for instance, be thought of in this regard, although such a method of interpretation may well be applied to more conventional funeral practices as well.[37] One of the more effective uses of such a mourning context developed from just such a manipulation of a funeral's power to define historical issues. With support from family members, and particularly her sister, Sara Moreno, Beatrice Longoría created what was to become a nationally and internationally reported struggle over how Mexicanos would be received in the post–World War II United States.[38]

The episode began with the death of Longoría's husband, Félix, in a battle that occurred in the Philippines during 1945. After being buried in a military cemetery in southeast Asia for nearly four years, the body was sent back to the United States for a proper funeral. However, when Beatrice pursued arrangements in Félix's hometown of Three Rivers, Texas, the manager of the Rice Funeral Home, T. W. Kennedy, Jr., refused to cooperate, claiming, "We just never made it a practice of letting them [Mexican Americans] use the chapel and we don't want to start now."[39] Rather than acquiescing to this discrimination, Beatrice Longoría stood her ground. Enlisting the aid of prominent friends, including Dr. Hector García, head of the GI Forum, she and her sister initiated contacts which quickly led to a publicity campaign that dramatically underscored the outrageousness of the funeral home's refusal. Although both Mexicanos and Anglos were horrified that an event like this could take place, the general reaction among Anglo-Texans in Three Rivers was defensive, if not outwardly belligerent and threatening—a fact underscored by the intense harassment received by Félix Longoría's father as the Anglo elite of the town moved to undercut the widow's power, trying but failing to get the father to sign a prepared statement denouncing her actions.[40] Later, when a Texas House of Representatives investigation was held, Beatrice Longoría and her family testified with the full awareness that their safety itself was precarious.[41] Although Senator Lyndon B. Johnson interceded early on in these affairs to offer Longoría a military funeral with full honors at Arlington National Cemetery, the impact of the case was far from played out. As Manuel Peña argues,

> The Longoría incident was thus important because, while it was by no means the first time that Mexicans had mobilized their resources to right what they considered a wrong committed against them, it did serve to highlight (to act as "catalyst" for) the intensifying civil rights activities that marked the post-war phase of the Mexican in the United States. (22–23)

With this courageous decision, one no doubt met initially with some fear by all involved, Beatrice Longoría and her supporters helped turn a seemingly local act of discrimination into an opportunity to coalesce an emergent Chicano political conscious (Peña 21). Groups including LULAC, the GI Forum, and the Community Service Organization found in Longoría's example support for a new method: "a strong emphasis on direct action—especially on active participation in politics" (Peña 22). Certainly any number of incidents might have played the "catalytic" role the Longoría case did; yet the Longoría situation was unique in its power to unite people in outrage and action.

This impact must in large part be ascribed to the special role of mourning as a social process. The funeral home director's statements were read by newspaper audiences of the time as more than a defense of a discriminatory custom with limited application. Instead, the nature of the mourning shared throughout the United States in this postwar period made it possible to rework, in whatever small way, the place of Mexicana worldviews vis-à-vis the society as a whole. A good portion of the dominant Anglo population was able, to a degree, to empathize with the Longoría family, and Beatrice in particular. At the same time, the extensive remaking of reality brought about by the postwar mourning created a context in which both Mexicanos and non-Mexicanos had a greater potential to conceive of new social dynamics, dynamics loosened, though certainly not freed, from a history of discriminatory "custom."

The corrido which developed around the Longoría incident, "Discriminación a un Mártir" (1949), offers an indication of a critical transformation in popular Chicano historiography as well, a change again reflecting the power of the mourning context manipulated by Beatrice Longoría and her collaborators. Detailing this transformation, Peña argues that the style of the Longoría corrido marks an important shift in the development of corrido rhetorical strategies. Contrasting "Discriminación a un Mártir" to the turn-of-the-century "El Corrido de Gregorio Cortez," Peña demonstrates a movement away from an earlier glorification of the epic hero and toward the representation of a group reaction to victimization, a group reaction which parallels the coalescing political strategies of organizations like LULAC.[42] While LULAC maintained essentially accommodationist or "melting pot–oriented" political strategies, we see in this artistic transition a mirroring of changing political approaches, approaches slowly moving toward new interventionist group dynamics that focus on the manipulation of legal rhetoric specifically.

Like all of the institutionally oriented interventions studied here, readings of the resistance associated with the Longoría episode must contend with co-optation, and specifically with the homosocial designs that have forced stories about women, like Beatrice Longoría and her sister, into the shadows of both "American" and Chicano histories. While Longoría's actions receive scant attention in such histories, if they receive attention at all, few of the documents that remain regarding the affair record much in the way of her more subtle motives. However, although her statements from this period are notable for their decorum, they remain steadfast assertions.[43] Hence, when the scandal hit full force and the Three Rivers elite as well as many noted Anglo-Texans attempted to save face by wooing the burial back to the town, Beatrice stood by her decision to have Félix honored at Arlington, thereby leaving the weight of the nation's criticism on the original racist actions.[44] Also, with regard to the resistance embodied in Longoría's actions, it should be noted that her original wish to make use of the funeral home for Félix's services was itself unusual, inasmuch as custom at the time usually placed such an event in the privacy of the Mexicano home (N. Williams 79–

82). Hence, from the outset Beatrice Longoría's actions were implicitly rebellious because they were marked by a potentially dangerous inroad into the public space of the Three Rivers chapel.

Stories like Longoría's come to our attention now primarily because of recent research efforts—a fact which brings us to the contemporary context and the fiction of Patricia Preciado Martín, a Chicana historian and short story author. I will focus on her story "The Ruins," collected in her *Days of Plenty, Days of Want* (1988), to explore its unique merging of mourning politics and historiographic concerns. The brief plot of this narrative follows a young Chicana, Alma Romero, as she pursues forbidden excursions to a ruined convent in her South Tucson barrio. Designated comically as the site of all manner of perversions, the former convent is portrayed as the home of temptation itself by Alma's mother, a woman whose Catholicism is valued for the strength it provides her even as those around her look to other sources of inspiration. Building on the Spanish meaning of her name, "soul," Alma's questing among the ruins revises the traditional Catholicism of her home and community. The ruins attract Alma not because she longs for a spiritual past but rather because she is interested in their new inhabitant, a character very much concerned with historical and political matters, including social protest. Working again in the allegorical vein, Preciado Martín names this character Doña Luz (roughly "Lady Illumination").

A potential source of inspiration for Alma, Doña Luz's history embodies resistance: "She had been, in her more youthful and vigorous days, a thorn in the side of several generations of bureaucrats and attorneys, having laid claim, with faded documents and dog-eared deeds, to several acres of land where the multi-story government complexes now stood in the heart of the city" (16). This image of resistance is reconfirmed in the story as the omniscient yet cordial narrator describes Doña Luz's subsequent attempts to save her ancestral family adobe from modern-day Anglo land-grabbing (the "progressive city council" had decided to make way for "a multi-level parking garage"). "In a last desperate show of defiance," Doña Luz had "thrown herself down in front of the wrecking ball," an act that provoked "a rash of negative publicity and a spate of sympathetic letters that had proved embarrassing to the city fathers" (15). Even though the demolition goes ahead, effectively ending the life of her elderly mother, there remains in Doña Luz a sense of struggle that is both historically and magically based. During one of Alma's secret journeys to the ruins, Doña Luz appears as if a ghost before her, yet a ghost with a notion of history more real than the city's own.

This ontological blending is of course a critical technique used by many of the Chicano artists I have considered, artists who wrestle with the dictates of institutional denial by creating transgressive stories linked to magical realist techniques. Again, Patricia Williams succinctly describes the evocative power of such blending when she argues that, despite the institutional denial of minority worldviews, issues of race always linger like apparitions that are maneuvered around even as they are "officially" disclaimed.[45] "The Ruins" supports the notion that two women also live a complex ontological existence and that the processes of mourning play a crucial role in the collaboration they fashion with regard to the fragments of elided Chicano history that circulate about them.

Doña Luz takes Alma to a small hovel in the ruins, a hovel that at first appears to be lined with white moths. On closer inspection, Alma begins to see instead small white scraps of paper on which are scrawled bits and pieces of Chicano history. As Doña Luz whispers to Alma,

> This is the history of our people which I have gathered together—the land grants and the homesteads and the property transfers; the place names of the mountains and the rivers and the valleys and the pueblos; the families and their names and their issue; the deeds, honorable and dishonorable; the baptisms, the weddings, the funerals; the prayers and the processions and the santos to whom they are directed; the fiestas, religious and secular; the milagros and the superstitions. (18)

Doña Luz builds on Alma's interest and brings her to the ruins precisely because she wishes to declare her final will and testament:

> "Tú estás encargada de todo esto. . . ." Alma, still grasping her bony hand and surveying with wonder the testament of Doña Luz, felt the warmth of that hand flow into her being like water being poured. . . . "This is my legacy. But I am old and failing. I entrust it to you lest it be lost and forgotten." (18)

Building on the practice of resistant Mexicana will and funeral construction, Preciado Martín presents a tale about the transmission of histories and about the potentially unifying mourning that is part of any historiography. In addition, the story revises the genealogy of resistant Chicana mourning I have attempted to sketch out here by making the work of the Chicana historian—Doña Luz—the narrative focus. Preciado Martín's own career as a historian adds to this symbolic level of meaning, inasmuch as "The Ruins" invites young Chicana readers to accept the legacy which is her project.

In this manner, the story may be reread as a kind of will in its own right—a testament to others who would likewise use mourning and historiography to remake reality. Taking up this legacy entails exploring lives and events that have been subjected both to forgetting and to pathological sublimation. The historian's work must thus contend with the often ambivalent successes afforded despite these institutional barriers. Hence, at the conclusion of the story,

> [W]ithout warning, a tornadolike gust blew open the unlocked door of Doña Luz's hovel. The airborne flakes blasted in with a ferociousness, and then Alma saw, helpless and aghast, that the shreds of precious paper, in an avalanche of blinding whiteness, had metamorphosed into giant white moths again. They quickened with life and took to the air in a dizzying funnel of flight. Blowing snow mingled with blowing paper and rose and fell and then eddied into a blizzard of memories. And then the memories and the spirit of Doña Luz fluttered out the open door in a thousand swirling fragments in the direction of the south wind somewhere west of Atzlán. (20)

The sense of loss that pervades this conclusion is charged with a variety of meanings. While the "actual" historical materials appear to be lost along with the doña, the self-consciously symbolic register of the story (what it has to say about how we interpret) suggests that Alma gains something crucial from this ancestral woman about the process of constructing history itself. It is thus possible to read "The Ruins" as a story about successful mourning, a story that asks its readers, and its Chicana readers in particular, to find, as Alma does, the essentially enriching nature of Doña Luz's relationship to her own past through something very much like a funeral.

An outcast, even at times within her own community, Doña Luz comes to represent a person who can live with her history, even as that history and the doña's reactions to it are pushed into a liminal (though not ahistorical) ontological existence. In Preciado Martín's story, then, we find one Chicana passing to another, not so much the fragments of history, not the stories themselves, but rather a lesson about how to read noncanonically, against the institutional grain. Here a space and a time is created for the construction of history (and the play of mourning) that is grounded in Chicana bonding, in the sharing of a sense of vocation.

Taken together, these different Mexicana and Chicana efforts to revise mourning suggest a political trajectory often elided or underdeveloped within masculine-focused Chicano culture and certainly within practices of mainstream institutions. Pursuing further the questions about desire and consent raised by authors like Ana Castillo, Cherríe Moraga, and Helena Maria Viramontes, we find that the methods of reading undertaken in this chapter significantly complicate our picture of legal-rhetorical practices—especially as grounded in Critical Legal and Critical Race studies—by demonstrating the diverse functions played by sexuality and gender as these affect political/resistant affiliations within communities. Reading the implications of the Chicana critique back through *Revolt of the Cockroach People* and *American Me,* we confront a tendency toward an "incestuous" male focus in Chicano studies in order to build on issues of "homosocial" dynamics. These issues, in turn, yield a better understanding of the "resistant" group affiliations modeled in the male works, affiliations that help define routes of access to patriarchal privilege.

In an overview of Chicana efforts to reformulate the function of mourning, we subsequently see how wills, testimonials, and funerals are manipulated to rethink processes of historiography and male-oriented activism. Overall, the arguments offered here demonstrate that the incestuous focus identified by Bruce-Novoa is actually better thought of as homosocial performance, in other words, as part of a larger "economy" of desire following the routes of legal-cultural rhetoric manipulated between men both inside and outside the Chicano communities. By contrast, in the Chicana efforts we find a complex and subtle history of resistance to these collaborations. Here we recognize that Chicanas have not tended to pursue representations of the more obvious legal interactions, including "benchmark" trials, but have instead developed insightful readings of the play of desire, rhetoric, and power.

Like the Mothers and the Grandmothers of the Plaza de Mayo in Argentina, the women contributing to this genealogy pursue "a process of reconstructing history, of recovering identity" not only of individuals but also of a people (Arditti and Lykes 465). As has been the case in Argentina in the wake of a legacy of "disappearances," the restitution modeled in the Mexicana and Chicana efforts "is an act which is psychically foundational, based upon the articulation of truth and justice" (Abuelas de Plaza de Mayo, qtd. in Arditti and Lykes 465). However, where "the fullest meaning" of restitution "is simply to cease being disappeared ones" in the Argentine context (Arditti and Lykes 465), a potentially more radical assertion with regard to mourning is at work in the Mexicana and Chicana projects. Here, a basic remaking of reality, suggested most explicitly in Preciado Martín's ontological blending, and an outright assertion of competing worldviews dominate the political horizon.

Conclusion

In the sociological study *The Bilingual Courtroom: Court Interpreters in the Judicial Process* (1990), Susan Berk-Seligson demonstrates the powerful role played by court translators, a role performed even as the official dynamic of the courtroom does everything it can to undercut a full recognition of these particular legal actors—who are, as it turns out, often women and frequently Latinas. In an extensive experiment re-presenting actual trial transcripts for mock jurors, Berk-Seligson found that by subtly altering a translator's linguistic habits—including the use of passive and active voice, interruptions, as well as politeness and formality markers—she could dramatically alter responses to testimony. All of the targeted linguistic alterations fit well within accepted variations of common courtroom practice, variations that are neither regulated during the trial nor taken into account during the training and certification of translators.[1] Even after the publication of *The Bilingual Courtroom*, the legal institution has done little to alter its use of translators, although we do hear more frequently the hardly practicable call to remove translators or bilingual jurors altogether. For instance, in a 1991 U.S. Supreme Court decision—perhaps the most ominous recent example—the justices voted 6–3 to allow a New York prosecutor to exclude "Hispanic" jurors from a trial involving Spanish-speaking witnesses "on the grounds that [the jurors] might not accept official English translations of Spanish testimony."[2]

While racism and classism no doubt contribute to the avoidance of the larger translation issue—the great majority of people affected are poor and Latino, as was the case among many of the original defendants in Berk-Seligson's study—the inaction is of course in keeping with the larger aims expressed in the law's "ideal" worldview. It may seem to many observers that an adjudication reoriented toward translation issues like that projected by Chicano artists and critics—one sensitive to conflicting worldviews and cultural issues—would be simply unworkable in an already overburdened court system; nevertheless, it may well be that the survival of the United States' legal culture as we know it depends on just such an accommodation. If the growing social striations of the 1970s, 1980s, and 1990s continue to disenfranchise racial groups at the rate they have—and there seems little reason to expect otherwise—then we are quite likely to see more wide-scale acts of civil disobedience akin to those I have noted in the Introduction, acts which continue to threaten an intensified disruption of socially constructed notions of what legitimately constitutes "criminality."

The ability of mainstream legal practitioners to avoid questions of translation—linguistic and cultural—is not accidental. As I suggested above, even CLS scholars have been caught in the larger distancing of translation issues. Hence, as Kimberlé Crenshaw points out, they have tended to "trash" civil rights activism because they see the law as a legitimating force that keeps everyone from understanding the true nature of social oppression. The CLS scholars in turn avoid the very different reception of the law by "minorities," thereby missing the point that the law's process of legitimation is, and always has been, aimed in good part at convincing the privileged that their actions are "just." Looking at Chicano narratives, we see that the rhetorical assumptions of legal culture do not necessarily mandate how Chicanos view their social conflicts, although they may certainly affect the structure of those views. When Luis Valdez focuses on the judge's manipulation of the defendants' appearance in *Zoot Suit*, there is certainly no sense that this is an exceptional discrimination. When Ana Castillo's characters work against their own indoctrination in patriarchal consensual dynamics, there is likewise little to find remarkable in their self-critical posture, particularly because they must contend with the consequences of these dynamics in virtually every aspect of their lives. In fact, in both works the much greater concern lies with how the characters will negotiate their circumstances and self-critical translations between worldviews in order to survive.

Throughout these Chicano narratives, we find that despite the mainstream and CLS claims, the illusion of effective neutrality in the legal system has little if any legitimacy. This very healthy skepticism is in part the product of a much more careful approach to linguistic assumptions, the kind of careful approach that virtually anyone in a radically subordinate position develops with regard to an overseer's pronouncements. Gerald López makes a similar point in *Rebellious Lawyering* when he notes:

> To meet their responsibility, workers must have more than would pass as an academically advanced understanding of the relationship of mandated terms to practices. They must have a handle on their superiors. To achieve this "handle," janitors, secretaries, and farm workers need to determine how their superiors make sense of the workplace—where mandated terms and actual practice converge. They must devise and deploy provisional strategies that will enable them (at least to appear) to work within the stories their superiors are living—to avoid triggering unwanted impressions, or to cull different positive meanings or (better still) storylines out of the same experience. . . . Without this painstaking effort to gain and effectively use elaborate knowledge of their superiors, subordinates will likely fail in their efforts to maintain their workplaces and keep their jobs. (59)

Being familiar with such working situations, Chicanos tend to share the sense that linguistic acts exist in a very close proximity with other more overtly political acts. As López goes on to argue, however, such skill in translation is often missed by academics and professionals who emphasize "what those subordinated by political and social life don't know how to do" (78).

If those of us who are teachers attend to this situation fully, we will invariably be challenged in the classroom inasmuch as the deep-seated antagonisms of Chicano films, novels, and poetry may well disrupt notions of artistic pleasure held dear by many of our students, and particularly our "privileged" students. Once again we are reminded that those most affected by the fantasy of such politically "neutral" assumptions tend to be those who benefit most by the illusion. Given this tendency, the work of understanding the critics and artists will no doubt be intimately bound with a more conflictual, dialogical approach to the politics of translation. In theoretical terms, questions of position must be confronted, questions which may contextualize our students' political assumptions in a rhetorical conflict less prone to a deferral of responsibility sanctioned by the transcendental norms of neutrality and meritocracy.

The law is of course not the only institutional route by which we might learn about failures of translation. For example, José Saldívar examines the manner in which the United States' mainstream publishing industry effectively barred Arturo Islas's *Rain God* (1984) by denying the novel's rich multivocality, its translation between cultures.[3] However, legal discourse will no doubt continue to play a dominant role as critics and artists tackle these problems, for legal culture most often defines "fair" or "just" social interaction. As I have suggested, Chicano attitudes about the law may convey a seeming ambivalence toward legal practices, an ambivalence clearly conditioned by historical circumstances. However, it is also crucial to remember that Chicanos hold a different relation to processes of legitimation; thus, their experiences have often enabled them to read through or translate legitimation in ways not necessarily available to others. It is exactly in this context that we may begin to understand best the often unrecorded yet strong wish to realize many of the promises held out by the law that is evident in Chicano legal critique. This ambivalence leads not to a latent weakness for utopian gestures but rather to a systematic exploration of how translation as a starting principle might reformulate interpretation.

One critic who may have a good deal to contribute to the study of this type of linguistic inquiry is Mikhail Bakhtin, whose Russian environment bore comparison to the Chicano context.[4] His works demonstrate a radically political process of conflict and negotiation in language, a process which according to Bakhtin is best revealed in artistic narrative.[5] In his arguments about how language functions, we find a pragmatic approach akin to speech act theory, an approach he described early in his career as "a philosophy of the deed." One mainstay of his oeuvre is the assumption that linguistic interaction is inherently multivocal. Thus, the exchange of language always carries with it the potential to create multiple habitations for the divergent worldviews of interlocutors. Inasmuch as such exchanges are conflictual, they expose what might be termed a rhetorical battlefield, a rhetorical strife that Bakhtin understood as a form of labor, as a form of work essential to linguistic interaction.[6] Speaking and listening, reading and writing, thus take on a physiological dimension fully in keeping both with Bakhtin's early philosophical revisions of Kant and his historical intellectual context, which found science and philosophy reaching new heights of collaboration.[7] Ultimately, Bakhtin's astute reading of linguistic interaction and the work constituted by this interaction yields a "theory" about how the labor may itself be appropriated.

Herein lies one distinct advantage of Bakhtinian analysis for Chicano studies. The historical disenfranchisement of Chicanos has been achieved by a unique dialectical blending of outright material coercion and more subtle hegemonic manipulation. Where the latter has been concerned, the law has played a fundamental role. From the Treaty of Guadalupe Hidalgo onward, Chicanos have been fighting for rights which were guaranteed yet not honored by the U.S. government; the systematic denial of Mexicano land-grant holdings is but the most obvious example. The law was "hegemonically" effective in these interactions because it maintained the promise, however attenuated, of a forthright dialogue when contested documents and events were being adjudicated. In hindsight, we can of course see these myriad legal decisions against Chicanos as a microprocess in which the larger aims of manifest destiny cemented Chicanos as a group into a role of social dependency in which legal interactions became again and again the most glaring forms of mock dialogue.

In the Chicano narratives themselves we discover a pattern of linguistic inquiry parallel to that undertaken by Bakhtin. Chicano artists have of course pursued this inquiry with the dictates of their own social context at the forefront of their efforts. Hence, their specific reworkings of historical events and legal culture have, among other things, posited legal rhetoric as a set of structuring principles for performances in which the Anglo society's racist actions may cloak themselves in postures of judicial neutrality. Contributing to our understanding of the original implications of this "neutrality" and the revisions they undergo in Chicano narratives, Bakhtin argues that particular rhetorical modes may truncate the multivocal receptiveness of language, positing instead what he terms "monological" discourse.

Monological discourse subverts an open habitation of language by restricting any accommodation that particular speech acts might make to potential interlocutors; thus, Bakhtin offers one model for understanding the play of power and the manipulation of linguistic labor in legal culture. Returning to Chicano treatments of legal culture, we find a corollary critique of "monological" practices. What the narratives reveal is not a stock condemnation of legal institutions but rather a much more guarded, complex inquiry open to the difficulties of cultural translation and in keeping with the diverse attitudes held by Chicanos toward the law. As I have noted of the narratives, we frequently find a retrial of the narrative subject matter; yet these retrials go far beyond a reversal of original court decisions and similar interpretations inasmuch as the monological assumptions enacted in the decisions are supplanted in the larger reinterpretation that the narratives themselves represent. Hence, illusions of judicial neutrality, for instance, are replaced by more dialogical notions of how understanding itself is created. In turn, works like *Zoot Suit,* "Cariboo Cafe," and *The Mixquiahuala Letters* are constructed to emphasize the active interpretive role the audience will have to play. In such examples, initial questions of guilt, innocence, or blame are put aside in large part to resurrect the fundamentally conflictual motivations masked precisely by the legal culture's façades of neutrality, freedom of consent, meritocracy, and so forth.

The subtleties of these legal dynamics, as they are represented in Chicano texts, may also be illuminated by Bakhtin's description of two predominant Western modes by which "understanding" itself is presumed to be achieved; these competing modes reveal much about the stakes involved in Chicano legal interventions. In an early, foundational text, Bakhtin argues that

> [i]n its naive and realistic interpretation, the word "understanding" always induces into error. It is not at all a question of an exact and passive reflexion, of a redoubling of the other's experience within me (such a redoubling is, in any case, impossible). . . . [Understanding is rather a] matter of translating the experience into an altogether different axiological perspective, into new categories of evaluation and formation. ("Author and Character" 22)

Throughout the studies of trial and legal culture found in Chicano narratives, we discover political interventions which parallel in fundamental ways the shift of method described here by Bakhtin. In the Chicano context, a similar turn to issues of translation becomes the key not only to reading specific historical events but also to developing much broader theories about border culture. The point lies in undercutting the law's simplistic notion of how understanding is won, a notion that condemns culturally rich events to the most abusive reductions in the court—a case supported by Berk-Seligson's analysis.

We should not underestimate the transgressive effect that the Chicano shift to a translation-oriented approach would have on mainstream legal practice and its worldview. This mainstream worldview is a very forceful legal projection, one assuming that individuals inhabit a place of "self-determined subjects, expressing consistent, unambivalent, and unexceptionable desires" (Kelman 290). As I have noted above, people in this mode presumably seek "their ends in a private world of voluntary transactions freed from force or nonnatural necessity by a state that imposes only clear rules against illicit force." In this dominant legal fantasy, the state imposes its "neutral" rules only "because it fears becoming forceful itself and because people should know precisely what is expected of them" (Kelman 290). As Mark Kelman has demonstrated, this legal fantasy supports the great majority of expectations in legal interactions. In other words, the issues that any given court will recognize need to fall within the boundaries of social interaction set out in this "naturalized" worldview. As CRS scholars have pointed out, this is hardly an innocent happenstance. By making certain modes of interpretation—for instance, those focusing on group interaction and institutional agency—fall outside the accepted rhetorical practices of the legal institution, the law simply makes certain race-focused solutions to problems harder to think; likewise, as we have seen throughout this study, alternatives that rely on consensual issues have commanded particularly high stakes, in large part because consensual dynamics tend to shift guilt and blame onto individualized victims in a particularly efficacious way.

The various critical "routes" explored in this study, including those concerning consensual issues, are of course limited to a certain extent by my initial decision to concentrate on institutional discourses, particularly legal culture. Even with these constitutive limitations, the implications of this study extend far beyond those routes explicitly mapped out. For instance, it would seem clear that we need to find ways to enhance coalition politics—within Chicano communities as well as among disenfranchised communities of various compositions. This study's approach to the manner in which group thinking and group agency are delegitimated by U.S. legal culture speaks directly to this need. It is therefore my hope that certain common grounds or intersections might be recognized as different groups take up and revise the methodologies offered here.

In addition, the rethinking of academic interpretive designs carried out in these pages might suggest ways to reformulate contemporary approaches to "multiculturalism" and ethnic studies, as well as the inevitable relations these fields of inquiry share with projects of imagining an "American" (U.S.) cultural history and a cultural history of the Americas. Ramón Saldívar offers an instructive lead. Saldívar poses an important objection to the linguistic assumptions animating arguments of revisionary historians, especially arguments which claim to chart "*the* cultural construction of ethnicity as embodied in American ethnic literature" (Saldívar's emphasis).[8] As Saldívar notes, efforts undertaken by such revisionists all sound

> wonderful, perhaps even after we notice that [their] key words, "consensus" and "consent," "dissensus" and "dissent," "integrative" and "integration," "legitimation" and "privilege" themselves ring with the unmistakable clarity of their origins in the liberal-democratic bourgeois political theories that form the foundations of the hegemonic American ideological consensus.
>
> The crucial factor here is that, often, these terms refer to consensus and dissent among the ruling groups alone and to their legitimacy as members of the ruling elite state apparatus. That is, consensus and dissensus do not apply to those *outside* the ruling group or their educational, cultural, and political state apparatuses: working-class people, people of color, gays and lesbians, women. (216)

What I would suggest is that the revisionary histories under consideration by Saldívar call out for exactly the legal-rhetorical scrutiny developed by the Chicano artists and critics. Such revisionary projects might reconsider their own participation in the consensual paradigms so effectively rethought by Chicano narratives, narratives which have a very sophisticated grasp of the mechanics of, and the denial embedded in, legal culture. Taking Saldívar's treatment of consensual dynamics a step further, it may also be necessary to reconsider the extent to which such notions associated with the "ruling elite" actually pertain, in striking complexity, to the everyday workings of Chicano culture as Chicanas and Chicanos alike go about their lives translating between both institutional designs and distinct group affiliations. Certainly there is tremendous evidence in these narratives, and the historical contexts they engage, that more work of the sort begun here would be beneficial, especially as critics attempt to develop more subtle readings of the interactions between institutional and artistic discourses.

Notes

INTRODUCTION

1. For a general appraisal of Chicano participation in the contemporary U.S. economic and political scenes, see Rudolfo Acuña, *Occupied America: A History of Chicanos*—especially part 2, "The Cementing of an Underclass: The Mexican in the United States." While virtually every institutional indicator reveals a steady overall decline in the institutional privileges engaged by Chicanos, Chicanos make up an inordinate percentage of the population labeled "criminal." According to Ronald Barri Flowers's recent study *Minorities and Criminality,* Latinos in general are arrested and convicted twice as often as Anglos (96).

2. Alfredo Mirandé, *Gringo Justice,* offers a very thorough study of the historical episodes (preceding the 1992 Los Angeles riots) and their reception; for a reading of Texas-Mexicano context, see Américo Paredes, *With His Pistol in His Hand,* which critically examines the celebrated historian Prescott Webb and his representation of Mexicano criminality.

3. According to Flowers, "An important factor often overlooked in causation or motivational approaches to Hispanic involvement in criminality is the mistreatment they and their ancestors have endured over the years, from an abusive, exploitative, prejudiced America, beginning with its early attitudes of Anglo-Saxon racial supremacy and superiority over Spanish colonists and any other ethnic or racial minorities, which manifested itself through colonialism, expansionism, and imperialism" (99).

Kimberlé Williams Crenshaw, in "Race, Reform, and Retrenchment: Transformation and Legitimation in Antidiscrimination Law," elaborates a theory about this constitutive relationship. Arguing that U.S. law has developed in a dialectical relationship with the systematic and unsystematic exercise of racism, she posits an intimate relationship between the two—one which remains largely unacknowledged by virtue of a larger economy of denial. See the extended discussion of Crenshaw below.

4. In an effort to reinforce the historical specificity of terms like *Chicano,* I will use varying, contextually appropriate names to designate the larger evolving communities that became "Chicano" primarily during the 1960s. These names include *Mexican-American, Pachuco, Latino,* and *Mexicano.* To

avoid confusion with regard to the latter term, I specify "Mexican national" for persons or groups claiming principal citizenship in Mexico.

5. A description of the inquiry may be found in "Police-INS Actions to Be Probed," *Los Angeles Times,* 20 May 1992: B3. See also "Estimates of Riot-related Arrests Deflated," *Los Angeles Times* 21 May 1992: B1, B4.

6. This action was of course being taken after the worst of the riots, when the agencies had remained at a distance from the self-destructing communities. The scrambling after the fact to explain this sort of inaction led the police department into yet another paradoxical posture, inasmuch as it was forced to create two conflicting narratives to explain what had taken place. In the first narrative, Chief Gates argued that the riots were initiated by specific and limited "gang" elements (the "flash point" theory). However, in defending his department's failure to intervene, he offered a second narrative in which the riots became an unrest exploding almost simultaneously throughout the affected parts of the city. These interpretive difficulties were subject to a predictable denial as other law enforcement agencies, notably the FBI, promptly attempted to build cases that would take advantage of the RICO statutes intended for the prosecution of widespread gang corruption and violence.

For a description of Gates's testimony and the inquiry made into the police department's inaction, see "After the Riots," *Los Angeles Times,* 13 May 1992: A18; the FBI's involvement is summarized in "Three Men Face Array of Federal, State Charges in Denny Beating," *Los Angeles Times,* 14 May 1992: B1, B16.

7. Valle and Torres (*Los Angeles Times,* 6 December 1992) are quick to point out that they are not interested in identifying a "sinister conspiracy." All the same, they find the general inability of the media to adequately handle the complex racial dynamics an outcome of English-speaking, North American disdain for "mestizo impurity." The outcome of such short-sightedness on the media's part has been a superficial attempt to interpret the events through the lens of "black versus white" race relations or similar limited "color codes"; these simply are not appropriate for understanding the full impact of the riots on Los Angeles's people of color.

8. In terms of this sort of institutional collaboration, readers will likely find José Angel Gutiérrez, "Chicanos and Mexicans under Surveillance: 1940–1980," interesting, though frightening, reading. Gutiérrez uses materials obtained through the Freedom of Information Act to summarize the variety of efforts undertaken by the CIA, the FBI, the military and local agencies to monitor and harass Chicanos, Mexicanos, and Mexican nationals. See chapter 1 for further discussion of Gutiérrez's findings.

9. See Alfredo Mirandé's study, "Fear of Crime and Fear of the Police in a Chicano Community." As both Flowers and Mirandé note, this fear leads to a significant underreporting of crimes perpetrated against Chicanos.

10. A number of Chicano writers have explored this awareness of underdevelopment; see, for instance, Mario García, *Mexican Americans,* Albert Camarillo, *Chicanos in a Changing Society,* and Gloria Anzaldúa, *Borderlands /*

La Frontera: The New Mestiza. Of those works pursuing this line of inquiry, however, José Saldívar's *Dialectics of Our America: Genealogy, Cultural Critique and Literary History* stands out as the most extended treatment of institutionally promoted dependency and its alternatives. Saldívar links the larger development of Chicano critiques of underdevelopment to a genealogy of "Calibanic" resistance centered in Havana's Casa de las Américas.

11. For a detailed reading of the ways in which legal rhetoric has contributed to this process, see Alan Freeman, "Legitimizing Racial Discrimination Through Antidiscrimination Law: A Critical Review of Supreme Court Doctrine," where he argues that antidiscrimination laws have actually helped to obscure injustices by perpetuating reading criteria that simply cannot account for institutional forces. One could well argue that class action works in a similar fashion, inasmuch as it assumes groups to be organized solely around discrete and circumscribed injuries.

12. See J. Saldívar, *Dialectics of Our America,* for treatments of Rolando Hinojosa, Arturo Islas, Gloria Anzaldúa, Ernesto Galarza, and Cherríe Moraga.

13. By defining the principal cultural work of these narratives as a resistance to Anglo hegemony, I am following the lead of Ramón Saldívar's groundbreaking study *Chicano Narrative: The Dialectics of Difference.* Saldívar's notion of resistance, elaborated with reference to Raymond Williams, has had a strong impact on this project.

14. As an example revealing the processes of legitimation, Archibald Cox's semiautobiographical study *The Court and the Constitution* is particularly interesting. Although I will examine this text in more detail later, I will note now that its aim—renewing a less politicized view of the law—leads Cox to pursue a "crisis of legitimation" argument that reinforces the need to maintain the explicitly formulated illusion of "powerless power" in the courtroom.

15. For years criminologists resisted linking studies of crime to studies of social reactions to crime. As Gary D. LaFree notes, this schism—once labeled the "great task of disconnection"—was initially complicated by the work of "labeling theorists" who disclosed in the 1960s that statistics and "criminal" behavior did not accurately correlate (109–11). Rather than fully exploring the connection between social relations and crime, mainstream criminologists have, according to LaFree, tended to follow two distinct paths: studying criminal etiology or studying criminal labeling. The mutually exclusive nature of these ventures has ensured that mainstream understandings of criminality, as they are figured over time, remain significantly incomplete. Because labeling theory assumes that "legal classification decisions are not necessarily the result of actual behavior, but represent stereotypes resulting from social interaction" (24), the approach has much to offer a larger critique of the law as that critique posits various official histories concerning Anglo/Chicano interactions.

16. In particular, Camarillo, *Chicanos in a Changing Society,* offers an in-depth view of this process by focusing on the disenfranchisement as it has

affected the Mexicano/Chicano communities of Santa Barbara in particular and southern California in general.

17. Genaro Padilla, "Recovery of Chicano Nineteenth-Century Auto-biography," has recently inspired much interest in the historical materials collected under Hubert Bancroft's auspices while he was researching his history of California. Despite the efforts made by Bancroft—hiring bi-lingual assistants to collect and record the Californio legacy—the Californio perspectives had little impact on his final *History of California* (1884–1890).

18. For an extended discussion of the unique position assumed by both Latin Americans and Chicanos, see J. Saldívar, *Dialectics of Our America,* and especially chapter 6, "The School of Caliban," in which he suggests a com-mon posture for resistant pan-American critics.

19. Focusing on this issue, Dominick LaCapra notes in "Criticism To-day" that "[w]riting or speaking as uses of language are not constitutive of pure theory in contrast to pure practice—a vision that easily lends itself to a hypostatized and simplistic opposition between the study and the streets. The comprehensive question is that of the ways in which the use of lan-guage as a material and as signifying practice is articulated with reference to related activities. This question is the larger frame for discourse analy-sis." Certain trends in critical legal studies follow a similar strategy, one which is perhaps best detailed in James Boyd White, "Judicial Criticism" (in *ILL*). Boyd White argues for a more performative approach to constitutional language by examining supreme court opinions that provide greater and lesser degrees of democratic engagement by all members of society.

20. See, for instance, the conclusion reached by Ramón Gutiérrez in "Community, Patriarchy, and Individualism: The Politics of Chicano His-tory and the Dream of Equality." A careful study of the dramatic changes lived by Chicano communities since the 1960s, this essay suggests (1) that the political strategies of the Chicano movement were significantly deficient because they tended to elide fundamental Chicano differences in the name of rejecting individualism and (2) that radically new approaches will have to be initiated if communities are to come to terms with the postmodern age.

21. For an excellent discussion of the limiting effects of the inclusion/exclusion approach to canonicity, see John Guillory, "Canonical and Non-Canonical: A Critique of the Current Debate."

22. See Carey McWilliams, *North from Mexico: The Spanish Speaking People in the United States,* for an elaboration of "the Spanish fantasy" as a concept denoting mainstream cultural amnesia with regard to Chicanos and their contributions.

1. LEGAL RHETORIC AND CULTURAL CRITIQUE

1. Below I discuss the term *meritocracy* at length; for now I use it to describe the manner in which people's work—work virtually always depen-

dent on collaborations and affiliations with others—is acknowledged only in the most constrained, individualized fashion. Within this ideologically conditioned paradigm, accomplishments have merit insofar as they confirm a "pull yourself up by the bootstraps" mentality and insofar as they do not raise larger social questions about one's relations (ameliorative or inhibitive) to particular groups.

2. Kimberlé Williams Crenshaw presents a striking reading of the law's "failure" in this regard in her essay "Demarginalizing the Intersection of Race and Sex: A Black Feminist Critique of Antidiscrimination Doctrine, Feminist Theory, and Antiracist Politics."

3. Both Patricia Williams and Kimberlé Crenshaw examine this assertion at length in their projects, although Crenshaw is the most explicit about the political efficacy of community building through activism. It should be noted that this particular premise marks an important departure from the larger movement of Critical Legal Studies, which tends to seek alternatives to the alienation and legitimation found in the law by turning away from rights discourse (see especially Crenshaw's "Race, Reform, and Retrenchment").

4. For an elaboration of these pedagogical concerns, see Kimberlé Williams Crenshaw, "Foreword: Toward a Race-Conscious Pedagogy in Legal Education."

5. In *Culture and Truth: The Remaking of Social Analysis*, Renato Resaldo tackles an analogous problem in the human sciences sphere by taking as the focus of his broader criticism the function of objectivism in anthropological and ethnographic studies.

6. As economic and educational indicators appear to confirm, reform efforts have tended to benefit most those in a position to take advantage of the new opportunities. Hence "the Chicano community" has become more polarized as a site of divisive hierarchical privilege.

For histories of these organizations, see Mario García, *Mexican Americans: Leadership, Ideology, and Identity, 1930–1960* (esp. 25–61), and Maurilio Vigil, "The Ethnic Organization as an Instrument of Political and Social Change: MALDEF, a Case Study."

7. Patricia Williams's *Alchemy of Race and Rights* as a whole acts as a response to these stylistic assumptions, challenging in its own manipulation of the autobiographical voice the law's refusal to acknowledge the necessary translation between different (cultural) frames of reference.

8. For a summary of the "neoconservative" rereading of the civil rights movement, including the role of the Heritage Foundation and Thomas Sowell, see Crenshaw, "Race, Reform, and Retrenchment" 1336–41.

9. This notion of an inescapable participation on a terrain vehemently not one's own builds on important contributions by feminist legal scholars, including Catharine MacKinnon. See in particular her argument about the place of feminist activism in patriarchy: "Feminism, Marxism, Method, and the State: Toward a Feminist Jurisprudence" 22.

10. For this notion I am indebted to José Saldívar, who has made available to me his manuscript "Border Matters," which explores at length the complex implications of shifting cultural narratives in just this fashion.

11. While Freeman does argue for the recognition of the victim's perspective, he too partakes of the larger CLS "trashing" of rights discourse. For a full treatment of Freeman's essay and its limitations, see Crenshaw, "Race, Reform, and Retrenchment" 1360–64.

12. See Henry Louis Gates, "Editor's Introduction: Writing 'Race' and the Difference It Makes," in which this "implicit presence" is mapped in terms of some of the forces which have shaped its history.

13. In my final chapters I will explore this Freudian dynamic more fully, but for now I will note that much work has been carried out on sociopsychological pathologies regarding failed mourning and the way such failure may come to be represented in charged references to ingestion disorders. At least one author, Mitchell Breitwieser, has suggested that American politics has been defined from very early by an uneasy institutional manipulation of grieving, one that may bear directly on current efforts to work through the legacies entailed by discrimination; see *American Puritanism and the Defense of Mourning: Religion, Grief, and Ethnology* in Mary White Rowlandson's *Captivity Narrative*.

14. See Bruce-Novoa's summary of González Echevarría's reaction to the controversy ("Canonical and Noncanonical Texts" 127).

15. In addition to Antonio Márquez's essay, see Francisco Lomelí and Donaldo Urioste's entry "Chicanesque Writings" in their *Chicano Perspectives in Literature: A Critical and Annotated Bibliography*.

16. At a talk by Henry Louis Gates, Jr., entitled "The Master's Pieces: On Canon Formation and the Black Tradition" (delivered 12 December 1988 at Cornell University), similar questions were raised about Gates's apparent elision of the problem of criteria by which to organize a black canon. During the discussion following the talk, Gates's response led to a description of the "democratic" construction of criteria which was being used for the *Norton Anthology of African-American Literature.* According to Gates (the head editor of the project), each period editor has been relatively free to choose texts by her or his own criteria. Gates develops a more pointed response to these particular issues in his recent work *Loose Canons: Notes on the Culture Wars* (1992).

17. Thanks to the efforts of Gates, among others, it is no longer common practice to use "race" as a self-evident category. These critics have demonstrated that race is a construct, functioning in a complex manner, both systematically and unsystematically. To the extent that such readings creatively construct systems for understanding the figure of race, they often replace the debilitating perception of anarchistic decentralization—identified in Bruce-Novoa's essay—with specific lines of thought to direct investigation.

18. See R. Saldívar, *Chicano Narrative,* Vernon E. Lattin, ed., *Contemporary Chicano Fiction: A Critical Survey,* and María Herrera-Sobek and Helena María Viramontes, eds., *Chicana Creativity and Criticism: Charting New Fron-*

tiers in American Literature, for examples of the influence that this set of assumptions maintains.

19. For a thorough discussion of La Malinche as a figure in Chicana writings, see Norma Alarcón, "Traddutora, Traditora: A Paradigmatic Figure of Chicana Feminism." Alarcón is also particularly effective in drawing out the male emphasis on bastardization, an emphasis which reads La Malinche's actions and victimization as a threat primarily to patriarchy.

20. See Ramón Gutiérrez, *When Jesus Came, the Corn Mothers Went Away: Marriage, Sexuality, and Power in New Mexico, 1500–1846,* especially the first section, in which Gutiérrez engages in a form of speculative history.

21. T. S. Eliot's formulation of the canonical identity as a gathering of great writers sealed off from time and space in an enclosed room perhaps best defines this insulation. However, something may be learned from an alternative etymology of the term offered by the *Oxford English Dictionary:* in music, a *canon* is "a species of musical composition in which the different parts take up the same subject one after another, either at the same or at a different pitch, in strict imitation." This definition, emphasizing sameness and repetition, is consonant with the univocality associated with canonicity in its traditional literary uses. It is exactly this tendency toward an insulated, monological mock dialogue that Chicano artists struggle against, both in their works and in their efforts to receive recognition from a publishing industry seemingly most interested in maintaining stereotypes (see especially José Saldívar's chapter on Arturo Islas in *The Dialectics of Our America*).

22. See Saldívar's statement in *Chicano Narrative* 173, and its citation in Fregoso's "Chicana Film Practices: Confronting the Many-headed Demon of Oppression," 189.

23. Revisiting Peter Brooks's term (as developed in *Reading for the Plot: Design and Intention in Narrative*), I will consider the cultural critic's project as one implicitly indebted to a notion of institutional designs, where *designs* signifies, as JanMohamed and Lloyd suggest, both formal qualities and historically situated desires.

24. Michel de Certeau has, of course, acted as a kind of patron saint for many critics who find in his theories of guerrilla mobility a much-needed response to the seeming lack of resistant agency prophesied by Michel Foucault in his studies of institutional power; see especially de Certeau, *The Practice of Everyday Life.*

25. For another example of this neoconservative retrenchment, see Dinesh D'Souza, *Illiberal Education.*

26. Even accepting Hirsch's essay on it own terms, interesting gaps open which reassert the conflict between institutional ideologies and less overt designs. According to Hirsch, "interpretation-as-communication" requires a principle of allegory as a means of positing distinct historically situated meanings, past and present. To check the arbitrary imposition of an interpretation, the allegorical process must be exposed to "valid" counterfactual propositions, which may be identified by their eternal applicability. For ex-

ample, in considering if Caesar would use the atom bomb, were he alive now, Hirsch argues that an interpreter must consider the timeless quality of "Caesar's character as a military tactician" (*ILL* 63). Ironically, Hirsch avoids answering the question on the grounds that he could take a definitive stand only if he had more knowledge than he has available. The deferral, however, supports an assertion: "[T]he validity of counterfactuals is like the validity of historical propositions. One has to have a lot of relevant knowledge." According to Hirsch, a reader should determine "relevant knowledge" by retaining fidelity to an agent's or author's dominant intentions; this imperative underscores Hirsch's definition of valid interpretation as "governed by, and consonant with, original meaning" (*ILL* 62).

To claim that historical interpretation may elide "nondominant" meanings presents some very serious problems. To retain a notion of historical change, a certain sensitivity to the possibilities of any given historical context seems inescapable; recent intellectual history has been quite explicit in this regard. Clearly, counterfactual logic can assist such historical speculation; however, a risk exists that, once without the security of assumed dominants, the proliferation of complexities will threaten both the rigid boundaries between "reality" and "phantasm" and the totalizing interpretations of historical events or artifacts. As I have noted, Hirsch tries to transcend these problems by defending the priority of the writer's dominant intention. However, inasmuch as Hirsch acknowledges the potential for migration between the assumed positions of writer and reader—he states he "wanted to avoid useless byways of polemics by conceding that interpretation-as-exploitation is also a tenable and tenanted position" (*ILL* 58)—it appears equally appropriate to apply the counterfactual logic Hirsch lauds to his own reading of reading, in turn asking how Hirsch may be acting in relation to institutional demands located firmly in the present, particularly the culture industry's challenge to the school's control of information.

27. The essentially liberal dynamic which constitutes the starting point for Hirsch limits forms of mediation between individual historical events and what he terms "transhistorical identities" by reproducing the same model of interaction I have noted with regard to the issue of affirmative action; this reproduction is inherited because of a relative failure to consider questions about the difficulties of moving beyond a liberal framework. Consequently, in Hirsch's model temporality is conditioned by the logic of synthetic individualism, where all relationships are understood through fixed contradictions reproduced by liberal, legitimated binaries describing the relations between particularities and universals. The limited historical parameters of contract law, functioning alongside the assumption of a judicial transhistorical objectivity, offer only one instance of such self-sustaining oppositions; these oppositions effectively defer more complexly mediated notions of repetition and change, as for example are implicit in considerations of the effects of institutional racism on the contract scenario. For an example of how complex these contract negotiations become in the CRS read-

ing, see Patricia Williams's chapter "The Pain of Word Bondage" in her *Alchemy of Race and Rights*.

28. For a summary of the Zamora trial, see Alice Greenfield, *The Sleepy Lagoon Case*.

29. See Charles Ramírez Berg's review of *Zoot Suit* in Keller, *Chicano Cinema*, 189–90.

30. José Angel Gutiérrez documents these efforts in his essay "Chicano and Mexicans under Surveillance." With regard to the Pachuco era, he notes that "the outbreak of the Spanish Civil War in 1936 caused authorities to look closer into the activities of persons of Mexican and Spanish ancestry residing in this country. The Federal Bureau of Investigation was wary of the Falangist Movement in Spain and its possible links to groups in the U.S. such as the Union Nacional Sinarquista which was founded in Mexico in 1937, but claimed 700 members in this country. The specter of a Fifth column among U.S. residents of Mexican ancestry was used by J. Edgar Hoover to order a national mobilization of intelligence gathering and surveillance of this community" (30).

31. In the play, El Pachuco's introduction of the intermission comes complete with an implicit extension of his gaze into the theater's hallways and bathrooms.

32. Ramón Saldívar begins his book on Chicano narrative by underscoring precisely this approach (see esp. 7, 10–11).

33. See Michel Foucault, *Discipline and Punish*, and particularly his discussion of disciplinary techniques as they coincide with the extension of Bentham's Panopticon (135–308).

2. MISSION DENIAL

1. Although Artenstein is not a Chicano, I treat this film as a Chicano production because it is clearly indebted to the larger participation of many Chicanos, including actors like Oscar Chavez, Maria Rojo, Tony Plana, and Pepe Serena and numerous others, like Lorena Parlee, supporting the project from behind the scenes. In addition, as a "period piece" with a comparatively small budget, this film depended more than most productions on the generous contributions of those most desirous of having González's story told. It is for these reasons that I choose not to treat Artenstein as an "auteur," although his part—from the original research onward—was obviously crucial.

2. In a preliminary documentary, *Ballad of an Unsung Hero* (directed by Artenstein [1983]), González describes each of these aspects of his life, including the near drowning he endured in a tank of raw sewage at San Quentin—tanks that he and other prisoners were subjected to for days at a time. Despite such treatment, González helped organize a hunger strike at the prison in 1939, a strike which won major reforms in living conditions.

3. Of note in this regard is the "Ballad of Juan Reyna," sung by González.

The song critiques a widely controversial trial in which Reyna was convicted of killing a Los Angeles police officer.

4. Among other roles, González has acted in recent years as the head of Revolutionary Veterans of California, an advocacy group for participants in the Mexican revolution who now reside in the United States.

5. Of course, it is now commonplace to challenge public/private distinctions like the one I am making use of here. Perhaps the most sophisticated of these critical approaches, Donna Haraway's "Manifesto for Cyborgs," makes a strong case for rethinking such public/private dichotomies by considering instead the myriad social, political, technological, and cultural affiliations which exist in the liminal space between anything we might term purely public and the purely private. Although I acknowledge Haraway's point, I still stand by the strategic purpose of revivifying the dichotomy when it appears to be pertinent to how particular groups read (or misread) their experience. Clearly the introduction of radio as a medium played a large part in challenging the dichotomy as it existed then, and on this score we might recognize that part of the threat posed by González was due to his role in very effectively mining this new liminal ground. Even while González might have gained strength precisely by manipulating this liminality, the responses he evoked from the Anglo establishment may be read as a retrenchment of, and battle over, public versus private domains.

6. Here amnesia is taken to be *an effort* not to remember something which nonetheless cannot be avoided and which, in turn, dramatically shapes psychological and interpretive activity.

7. The psychoanalytic term *working through* is used here in order to suggest a mode of interacting with particularly charged or critical social issues. Drawing from the works of Freud and Dominick LaCapra, I adopt this term to denote a process whereby charged issues (or "materials" in the Freudian lexicon) are engaged in such a manner as to produce alternative perspectives or options that allow a distance from the simple repetition of the initial issue (or the assumptions which dominated its discussion). Such "salutary" options, in turn, allow affected people to find new models of dealing with problems.

8. I would like to thank Amy Rabbino, who has noted in seminar that the English subtitles which appear in the midst of the fight between the official and González take on an irony that is furthered both by their glaring presentation and by their often obvious inadequacy. Ultimately the subtitles, like the other forms of stylization discussed above, highlight the politics of the medium. In this sense, the necessary reduction of text that accompanies the use of subtitles itself becomes an ironic mirror for the Anglo refusal of cultural translation depicted by the film's narrative.

9. For an example of this scapegoating mechanics, see Gary Imhoff and Gerda Bikales, "The Battle over Preserving the English Language," *USA Today* 115, no. 2,500 (January 1987): 63–65. These proponents of English-Only open their article by claiming that "the political forces behind bilingual education are those which promote cultural separatism" (63). The ar-

ticle proceeds by supposing that the promotion of biculturalism will create political chaos in this country, dissolving the glue which holds it together, an approach clearly reminiscent of E. D. Hirsch's in *Cultural Literacy.*

10. No doubt the reaction to European immigration which took place in the 1920s set the stage for the present English-only movement. Not only was bilingual education in existence prior to World War I, but it was often looked on as a national resource. With the 1920s and the Great Depression, however, a growing concern over immigration made it possible for provincialists to sway public opinion against bilingualism by emphasizing the need for national unity. For an overview of attitudes toward U.S. language policy, see Dennis Baron, *The English Only Question: An Official Language for Americans?*

11. For summaries of these battles, see Reynaldo F. Macías, ed., *Are English Language Amendments in the National Interest? A Policy Analysis of Proposals to Establish English as the Official Language of the United States,* and Antonio J. Califa, "Declaring English the Official Language: Prejudice Spoken Here."

12. See Baldwin, "In Search of a Majority" (233), for an elaboration of this point. Within the specific context of the English-only movement, proponents of the law—including, until recently, Linda Chavez, who quit U.S. English when a memo was leaked revealing the organization's politically oriented anti-Latino agenda—argue that forced assimilation will improve the economic status of the groups involved. However, both sides agree that none of the studies of education has shown a linguistic advantage to the English-only approach, otherwise known as the immersion technique; to date it is not apparent that a distinct advantage exists to monolingual over bilingual ESL programs, although there are certainly many practitioners who feel that bilingual education has never had a sufficient chance to prove itself. Meanwhile, the bill's detractors argue that standards beyond English proficiency need to be considered. They ask, How does one measure the loss of science and math instruction in an immersion program? How does one measure the student's sense of self-worth or the student's relationship with family and culture? At the very least we need to be aware that short-term gains may have subtle, long-term effects.

13. As Mike Davis notes in *City of Quartz: Excavating the Future in Los Angeles,* neither oil nor oranges nor movies "provided an adequate economic foundation for Los Angeles's dramatic ascent during the 1920s. . . . Homegrown wealth and commerce were insufficient to support the region's lavish superstructures of consumption" (117–18). The creation of the All Year Club in the 1920s—a business venture promoting retirement and travel in California—attempted to sustain absolutely necessary growth by convincing people, primarily Easterners, that life in the Golden State could be both comfortable and culturally rich. Santa Barbara did its part to convince visitors of the latter by initiating the first city laws in the West dictating "Mission style" architecture for its downtown tourist district.

14. For a summary of the policies and their apparent motivations, see Valerie Mathes, *Helen Hunt Jackson and Her Indian Reform Legacy,* 56.

15. The historical legacy of such activist mourning will be pursued at length in chapter 5.

16. For a reading of this aspect of African-American slave narratives, see H. Bruce Franklin, *Prison Literature in America: The Victim as Criminal and Artist,* and especially chapter 1, devoted to Frederick Douglass and Linda Brent.

17. The Los Angeles History Project develops this argument in its video production *Ramona: A Story of Passion and Protest.*

18. See Mary Dearborn's elaboration of this argument in her *Pocahontas's Daughters: Gender and Ethnicity in American Culture,* 131–58.

19. Prescott Webb's work (see esp. *The Great Plains* and *The Texas Rangers*) is perhaps the most infamous example; however, Chicana historiography is now uncovering a systematic manipulation of such stereotypes that infuses Anglo/Mexican relations from well before the Mexican-American War. For example, see the work of Antonia Castañeda (discussed below).

20. Ramón Gutiérrez documents these aspects of colonial life in the first chapters of his latest study, *When Jesus Came, the Corn Mothers Went Away.*

21. See, for instance, the photograph of the Reata barbecue used in a full two-page reproduction by Donald Richie in his *George Stevens: An American Romantic,* 74–75.

22. Stevens was interviewed on this point by Richard Dyer MacCann; see his "Giant in Preparation: George Stevens Bringing Novel on Texas to Screen," *Christian Science Monitor,* 18 September 1956.

23. The interview with Joe Hyams is cited in Bruce Petri, *A Theory of American Film* (185).

24. For a brief summary of Stevens's career, see the introduction to Petri.

25. Fred Hift's article from *Variety* offers an example of this positive critical response (qtd. in Petri 186). The elaborate editing process is also detailed in Petri (185).

26. Petri sums up the situation and Stevens's response when noting, "Because of the frantic efforts in Hollywood to offer wide-screen entertainment that could not be approximated by television, Stevens was under immense pressure to photograph *Giant* in Cinemascope, or a similar process. In fact, the initial publicity for the film announced that it would be filmed in Warner SuperScope. Although the vast sweep of the novel would seem to make it a natural for the wide screen, Stevens held out against the pressure" (187).

27. Arnold García, Jr., records this relationship in his newspaper article "Hispanic Champion Battles Against Bias: Passion for Equality Burns in Hector García," *Austin American-Statesman,* 15 December 1985: D1, D12.

28. The fight over the burial of Félix Longoría in Three Rivers, Texas, will be discussed at length in the final chapter.

3. "RANCHO MEXICANA, USA" UNDER SIEGE

1. On dependency theory, see Wallerstein, *The Capitalist World Economy,* and Cardoso and Faletto, *Dependency and Development in Latin America.*

2. See George Mariscal's discussion of this approach and his citation of Frederic Jameson in "Alejandro Morales in Utopia" (80).

3. For an explicit indication of the relationship between Yates's work and Fuentes's novel, see the preface to *Terra nostra* (Spanish edition).

4. Mario García develops this argument in his essay "History, Literature, and the Chicano Working-Class Novel: A Critical Review of Alejandro Morales' *The Brick People*."

5. Houston Baker, for instance, explores a methodology informed by African-American music in his *Blues, Ideology, and Afro American Literature: A Vernacular Theory*. With reference to *Invisible Man*, see especially 172–99.

6. See Ralph Ellison's introduction to *Invisible Man* (1990 edition) for an extended discussion of the various political contexts he is engaging (including his dialogue with Richard Wright) and for an explanation of how his novel's structure attempts to remedy the earlier tendency to make African Americans into relatively simplistic reactions to, or symptoms of, social problems. For an explicit discussion of institutionally based manipulation, see Michel Foucault, *Discipline and Punish: The Birth of the Prison*, especially the sections "Correct Training" and "Panopticism" (170–308).

7. Brian McHale's theorization of "worlds" or "zones" in *Postmodernist Fiction* emphasizes the dominant ontological trend in postmodernist experiments and offers one interesting context for considering how political strategies may be constructed through the combative juxtaposition of "core" and "periphery" worldviews.

8. For further information about the Casa de las Américas enterprise, see Judith A. Weiss, *Casa de las Américas: An Intellectual Review of the Cuban Revolution*.

9. Note, for instance, Roberto González Echevarría's undervaluation of the form, and particularly its institutional implications, in "Carpentier y lo real maravilloso."

10. González Echevarría comes to a similar point in his more recent study of Latin American literary history, *Myth and Archive: A Theory of Latin American Narrative*. In this work González Echevarría claims that a new relationship to the mythical is taken up by contemporary Latin American authors, a relationship which allows works to exploit tensions between differing worldviews. Echevarría understands these combative worldviews as fitting into two categories: the first, termed the *archive*, is constituted by the discourses of hegemonic Western institutions, especially the legal. The second, termed the *mythic*, exploits a variety of extrahistoric origin narratives. There is an assumption here that New World exceptionalism is in itself a defining force in terms of the development of the magical. Taking up Fuentes's work as well, we thus find more support for José Saldívar's larger claim in *Dialectics of Our America* that the magical has a defining link to political contexts, and the underdevelopment tending toward despotic institutions, that have helped shape Latin America's specific colonial history.

11. Genaro Padilla describes the doña's manuscript in "The Recovery of

Chicano Nineteenth-Century Autobiography." Recalling the Fuentes epigraph, the Doña Eulalia memoir and its re-presentation by Morales may be read as yet another exploitation of ontological frames for resistant purposes.

12. The rapid growth in the Latino population is detailed in Robert Pear, "Hispanic Population Growing Five Times as Fast as Rest of U.S.," *New York Times*, 11 September 1987: 1.

13. In a scene indicative of this new consumerism, one of the husbands, Pedro Gonzalo, forestalls the interpretive battle over the photo by promising to buy the family a car (120).

14. A reevaluation of these aspects of daily life is undertaken in de Certeau, *Practice of Everyday Life* (xiv), LaCapra, *Soundings in Critical Theory* (20–21), and Hall, "Cultural Studies: Two Paradigms" (71).

15. As I have noted with regard to the term *working through*, I use it to suggest a process of actively engaging emotionally charged historical material which has been occluded through denial or otherwise significantly displaced by various cognitive-rhetorical mechanisms. For a full development of the term in this context, see Dominick LaCapra, *Soundings in Critical Theory* (esp. 30–66).

16. Probably one of de Certeau's clearest examples of the tactic may be found in his discussion of *la perruque:* "the worker's own work disguised as work for his employer" (*Practice of Everyday Life* 25). De Certeau offers this pilfering, or what he more frequently calls "poaching," as an operational model of popular culture which might displace traditional modes of study which have emphasized "the past, the countryside, or primitive peoples" (25).

17. Although de Certeau would read perruque as a form of resistance in which the worker is able to "signify his own capabilities through his *work* and to confirm his solidarity with other workers or his family through *spending* time in this way" (*Practice of Everyday Life* 25–26), a certain breakdown between tactic and strategy may be evident in that de Certeau notes how such improvisation may well take place with the knowledge of the boss, who has chosen to turn a not-so-blind eye. Since the boss may continue to exercise a control over the situation by dictating the limits of the "blindness," perruque may also, therefore, be read as an escape valve, an enclave in which the worker is permitted to fantasize liberty. In any case, the distinction between tactic and strategy may require more caution than de Certeau admits. As Rosa Linda Fregoso notes in "The Discourse of Difference," such questions have subtle implications for the Chicano critic, who, by virtue of participation in the academy, is involved in the "representation" of culture.

18. The originally psychoanalytic concept of *working through* has become a dominant trope for a number of the cultural critics working in the wake of Foucault and the radical historical breaks he suggests; these critics include Hall ("Cultural Studies" 68), LaCapra (*Soundings in Critical Theory* 30–66), and Mailloux (*ILL* 345–63).

19. Such a project would need to consider the institutional implications of Freud's later works, including *Civilization and Its Discontents,* in which he begins to develop more social forms of analysis. A number of critics have already begun exploring this terrain, including Samuel Weber (*Legend of Freud*), Dominick LaCapra, and Mitchell Breitwieser.

20. Mark Kelman is paraphrasing here the work of Roberto Unger, in particular his *Knowledge and Politics* 81–83.

21. For a brief summary of *Washington v. Davis* and its impact, see Freeman, "Legitimizing Racial Discrimination."

22. This point is one focus of Williams's chapter "The Pain of Word Bondage," in *Alchemy of Race and Rights* 146–65.

23. The dedication to his parents and their final silencing in the text reinforce the suggestion that this sacrifice is a continuation of Rodriguez's active resentment rather than a form of existential reconciliation occurring after he has lost contact with them.

24. For a summary of Kennedy's essay "The Structure of Blackstone's Commentaries," see Kelman 275.

25. Freeman offers an extended discussion of these legal manipulations in "Legitimizing Racial Discrimination."

26. The fact that de Certeau describes Foucault's study in spatial terms ("landscape"), terms associated with "the strategic," suggests a potentially fundamental power in such "homeopathic" projects.

27. This take on the movement echoes the findings of Ramón Gutiérrez in his "Community, Patriarchy, and Individualism: The Politics of Chicano History and the Dream of Equality."

28. This in fact is one implicit premise behind García's project in *Mexican Americans.*

29. As Acuña notes in his most recent preface to *Occupied America,* a fundamental split between haves and have-nots now typifies Chicano communities.

30. Ironically, *The Practice of Everyday Life,* which began as a counter to Foucault, becomes a repetition of the "homeopathic" panopticism that de Certeau later identifies in Foucault's work, a method which uses "panoptical discourse as a mask for tactical interventions." See de Certeau, *Heterologies,* for a discussion of this process of "panoptic fiction" (191).

4. CONSENSUAL FICTIONS

1. Genaro Padilla suggests something similar when he notes that Vallejo, in his *Recuerdos históricos tocante a la alta California,* tactically played on his lost institutional power by extending a public, personal, and verbal eloquence befitting his former station in society (299–300).

2. On the distinct era of Mexican-American politics, see García, *Mexican Americans.*

3. See, for instance, Kammen, *Sovereignty and Liberty: Constitutional Dis-*

course in American Culture (esp. 3–42), as well as Bercovitch, "The Rites of Assent: Rhetoric, Ritual, and the Ideology of American Consensus."

4. I will develop the notion of "homosocial desire" at length in the following chapter; for now, though, I propose the concept as a means of understanding the play of desires among men within patriarchy. This very efficacious play of desires taps the wide range that exists between the "officially" recognized poles of heterosexual and homosexual orientations in order to solidify affiliations and entitlements among men and at the strategic expense of women's interests.

5. Cynthia Gillespie takes up a discussion of this inaction in *Justifiable Homicide: Battered Women, Self-Defense and the Law* 136–39.

6. Tiffany Lopez offered a reading of this incest dynamic in "Silencio Nunca Mas: Incest and Child Sexual Abuse in Cherrie Moraga's *Giving Up the Ghost*," MLA Convention, December 1991.

7. For examples of work tracing this legal interest, see Deena González, "The Widowed Women of Santa Fe," and Angelina Veyna, "Women in Early New Mexico" (discussed below).

8. The law is obviously not monolithic in this regard; however, a clear tendency toward authoritarian modes of argumentation has been identified by CLS scholars. For a reading of how both authoritarian and more "democratic" modes of argument are played out in a particular case, see James Boyd White, "Judicial Criticism" (*ILL* 339–410).

5. A SOCIAL CONTEXT FOR MOURNING AND MOURNING'S SUBLIMATION

1. For a summary of trends in litigation at this time, see Guadalupe San Miguel, Jr., "Mexican American Organizations and the Changing Politics of School Desegregation in Texas, 1945 to 1980."

2. As part of his strategy, Acosta carefully detailed the legal precedents which affirmed that grand jury selection committees must "be mindful of the need for making nominations from various geographical locations within the County, the different racial groups, and all economic levels" (1962 Los Angeles County Policy Statement, cited in Acosta, brief, p. 25); from this material, Acosta successfully argued in his appeals case (*Montez v. Superior Court*, 1970) that the statistics and testimonies of the nominating judges demonstrated a process of systematic discrimination against Chicanos. Acosta summarized his case before the appeals court by noting that

> [t]he net effect of the nomination/selection process during the past eleven years has been the total exclusion of the Spanish-surnamed Mexican American—who constitute 12.9% of the County population—from eight of the last eleven Grand Juries. Or, if "averages" are preferred, only 1.7% of the ultimately selected Grand Jurors over the past eleven years have been of the Mexican American ethnic minority. Whether one counts nominees (approximately five to one) or Grand Jurors (approximately 7.5 to 1), at the very least there has been a striking and long-standing disparity between population and Grand Jury representation. (brief, p. 25)

Beyond "quashing" (or negating) the original grand jury's indictment against his clients—Chicanos who purportedly disrupted a speech by then Governor Ronald Reagan—this decision confirmed a new course for Chicano litigation in the sense that it built its argument not on the immediate details of the case but rather on the larger process through which adjudication has been forced to contend with political bias; here I am thinking primarily of the subsequent dependence upon the Voting Rights Act of 1965, a document that was essential for Acosta as well.

3. See San Miguel's essay for a fully detailed reading of the divergent strategies followed by these organizations.

4. For a sense of this rhetorical awareness, see Héctor Calderón's approach to the novel as satire: "To Read Chicano Narrative: Commentary and Metacommentary."

5. See Acosta's position paper, "Challenging Racial Exclusion on the Grand Jury" (7–9). See also the brief for *Montez v. Superior Court* (p. 19).

6. See the conclusion of Alurista's essay, "Acosta's *Revolt*: The Case, the Novel, and History" (94–95).

7. Consider, for instance, the rhetorical situation Acosta creates in "Challenging Racial Exclusion" when he makes Chicana protest an echo of machismo (1). Finding himself in a situation where he fears his own participation in hegemonic designs as a sort of ventriloquist's puppet—a point I will elaborate on shortly—Zeta, the narrator, likewise seems to be locked into a struggle that defines success as discovering one's own desires voiced through "consenting" others.

8. The whole episode is even more disturbing because of the aura of militaristic discipline. Inasmuch as all three women until this point are treated as though they "belonged" to Zeta (they are said to be Zeta's "rukas"), the prospect of additional male partners clearly signals a taboo which Zeta must disavow before the orgy can commence; hence, "No one speaks for a moment. They await my [Zeta's] instructions" (130). Given that the exchange starts with the celebration of a paramilitary action—the bombing of a Safeway store—and that the language of military discipline is satirically in the air, the exchange of women emphasizes Zeta's power, even as he uses his privilege to defer it.

9. In considering this "economic" manipulation, Sedgwick, in *Epistemology of the Closet*, suggests that "coming out" itself may reinforce the system of entitlements (67) even while such an act may also open a new epistemological space (77–78).

10. Through a reading of Henry James's "Beast in the Jungle," Sedgwick highlights the rise of "bachelor" culture as a response to the growing heterosexist rigors of the oedipal family in the nineteenth century, noting the way in which bachelor-oriented texts play on the anxieties evoked by the homosexual implications of the bachelor alternative.

11. It is interesting to note that despite Acosta's important role in the legal scene of the late 1960s, he is entirely ignored by both Acuña and Mirandé as they write their histories. Even when Acosta has been noticed, the

tendency has been to resurrect his revolutionary aspects as if his sexism were ancillary; see, for instance, Ramón Saldívar's claim in *Chicano Narrative* that it is the legal critique and not the sexual attitudes that constitutes the greatest transgression in the novel.

12. See the first chapter of Sedgwick's *Epistemology* for a full account of the oedipal family in this regard.

13. On these group dynamics, see Robin Warshaw, *I Never Called It Rape: The Ms. Report of Recognizing, Fighting, and Surviving Date and Acquaintance Rape*. As Warshaw notes, one of the distinguishing features of group acquaintance rape is "the use of rape as a reinforcing mechanism for membership in the group of men." In such situations, these men "experience a special bonding with each other, a unity of purpose that comes from the pride they feel in reducing their victim to nothing more than a vessel for their masculinity" (101).

14. For more about Salazar's role as a media personality and his death at the hands of the Los Angeles police department, see Acuña 345–50.

15. The great irony here is that the film *Viva Zapata* in fact portrays Zapata achieving both ends simultaneously during his wedding night. Once again Acosta appears to condemn his protagonist to an inevitably shameful situation in which he must reject either his political commitments or his sexual affiliations with his community. (In both cases, rejection would be taken as evidence of a cultural affront.)

16. Sublimation has been a key concept in the literature devoted to psychoanalysis, yet as J. Laplanche and J.-B. Pontalis note in *The Language of Psychoanalysis*, it remains a "lacuna in psychoanalytic thought" because no comprehensive theory exists about its range and functions (432–33). In his later work Freud used the notion of sublimation to describe the "desexualized energy" which had been freed from the libido for service as ego energy, or as energy displaced onto nonsexual activities (art and intellectual pursuits were two of Freud's more famous examples). Breitwieser's use of the term, one I will follow, delineates an important twist on this reading, inasmuch as it suggests a specific process by which more primitive forms of energy are bound up in "sublime" cultural efforts; here religion, nationalism, and the law would become central. Viewed as a process that may be affected by institutional dictates like those evidenced in the Puritan political economy, sublimation thus reveals a pathological potential, one which may block the work of the more primitive energies (including mourning) bound up in its projects. Hence, Breitwieser argues that nation-states and their war machines gain mastery over a diverse source of nonaligned energies by manipulating situations of mourning so as to trick people into a sense of closure that is too easily won (that is, a sense of having finished with the lost loved one by finding a higher object of affection, one that can make sense of the more primary loss). Instead of proceeding with the full "work of mourning," work that involves coming to terms with each of the independently arising memories that make up one's complex relationship

with the dead, this sublimating mechanism thus offers a quick fix, a means of transferring the obligation to do this work onto a set of sublime social relations. In this way, one love (the love for the larger social cause) replaces another (the love lost), but in a manner that purposefully leaves the original wound incompletely treated, a situation that can drive the affected population all the more desperately into the sublimation. (As Breitwieser notes [112], Puritanism was itself "overefficient" in this way.)

17. Although it might be tempting to consider Acosta's representations of the courtroom an aberration which reflects certain biases, sociological analysis of bilingual courtrooms, and particularly the role of the predominantly female translators, confirms a whole set of factors affecting jury decisions which are elided as the court attempts to make these translators purely passive entities. See Susan Berk-Seligson, *The Bilingual Courtroom: Court Interpreters in the Judicial Process,* for a particularly careful study of the ways in which these translators often have a very significant impact, acting as a kind of symbolic jury which is then read by the actual jury for cues about the case being tried.

With regard to Acosta's own manipulation of a "feminized" audience, we may recall Zeta's continual fixation on the seduction of the women jurors, a seduction consummated after one central case.

18. See particularly Paz, *Labyrinth of Solitude.* My thanks to Norma Alarcón for pointing out this connection.

19. Theodore Davidson's *Chicano Prisoners: The Key to San Quentin* is a valuable study of the intricate economic system formed by Chicano prisoners. As Davidson argues, and Olmos emphasizes, it was exactly the move to establish continuity on both sides of the wall that allowed La Eme to achieve economic success. See also Alfredo Mirandé's discussion of La Eme in *Gringo Justice,* where he takes issue with the larger tendency to single out the relationship between gang and community when Chicanos specifically are the subject of study (as if the Chicano community were somehow inherently more accepting of gang violence, etc.).

20. For summaries of these various histories, see Davidson, Kahn, and Mirandé, *Gringo Justice.*

21. As Davidson points out (84), gangs like La Eme are often much smaller than imagined by outsiders, so that the entire "official" membership might number well under three hundred for the whole California prison system at any given time. The power the gangs wield is thus a matter of their ability to control myriad negotiations through a variety of affiliates.

22. My thanks to Deena González for her criticism with regard to these limitations.

23. These comments are recorded in Terry Pristin, "Olmos Puts Warning Out to Gang Members," *Los Angeles Times,* 24 February 1992: F1, F7, F9.

24. Alarcón details latently misogynistic tendencies with regard to Paz in "Traddutora, Traditora" (65–66).

25. Chief Justice Warren Burger's argument is recounted by Hellen Pors-

dam in "Doing What Comes Naturally? Fish, Posner, and the Law and Literature Enterprise" (494); for further reference to Burger's statements, see his essay, "Isn't There a Better Way?"

26. My thanks to Dan Gunter for pointing out the manner in which my summary of this argument might lead readers to believe that Breitwieser is relying on an overly simple notion of the "natural" processes of mourning. As Gunter has noted, such processes are always culturally determined, and hence no natural mode of mourning preexists the Puritan manipulations. Breitwieser is more sophisticated on this issue than my reading allows, and without trying to fully recover his subtlety, I would simply reinforce that the "unsatisfied mourning" or melancholia that I am describing in the Chicano context is perhaps best thought of as one result of larger, ongoing social and cultural conflicts that have affected in a variety of ways the numerous tools which communities use to contend with loss.

27. With regard to Olmos's title, it should be noted that Beatrice Griffith published a book by the same name in 1947. Although the link between the two works would seem fairly obvious—for both, the zoot suit riots have a privileged place in the interpretation of the contemporary Chicano social situation—more subtle correspondences exist which support the notion that the play of sexual desire is central to Olmos's interests. I am thinking particularly of Griffith's short story included in the volume and sharing its title. This version of "American Me" is told from the perspective of a young Chicana as she goes to a carnival with her boyfriend, only to see the event turn into a race riot. The moral of the story is pertinent to my reading inasmuch as the young Chicana announces that in spite of the tensions, her boyfriend knows how to turn the evening into a romantic affair (he bestows their first kiss). Like the rap song that concludes Olmos's film, the implicit message here is that the all-important heterosexual connection must not be lost despite the larger social context.

28. While shame is not generally associated with expressions of melancholia (melancholiacs are in fact notable for the exhibitionism which attends their moral contrition), there may well exist a process by which mourning, when bound with the historical pressures I am describing, alters shame significantly, turning it inward in a manner that allows a certain overcoming of its original prohibitions.

29. My appreciation to Norma Alarcón for bringing this possibility to my attention.

30. The response, detailed in the *Los Angeles Times* story "Olmos Puts a Warning Out to Gang Members" (24 February 1992: F1, F7, F9), suggests that the director's oeuvre should be taken as a whole.

31. For a summary of traditional Mexicano funeral practices, see Norma Jean Williams, *Changing Patterns in the Mexican American Family,* and specifically her discussion of funerals in the chapter "Changes in Life Cycle Rituals Within the Working Class Group" (79–82).

32. See José Limón, "La Llorona, the Third Legend of Greater Mexico:

Cultural Symbols, Women, and the Political Unconscious," and Monica Palacios, "La Llorona Loca: The Other Side."

33. This work is discussed by Rosa Linda Fregoso in "Chicana Film Practices" (201).

34. The Mothers of the Plaza de Mayo protest against the Argentine government and for restitution by carrying photos of their disappeared children in regular rallies that will not let officially sanctioned institutional forgetting (taking the form of two amnesty laws, Punto Final, 1986, and Obediencia Debida, 1987) sublimate the losses. These women and their associates, the Grandmothers of the Plaza de Mayo, "see their work as part of a process of reconstructing history"—the recovery of individual children, but also the recovery of Argentina as a whole (see Rita Arditti and M. Brinton Lykes, "Recovering Identity: The Work of the Grandmothers of the Plaza de Mayo" 465). In developing a link between the Argentine activities and the Chicana practices I study below, I follow a line of thought also suggested by the Chicana filmmakers Susana Muñoz and Lourdes Portillo, who have collaborated to produce an extended documentary, *Las Madres: The Mothers of the Plaza de Mayo*. Readers wanting to pursue the Argentine context may also be interested in *Nunca Mas—The Report of the Argentine National Commission on the Disappeared*.

35. See Veyna, "Women in Early New Mexico," for a more general assessment of these documents and their likely role in the society of their time.

36. In one exemplary case cited by González, that of the widow Chavez, hegemony and coercion come together in a most obvious form as Chavez's priest (in collusion with her law clerk) threatens to excommunicate her if she does not comply with a falsified will cheating her heirs out of her property; see González, "Widowed Women of Santa Fe" (42–43), for a recounting of the story.

37. For an excellent reading of the language of funerals (and mourning in general) in the context of the gay community's response to AIDS deaths and government policy, see Douglass Crimp, "Mourning and Militancy."

38. This summary of the Longoría episode is much indebted to Manuel Peña, "Folksong and Social Change: Two Corridos as Interpretive Sources."

39. See Kennedy's letter to Beatrice Longoría dated 12 January 1949. My thanks to the Hector P. Garcia Archives at Corpus Christi State University for making available the various correspondences I cite with regard to the Longoría affair.

40. In a notarized statement, Félix's father, Guadalupe Longoría, Sr., documented this harassment and his full support of his sister-in-law's actions and her right to choose the method and place of burial.

41. For a description of the threatening atmosphere around the investigation hearings, see Peña 21.

42. This parallel is at the core of Peña's argument in "Folksong and Social Change."

43. See, for instance, Beatrice Longoría's statement, dated 9 February 1949. Given the sorts of threats the family was living with at the time, it seems clear that the deferential tone here is a necessary facet of both surviving and resisting Anglo control.

44. For a sense of the pressure being placed on the family and its supporters, see the letter sent to Dr. Hector García by R. E. Smith (17 January 1949), the chairman of the Good Neighbor Commission, in which Smith claims that "all Texans and the children of Texans now living will feel the effect of the criticism [ensuing from the affair] and we all know that none of them had anything to do with it." Elsewhere, the author notes, "we must bear in mind that the reputation of Texas will be at stake in history's recording of our handling of this very delicate matter."

45. See Williams, *Alchemy of Race and Rights,* and particularly the chapter "The Pain of Word Bondage."

CONCLUSION

1. For a discussion of these specific translation dynamics, see Berk-Seligson's chapter "The Impact of the Interpreter on Mock Juror Evaluations of Witnesses" (146–97). See also Berk-Seligson's summary of the training and certification of federal court interpreters (36–42).

2. For a summary of the decision in *Hernandez v. New York,* see "Court Backs Jury Barring of Hispanics" *Santa Barbara News Press,* 29 May 1991: A1, A7.

3. See Saldívar, *Dialectics of Our America* ch. 5.

4. Clearly it is a large step to bring together the Russian and Chicano cultural contexts. Even so, there exist strong parallel concerns which could act as a bridge: for instance, questions of political suppression, revolutionary promise, and more effective democratic participation. Looking at Bakhtin's work itself, we find another possible reason for the missed connection in the fact that Bakhtin "rarely discusses the specific events of class and group conflict in a given region or locality" (White 235). No doubt a result of the political suppression under which he worked, this lack of specificity leaves Bakhtin somewhat weak on questions of institutional power, particularly when race and gender issues are the focus. Nevertheless, his notions about processes of translation may help contextualize the political stakes of Chicano/legal interaction in quite significant ways.

5. I have in mind here the work available in *The Dialogic Imagination, Rabelais and His World,* and *Problems of Dostoevsky's Poetics.* For an overview of Bakhtin's contributions, see Morson and Emerson, *Mikhail Bakhtin: Creation of a Prosaics.*

6. Allon White develops this argument in "The Struggle over Bakhtin: Fraternal Reply to Robert Young."

7. Bakhtin's intellectual history is recounted by Morson and Emerson in "The Shape of a Career," part of their larger study *Mikhail Bakhtin.*

8. The comment is taken from Werner Sollors, *The Invention of Ethnicity,* and is quoted by Saldívar in his *Chicano Narrative* (216).

Works Cited

Abuelas de Plaza de Mayo. *Missing Children Who Disappeared in Argentina Between 1976 and 1983.* Buenos Aires: Abuelas de Plaza de Mayo, 1988.

Acosta, Oscar Zeta. *Autobiography of a Brown Buffalo.* San Francisco: Straight Arrow, 1972.

———. "Challenging Racial Exclusion on the Grand Jury." *Caveat* 7 (1970): 7–9.

———. Legal briefs, 1969–1971. Colección Tloque Nahuaque. U of California, Santa Barbara.

———. *The Revolt of the Cockroach People.* New York: Random, 1973.

Acuña, Rudolfo. *Occupied America: A History of Chicanos.* New York: Harper, 1988.

Alarcón, Norma. "Traddutora, Traditora: A Paradigmatic Figure of Chicana Feminism." *Cultural Critique* 13 (fall 1989): 57–88.

Alurista. "Acosta's Revolt: The Case, the Novel, and History." *Contemporary Chicano Fiction.* Ed. Vernon E. Lattin. Binghamton: Bilingual Review, 1986. 94–104.

Anzaldúa, Gloria. *Borderlands / La Frontera: The New Mestiza.* San Francisco: Spinsters / Aunt Lute, 1987.

Arditti, Rita, and M. Brinton Lykes. "'Recovering Identity': The Work of the Grandmothers of the Plaza de Mayo." *Women's Studies International Forum* 15 (1992): 461–71.

Argentina. Comisión Nacional sobre la Desaparición de Personas. *Nunca Mas: The Report of the Arentine National Commission on the Disappeared.* New York: Farrar, Straus and Giroux, 1986.

Artenstein, Isaac, dir. *Ballad of an Unsung Hero.* Cinewest, 1983.

———. *Break of Dawn.* Platform Releasing, 1988.

Baca Zinn, Maxine. "Chicanas: Power and Control in the Domestic Sphere." *De Colores: Journal of Emerging Raza Philosophies* 2.3 (1975): 19–31.

Baker, Houston. *Blues, Ideology, and Afro-American Literature: A Vernacular Theory.* Chicago: U of Chicago P, 1984.

Bakhtin, Mikhail. "Author and Character in Aesthetic Activity." *Mikhail Bakhtin: The Dialogic Principle.* Trans. Tzvetan Todorov and Wlad Godzich. Minneapolis: U of Minnesota P, 1984. 22.

———. *The Dialogic Imagination.* Trans. Caryl Emerson and Michael Holquist. Austin: U of Texas P, 1981.

————. *Problems of Dostoevsky's Poetics.* Ed. and trans. Caryl Emerson. Minneapolis: U of Minnesota P, 1984.

————. *Rabelais and His World.* Trans. Hélène Iswolsky. Cambridge: MIT P, 1968.

Baldwin, James. "In Search of a Majority." *The Price of the Ticket.* New York: St. Martin's / Marek, 1985. 229–36.

Bancroft, Hubert Howe. *History of California.* San Francisco: History Company, 1884–1890.

Banham, Reyner. *Los Angeles: The Architecture of Four Ecologies.* New York: Penguin, 1971.

Baron, Dennis. *The English-Only Question: An Official Language for Americans?* New Haven: Yale UP, 1990.

Bercovitch, Sacvan. "The Rites of Assent: Rhetoric, Ritual, and the Ideology of American Consensus." *The American Self: Myth, Ideology, and Popular Culture.* Ed. Sam Girgus. Albuquerque: U of New Mexico P, 1981. 5–42.

Berk-Seligson, Susan. *The Bilingual Courtroom: Court Interpreters in the Judicial Process.* Chicago: U of Chicago P, 1990.

Bourdieu, Pierre. *La Distinction: Critique sociale du jugement.* Paris: Éditions de Minuit, 1979.

Breitwieser, Mitchell Robert. *American Puritanism and the Defense of Mourning: Religion, Grief, and Ethnology in Mary White Rowlandson's Captivity Narrative.* Madison: U of Wisconsin P, 1990.

Brooks, Peter. *Reading for the Plot: Design and Intention in Narrative.* New York: Random-Vintage, 1984.

Bruce-Novoa, Juan. "Canonical and Noncanonical Texts." *Américas Review* 14.3–4 (1986): 119–35.

Bumiller, Kristin. "Fallen Angels: The Representation of Violence Against Women in Legal Culture." *At the Boundaries of the Law: Feminism and Legal Theory.* Ed. Martha Albertson Fineman and Nancy Sweet Thomadsen. New York: Routledge, 1990. 95–112.

Brownmiller, Susan. *Against Our Will: Men, Women, and Rape.* New York: Simon, 1975.

Burger, Warren. "Isn't There a Better Way?" *American Bar Association Journal* 68 (1982): 274–77.

Calderón, Héctor. "To Read Chicano Narrative: Commentary and Metacommentary." *Mester* 13.2 (1983): 3–14.

Califa, Antonio J. "Declaring English the Official Language: Prejudice Spoken Here." *Harvard Civil Rights–Civil Liberties Law Review* 24 (1989): 294–348.

Camarillo, Albert. *Chicanos in a Changing Society: From Mexican Pueblos to American Barrios in Santa Barbara and Southern California, 1848–1930.* Cambridge: Harvard UP, 1979.

Cardoso, Fernando, and Enzo Faletto. *Dependency and Development in Latin America.* Trans. Marjory Muttingly Urquidi. Berkeley: U of California P, 1979.

Castañeda, Antonia. "The Political Economy of Nineteenth Century Stereo-types of Californianas." Del Castillo, *Between Borders* 213–36.

Castillo, Ana. *The Mixquiahuala Letters.* Binghamton: Bilingual Press / Editorial Bilingüe, 1986.

———. *My Father Was a Toltec: Poems.* Novato, Calif.: West End Press, 1988.

———. *Sapogonia.* Tempe: Bilingual Press / Editorial Bilingüe, 1990.

———. *Women Are Not Roses.* Houston: Arté Público, 1984.

Castillo, Debra. "Double Zero Place: A Discourse on War." MLA Convention. San Francisco, 30 December 1987.

———. *Talking Back: Toward a Latin American Literary Feminist Criticism.* Ithaca: Cornell UP, 1992.

Cox, Archibald. *The Court and the Constitution.* Boston: Houghton, 1987.

Crenshaw, Kimberlé Williams. "Demarginalizing the Intersection of Race and Sex: A Black Feminist Critique of Antidiscrimination Doctrine, Feminist Theory, and Antiracist Politics." Katharine Bartlett and Rosanne Kennedy, eds. *Feminist Legal Theory: Readings in Law and Gender.* San Francisco: Westview, 1991. 57–80.

———. "Foreword: Toward a Race-Conscious Pedagogy in Legal Education." *National Black Law Journal* 11.1 (1989): 1–14.

———. "Race, Reform, and Retrenchment: Transformation and Legitimation in Antidiscrimination Law." *Harvard Law Review* 101 (1988): 1331–87.

Crimp, Douglass. "Mourning and Militancy." *October* 51 (winter 1989): 3–18.

Davidson, Theodore. *Chicano Prisoners: The Key to San Quentin.* New York: Holt, 1974.

Davis, Mike. *City of Quartz: Excavating the Future in Los Angeles.* New York: Random-Vintage, 1990.

Dearborn, Mary. *Pocahontas's Daughters: Gender and Ethnicity in American Culture.* New York: Oxford UP, 1986.

De Certeau, Michel. *Heterologies: Discourse on the Other.* Trans. Brian Massumi. Minneapolis: U of Minnesota P, 1986.

———. *The Practice of Everyday Life.* Trans. Steven Rendall. Berkeley: U of California P, 1984.

Del Castillo, Adelaida R., ed. *Between Borders: Essays on Mexicana / Chicana History.* Encino: Floricanto Press, 1990.

D'Souza, Dinesh. *Illiberal Education: The Politics of Race and Sex on Campus.* New York: Free Press, 1991.

Dworkin, Andrea. *Intercourse.* New York: Free Press, 1987.

Ellison, Ralph. *Invisible Man.* New York: Random-Vintage, 1990.

Ferber, Edna. *Giant.* New York: Doubleday, 1952.

Flowers, Ronald Barri. *Minorities and Criminality.* New York: Praeger, 1988.

Foucault, Michel. *Discipline and Punish: The Birth of the Prison.* New York: Random-Vintage, 1979.

Franklin, H. Bruce. *Prison Literature in America: The Victim as Criminal and Artist.* New York: Oxford UP, 1989.

Freeman, Alan. "Legitimizing Racial Discrimination Through Antidiscrimination Law: A Critical Review of Supreme Court Doctrine." Hutchinson, *Critical Legal Studies* 120–36.

Fregoso, Rosa Linda. "Chicana Film Practices: Confronting the Many-headed Demon of Oppression." Noriega, *Chicanos and Film,* 168–82.

———. "The Discourse of Difference: Footnoting Inequality." *Crítica* 2.2 (1990): 182–87.

Freud, Sigmund. *Civilization and Its Discontents.* Trans. Joan Riviere. London: Hogarth, 1930.

———. "Mourning and Melancholia" (1917). *The Complete Psychological Works of Sigmund Freud.* Trans. James Strachey. London: Hogarth, 1953. 14:243–58.

Fuentes, Carlos. *Terra nostra.* Barcelona: Editorial Seix Barral, 1975. Trans. Margaret Sayers Peden. New York: Farrar, 1976.

García, Hector P. Statement, 9 February 1949. Hector Perez Garcia Archives, Corpus Christi State University Library.

García, Mario T. *Desert Immigrants: The Mexicans of El Paso, 1880–1920.* New Haven: Yale UP, 1981.

———. "History, Literature, and the Chicano Working-Class Novel: A Critical Review of Alejandro Morales' *The Brick People." Crítica* 2.2 (1990): 188–201.

———. *Mexican Americans: Leadership, Ideology, and Identity, 1930–1960.* New Haven: Yale UP, 1992.

Gates, Henry Louis, Jr. "Editor's Introduction: Writing 'Race' and the Difference It Makes." *Critical Inquiry* 12.1 (1985): 1–20.

———. *Loose Canons: Notes on the Culture Wars.* New York: Oxford UP, 1992.

———. "The Master's Pieces: On Canon Formation and the Black Tradition." (Lecture.) Cornell University, 12 December 1988.

———, ed. *Norton Anthology of African-American Literature.* New York: Norton, forthcoming.

Gillespie, Cynthia. *Justifiable Homicide: Battered Women, Self-Defense, and the Law.* Columbus: Ohio State UP, 1989.

González, Deena F. "The Widowed Women of Santa Fe: Assessments on the Lives of an Unmarried Population, 1850–1880." *On Their Own: Widows and Widowhood in the American Southwest, 1848–1939.* Ed. Arlene Scardon. Urbana: U of Illinois P, 1988. 65–90.

González-Berry, Erlinda. "Alejandro Morales." *Chicano Literature: A Reference Guide.* Ed. Francisco A. Lomelí and Julio A. Martínez. Westport: Greenwood, 1985. 299–309.

González Echevarría, Roberto. "Carpentier y lo real maravilloso." *Otros mundos, otros fuegos.* Ed. Donald Yates. Pittsburgh: Michigan State U Latin American Studies Center, 1975. 221–32.

———. *Myth and Archive: A Theory of Latin American Narrative.* Cambridge: Cambridge UP, 1990.

González v. Superior Court. 35 *Pacific Reporter* (2d ser.) 556.

Gramsci, Antonio. *Prison Notebooks.* Trans. Joseph Buttigieg and Antonio Callari. New York: Columbia UP, 1992.

Greenfield, Alice. *The Sleepy Lagoon Case: A Pageant of Prejudice.* Los Angeles: Citizen's Committee for the Defense of the Mexican-American Youth, 1942.

Griffith, Beatrice. *American Me.* Boston: Riverside, 1947.

Guillory, John. "Canonical and Non-Canonical: A Critique of the Current Debate." *English Literary History* 54 (1987): 483–527.

Guiol, Fred, and Ivan Moffat. *Giant: Screenplay.* Hollywood: Script City, 1987.

Gutiérrez, José Angel. "Chicanos and Mexicans under Surveillance: 1940–1980." *Renato Rosaldo Lecture Series Monograph* 2 (spring 1986): 28–57.

Gutiérrez, Ramón A. "Community, Patriarchy, and Individualism: The Politics of Chicano History and the Dream of Equality." Chicano Cultural Studies Conference. U of California, Santa Barbara, 25 May 1990.

———. *When Jesus Came, the Corn Mothers Went Away: Marriage, Sexuality and Power in New Mexico, 1500–1846.* Stanford: Stanford UP, 1991.

Hall, Stuart. "Culture Studies: Two Paradigms." *Media, Culture, and Society* 2 (1980): 55–72.

Haraway, Donna J. "Manifesto for Cyborgs: Science, Technology, and Socialist Feminism in the 1980s." *Socialist Review* 80 (1985): 65–108.

Herrera-Sobek, María. *The Mexican Corrido: A Feminist Analysis.* Bloomington: Indiana UP, 1991.

Herrera-Sobek, María, and Helena María Viramontes, eds. *Chicana Creativity and Criticism: Charting New Frontiers in American Literature.* Houston: Arté Público, 1988.

Hirsch, E. D., Jr. *Cultural Literacy: What Every American Needs to Know.* New York: Random, 1988.

Hutchinson, Allan, ed. *Critical Legal Studies.* Totowa, NJ: Rowman and Littlefield, 1989.

Imhoff, Gary, and Gerda Bikales. "The Battle over Preserving the English Language." *USA Today* 115, no. 2,500 (January 1987): 63–65.

Islas, Arturo. *The Rain God.* Palo Alto: Alexandrian, 1984.

Jackson, Helen Hunt. *A Century of Dishonor: A Sketch of the United States Government's Dealings with Some of the Indian Tribes.* Boston: Roberts Brothers, 1881.

———. *Ramona.* New York: Roberts Brothers, 1884. Rpt. New York: Avon, 1970.

JanMohamed, Abdul R., and David Lloyd. Introduction. *Cultural Critique: The Nature and Context of Minority Discourse* 6 (spring 1987): 5–12.

Kahn, Brian. *Prison Gangs in the Community: A Briefing Document for the Board of Corrections.* Sacramento: California Board of Corrections, 1978.

Kammen, Michael. *Sovereignty and Liberty: Constitutional Discourse in American Culture.* Madison: U of Wisconsin P, 1988.

Keller, Gary D. *Chicano Cinema: Research, Reviews, and Resources.* Binghamton: Bilingual Review, 1985.

Kelman, Mark. *A Guide to Critical Legal Studies.* Cambridge: Harvard UP, 1987.

Kennedy, Duncan. "The Structure of Blackstone's Commentaries." Hutchinson, *Critical Legal Studies* 139–47.

Kerouac, Jack. *On the Road.* New York: Viking, 1959.

Kolodny, Annette. *The Lay of the Land: Metaphor as Experience and History in American Life and Literature.* Chapel Hill: U of North Carolina P, 1975.

LaCapra, Dominick. "Criticism Today." *The Aims of Representation: Subject, Text, History.* Ed Murray Krieger. New York: Columbia UP, 1987. 235–56.

———. *Soundings in Critical Theory.* Ithaca: Cornell UP, 1989.

LaFree, Gary D. *Rape and Criminal Justice: The Social Context of Sexual Assault.* Belmont, Calif.: Wadsworth, 1989.

Laplanche, J., and J.-B. Pontalis. *The Language of Psychoanalysis.* Trans. Donald Nicholson-Smith. New York: Norton, 1973.

Lattin, Vernon E. *Contemporary Chicano Fiction: A Critical Survey.* Binghamton: Bilingual Review/Press, 1986.

Lau v. Nichols, 414 US 563 (1974).

Levinson, Sanford, and Steven Mailloux, eds. *Interpreting Law and Literature; A Hermeneutic Reader.* Evanston: Northwestern UP, 1988.

Limón, José. "La Llorona, the Third Legend of Greater Mexico: Cultural Symbols, Women, and the Political Unconscious." *Renato Rosaldo Lecture Series* 2 (1984–85): 59–93.

Lomelí, Francisco, and Donaldo Urioste. "Chicanesque Writings." *Chicano Perspectives in Literature: A Critical and Annotated Bibliography.* Ed. Francisco Lomelí and Donaldo Urioste. Albuquerque: Pajarito, 1976. 107–10.

Longoría, Beatrice. Letter addressed to Mr. Kennedy, Director of the Rice Funeral Home, 14 January 1949. Hector Perez Garcia Archives, Corpus Christi State University Library.

———. Statement, 9 February 1949. Hector Perez Garcia Archives, Corpus Christi State University Library.

Longoría, Guadalupe, Sr. Statement, 20 February 1949. Hector Perez Garcia Archives, Corpus Christi State University Library.

López, Gerald P. "The Idea of a Constitution in the Chicano Tradition." *Journal of Legal Education* 37 (June 1987): 162–66.

———. *Rebellious Lawyering: One Chicano's Vision of Progressive Law Practice.* Boulder: Westview, 1992.

McHale, Brian. *Postmodernist Fiction.* New York: Methuen, 1987.

Macías, Reynaldo, ed. *Are English Language Amendments in the National Interest? A Policy Analysis of Proposals to Establish English as the Official Language of the United States.* Claremont, Calif.: The Center, 1989.

MacKinnon, Catharine A. "Feminism, Marxism, Method, and the State: Toward Feminist Jurisprudence." *Signs: Journal of Women in Culture and Society* 8 (1983): 635–58.

McWilliams, Carey. *North from Mexico: The Spanish-Speaking People of the United States.* New York: Praeger, 1948.

Mariscal, George. "Alejandro Morales in Utopia." *Confluencía* 2.1 (1986): 78–83.

Márquez, Antonio. "Literatura Chicanesque." *A Decade of Chicano Literature (1970–1979): Critical Essays and Bibliography.* Ed. Luis Leal et al. Santa Barbara: Editorial la Causa, 1982. 73–82.

Mathes, Valerie Sherer. *Helen Hunt Jackson and Her Indian Reform Legacy.* Austin: U of Texas P, 1990.

Menendez, Ramón, dir. *Stand and Deliver.* Warner Brothers, 1988.

Mirandé, Alfredo. *The Chicano Experience: An Alternative Perspective.* Notre Dame: U of Notre Dame P, 1985.

———. "Fear of Crime and Fear of the Police in a Chicano Community." *Sociology and Social Research* 64 (1980): 528–41.

———. *Gringo Justice.* Notre Dame: U of Notre Dame P, 1987.

Montez v. Superior Court, 10 Cal. App. 3d 343 (1970).

Moraga, Cherríe. *Giving Up the Ghost: Teatro in Two Acts.* Los Angeles: West End, 1986.

Morales, Alejandro. *The Brick People.* Houston: Arté Público, 1988.

———. *Reto en el paraíso.* Ypsilanti, Mich.: Bilingual Press / Editorial Bilingüe, 1983.

Morson, Gary Saul, and Caryl Emerson. *Mikhail Bakhtin: Creation of a Prosaics.* Stanford: Stanford UP, 1990.

Muñoz, Susana, and Lourdes Portillo. *Las Madres: The Mothers of the Plaza de Mayo.* Los Angeles: Direct Cinema Limited, 1986.

Nichols, John. *The Milagro Beanfield War.* New York: Ballantine, 1974.

Noriega, Chon A. *Chicanos and Film: Essay on Chicano Representation and Resistance.* New York: Garland, 1992.

Olmos, Edward James, dir. *American Me.* Universal Studios, 1992.

Olmstead v. United States, 277 US 438 (1928).

Padilla, Genaro M. "The Recovery of Chicano Nineteenth-Century Autobiography." *American Quarterly* 40.3 (September 1988): 286–306.

———. "Self as Cultural Metaphor in Acosta's *Autobiography of a Brown Buffalo.*" *Journal of General Education* 35 (1984): 242–58.

Palacios, Monica. "La Llorona Loca: The Other Side." *Chicana Lesbians: The Girls Our Mothers Warned Us About.* Ed. Carla Trujillo. Berkeley: Third Woman, 1991. 49–51.

Paredes, Américo. *With His Pistol in His Hand: A Border Ballad and Its Hero.* Austin: U of Texas P, 1958.

Paredes, Raymund. "The Evolution of Chicano Literature." *Three American Literatures.* Ed. Houston Baker, Jr. New York: MLA, 1982. 33–79.

Parlee, Lorena, and Paul Espinoza. "Ballad of an Unsung Hero." *Caminos* 5.11 (1983): 35–37.

Paz, Octavio. *Labyrinth of Solitude.* New York: Grove, 1985.

Peña, Manuel H. "Folksong and Social Change: Two Corridos as Interpretive Sources." *Aztlán* 13.1–2 (1982): 12–42.

Petri, Bruce. *A Theory of American Film: The Films and Techniques of George Stevens.* New York: Garland, 1987.

Porsdam, Helle. "Doing What Comes Naturally? Fish, Posner, and the Law and Literature Enterprise." *American Quarterly* 44 (1992): 494–505.

Preciado Martín, Patricia. *Days of Plenty, Days of Want.* Houston: Arté Público, 1988.

Ramona: A Story of Passion and Protest. (Videotape.) Princeton: Films for the Humanities, 1990.

Rebolledo, Tey Diana. "The Politics of Protest: Or, What Am I, a Critic, Doing in This Text Anyhow"? Herrera-Sobek and Viramontes, *Chicana Creativity and Criticism* 129–38.

Rechy, John. *The Sexual Outlaw: A Documentary.* New York: Grove, 1985.

Richie, Donald. *George Stevens: An American Romantic.* New York: Museum of Modern Art, 1970.

Rodriguez, Richard. *Hunger of Memory: The Education of Richard Rodriguez.* New York: Bantam, 1982.

Rosaldo, Renato. *Culture and Truth: The Remaking of Social Analysis.* Boston: Beacon, 1989.

Saldívar, José. *The Dialectics of Our America.* Durham: Duke UP, 1991.

Saldívar, Ramón. *Chicano Narrative: The Dialectics of Difference.* Madison: U of Wisconsin P, 1990.

———. "A Dialectic of Difference: Toward a Theory of the Chicano Novel." *Contemporary Chicano Fiction: A Critical Survey.* Ed. Vernon E. Lattin. Binghamton: Bilingual Press / Editorial Bilingüe, 1986. 13–31.

———. "Ideologies of the Self: Chicano Autobiography." *Diacritics* 15.3 (1985): 25–33.

San Miguel, Jr., Guadalupe. "Mexican American Organizations and the Changing Politics of School Desegregation in Texas, 1945 to 1980." *Social Science Quarterly* 63 (December 1982): 701–15.

Santiago, Danny. *Famous All over Town.* New York: Simon, 1983.

Scarry, Elaine. *The Body in Pain.* New York: Oxford UP, 1985.

Sedgwick, Eve Kosofsky. *Between Men: English Literature and Male Homosocial Desire.* New York: Columbia UP, 1985.

———. *Epistemology of the Closet.* Berkeley: U of California P, 1992.

Smith, R. E. Letter addressed to Dr. Hector P. Garcia, 17 January 1949. Hector Perez Garcia Archives, Corpus Christi State University Library.

Sollors, Werner. *The Invention of Ethnicity.* New York: Oxford UP, 1989.

Stallybrass, Peter, and Allon White. *The Politics and Poetics of Transgression.* Ithaca: Cornell UP, 1986.

Stevens, George, dir. *Giant.* Warner Brothers Studio, 1956.

Trujillo, Carla. *Chicana Lesbians: The Girls Our Mothers Warned Us About.* Berkeley: Third Woman, 1991.

Unger, Roberto. *Knowledge and Politics.* New York: Free Press, 1975.

Valdez, Luis. *Zoot Suit.* Unpublished play manuscript. California State University, Northridge, 1978.

———, dir. *Zoot Suit.* Swank Film Company, 1981.

Veyna, Angelina F. "Women in Early New Mexico: A Preliminary View." *Chicana Voices: Intersections of Class, Race and Gender.* Ed. Teresa Cordova. Austin: Center for Mexican American Studies, U of Texas, 1986. 120–35.

Vigil, Maurilio. "The Ethnic Organization as an Instrument of Political and

Social Change: MALDEF, a Case Study." *Journal of Ethnic Studies* 18.1 (1990): 15–31.

Viramontes, Helena María. *The Moths and Other Stories*. Houston: Arté Público, 1985.

Wallerstein, Immanuel. *The Capitalist World Economy*. Cambridge: Cambridge UP, 1979.

Warshaw, Robin. *I Never Called It Rape: The Ms. Report of Recognizing, Fighting, and Surviving Date and Acquaintance Rape*. New York: Harper and Row, 1988.

Washington v. Davis, 426 US 229 (1976).

Webb, Walter Prescott. *The Great Plains*. Boston: Ginn, 1931.

———. *The Texas Rangers*. Cambridge: Houghton, 1935.

Weber, Samuel. *The Legend of Freud*. Minneapolis: U of Minnesota P, 1982.

Weisberg, Richard. "Law in and as Literature: Self-Generated Meaning in the "Procedural Novel." *The Comparative Perspective on Literature: Approaches to Theory and Practice*. Ed. Clayton Koelb and Susan Noakes. Ithaca: Cornell UP, 1988. 224–32.

Weiss, Judith. *Casa de las Américas: An Intellectual Review of the Cuban Revolution*. Chapel Hill: Estudios Hispanofila, 1977.

White, Allon. "The Struggle over Bakhtin: Fraternal Reply to Robert Young." *Cultural Critique* 8 (winter 1987–88): 217–41.

Williams, Norma Jean. *Changing Patterns in the Mexican American Family*. Ann Arbor: University Microfilms International, 1988.

Williams, Patricia. *The Alchemy of Race and Rights: Diary of a Law Professor*. Cambridge: Harvard UP, 1991.

Yates, Frances. *The Art of Memory*. Chicago: U of Chicago P, 1966.

Young, Robert, dir. *The Ballad of Gregorio Cortez*. Embassy Pictures, 1982.

Index

Academic discourse: and archival work, 29, 152; and Chicana/Mexicana mourning practices, 152, 153; decontextualization of, 16; and figurative exploitation, 22; legal sphere engaged by, 19–20, 37; and multiculturalism, 171–72; and nationalism, 20; and patriarchy, 103, 118; and pluralism, 6, 31; and reading practices, 22, 25; and social agency, 21; and utopianism, 103. *See also* Canon formation

Academic institutions: and cultural capital, 34; and law schools, 12; and reformism, 9, 11–12; and silencing of Chicana culture, 119, 123

Acculturation, 96–98, 118

Acosta, Oscar Zeta: legal activism of, 125–26, 188–89n2, 189n11; literary works of, 8, 24, 42, 43, 84, 101, 124–39

Activism: Acosta's novelistic representation of, 125, 128, 133, 134, 135–38; Artenstein's documentary film on, 50–56; and Chicana/Mexicana mourning practices, 8, 150–63; and civil rights, 3, 17–18, 125, 166; and community lawyers, 16; and critique of political agency, 5; and direct action, 157; and institutional reform, 11; and male power, 105, 122, 129–38; and minority worldviews, 14, 18; and passivity, 15; and prison reform, 181n2; and public opinion, 106; and struggle for public voice, 50–56. *See also* Chicano movement; Militants, Chicano; Reformism

Acuña, Rudolfo, 125, 173n1, 187n29, 189n11

Affirmative action, 9, 15, 95, 98

African Americans, 16–17, 18, 45, 178n16; slave narratives of, 31, 65; social-realist literature by, 83–84

Agency, social: and academic discourse, 21; and collective action, 15, 83, 90, 102; de Certeau's analysis of, 91; Foucault's analysis of, 5, 90, 91; and legal rhetoric, 9–10, 171; and legal system, 10, 15; and liberalism, 9, 15, 21, 96; and Native American legal struggles, 60; and sexual identity, 112; and synthetic individualism, 15. *See also* Group analysis, in legal argumentation

Agency, social, representations of: in Jackson's *Ramona*, 65, 67; in Morales's *Brick People*, 67; in Valdez's *Zoot Suit*, 67

Alarcón, Norma, 109, 110, 118, 130, 149, 150, 179n19

Alchemy of Race and Rights (Williams), 16–17, 177n1

Alienation, 130, 177n3

American Me (Olmos), 8, 124, 139–44, 147–52, 162, 192n27

Amnesia, 7, 53, 55, 60, 69, 79, 82, 100, 176n22, 182n6

Anarchism, 178n17, 181n30

Antidiscrimination laws, 12

Anzaldúa, Gloria, 27, 118–19

Architecture, Mission Revival, 57, 78, 183n13

Archival work, 29, 152

Arditti, Rita, 163

Argentina, Mothers of the Plaza de Mayo in, 153–54, 163, 193n34

Art and artists, Chicano: and dialectical criticism, 14; and historical criticism, 6, 41–42; interdisciplinary approach of, 5, 7; legal sphere engaged by, 3–4, 9, 11, 14, 19, 31, 41–42, 172; and magical realism, 160; and public discourse, 56; and significance of Chicana work, 29, 123, 152; and social dependency, 5, 6; and theoretical discourse, 29; and translation dynamics, 166, 167

The Art of Memory (Yates), 82

Artenstein, Isaac, 50, 181n1

Compositor: Graphic Composition, Inc.
Text: 10/13 Palatino
Display: Palatino
Printer: BookCrafters
Binder: BookCrafters